T0355541

Joan, the Fair Maid of Kent

Joan, the Fair Maid of Kent

A Fourteenth-Century Princess and her World

·: *Anthony Goodman* :·

THE BOYDELL PRESS

First published 2017
The Boydell Press, Woodbridge
ISBN 978 1 78327 176 4

The Boydell Press is an imprint of Boydell & Brewer Ltd
PO Box 9, Woodbridge, Suffolk IP12 3DF, UK
and of Boydell & Brewer Inc.
668 Mt Hope Avenue, Rochester, NY 14620–2731, USA
website: www.boydellandbrewer.com

A catalogue record for this book is available from the British Library

The publisher has no responsibility for the continued existence
or accuracy of URLs for external or third-party internet websites
referred to in this book, and does not guarantee that any content
on such websites is, or will remain, accurate or appropriate

This publication is printed on acid-free paper

Designed and typeset in Adobe Jenson Pro by
David Roberts, Pershore, Worcestershire

To Jackie
Without whom this book would never have been completed

Contents

Illustrations

The author and publishers are grateful to all the institutions and individuals listed for permission to reproduce the materials in which they hold copyright. Every effort has been made to trace the copyright holders; apologies are offered for any omission, and the publishers will be pleased to add any necessary acknowledgement in subsequent editions.

Abbreviations

Anon. Chron. 1333–81	*The Anonimalle Chronicle, 1333–1381*, ed. V. H. Galbraith (Manchester, 1927)
Baker	Geoffrey le Baker, *Chronicon Galfridi le Baker de Swynebroke*, ed. E. M. Thompson (Oxford, 1889)
BL	London, British Library
BM	London, British Museum
BPR	*Register of Edward the Black Prince*, ed. M. C. B. Dawes, 4 vols (London, 1930–33)
CCR	*Calendar of Close Rolls, Edward II–Richard II*, 24 vols (London, 1892–1927)
CFR	*Calendar of Fine Rolls, Edward II–Richard II*, 10 vols (London, 1912–29)
CIPM	*Calendar of Inquisitions Post Mortem, Edward I–Richard II*, 17 vols (London, 1904–88)
Complete Peerage	G. E. Cokayne, *The Complete Peerage of England, Scotland, Ireland, Great Britain and the United Kingdom*, rev. V. Gibbs et al., 13 vols (London, 1910–59)
CPL	*Calendar of Entries in the Papal Registers Relating to Great Britain and Ireland: Papal Letters*, ii–iv (London, 1895–1902)
CPP	*Calendar of Entries in the Papal Registers Relating to Great Britain and Ireland: Petitions to the Pope, 1342–1419* (London, 1896)
CPR	*Calendar of Patent Rolls, Edward II–Richard II*, 27 vols (London, 1894–1916)
DL	Duchy of Lancaster
EHR	*English Historical Review*
Eulogium	*Eulogium Historiarum*, ed. F. S. Haydon, 3 vols, RS 9 (London, 1858–63)
Foedera	*Foedera, Conventiones, Literae et Cujuscunque Generis Acta Publica*, ed. T. Rymer, 3 vols in 6 parts (London, 1816–30)

Froissart, Œuvres	J. Froissart, Œuvres complètes: Chroniques, ed. J. M. B. C. Kervyn de Lettenhove, 25 vols (Brussels, 1867–77)
Froissart, trans. Brereton	Froissart, J., Chronicles, trans. G. Brereton (Harmondsworth, 1968)
JGR 1371–75	John of Gaunt's Register, 1371–1375, ed. S. Armitage-Smith, 2 vols, Camden Third Series, 20–1 (London, 1911)
JGR 1379–83	John of Gaunt's Register, 1379–1383, ed. E. C. Lodge and R. Somerville, 2 vols, Camden Third Series, 56–7 (London, 1937)
JMH	Journal of Medieval History
King's Works	R. A. Brown, H. M. Colvin and A. J. Taylor, The History of the King's Works: The Middle Ages, 2 vols (London, 1963)
le Bel	Chronique de Jean le Bel, ed. J. Viard and E. Déprez, 2 vols, SHF (Paris, 1904–5)
ODNB	The Oxford Dictionary of National Biography, ed. H. C. G. Matthew and B. H. Harrison, 60 vols (Oxford, 2004)
RHS	Royal Historical Society
RP	Rotuli Parliamentorum, 6 vols (London, 1767–77)
RS	Rolls Series
St Albans	T. Walsingham, The St Albans Chronicle: The Chronica Maiora of Thomas Walsingham, ed. J. Taylor, W. R. Childs and L. Watkiss, 2 vols (Oxford, 2003–11)
SHF	Société de l'Histoire de France
Test. Ebor.	Testamenta Eboracensia, 6 vols, Surtees Society, 4, 30, 45, 53, 79, 106 (1836–1902)
Test. Vet.	Testamenta Vetusta, ed. N. H. Nicolas, 2 vols (London, 1826)
TNA	Kew, The National Archives
West. Chron.	The Westminster Chronicle, 1381–1394, ed. L. C. Hector and B. F. Harvey (Oxford, 1982)

England and Wales in the later fourteenth century

La Coruña

Oviedo

ASTURIAS

VIZCAYA

Santiago

GALICIA

León

Orense

Valencia de Don Juan

LEÓN

Valderas

Benavente

Ponte do Mouro

Braganca

Villalobos

Alcañices

Zamora

Oporto

Ledesma

Trancoso

Salamanca

Ciudad Rodrigo

Coimbra

Batalha

Toledo

Aljubarrota

PORTUGAL

Lisbon

Carmona

Seville

GRA

Grar

Algeciras

Bu

Dax
GASCONY
Bayonne
Peyrehorade
St Jean Pied de Port
VA
alvatierra
Roncesvalles
Vitoria
Pamplona
oño
NAVARRE
Najera

CATALONIA

ARAGON

Barcelona

VALENCIA

Murcia •

The Iberian Peninsula in the later
fourteenth century

FRIESLAND

HOLLAND

GUELDERS

ZEALAND

BRABANT

Damme
Sluys
Gravelines
Bruges Ghent
Calais Bourbourg
FLANDERS Cortenberghe
Ypres

NAMUR

HAINAULT

LUXEMBOURG

Amiens

Reims

Paris

Troyes

COUNTY
OF
NEVERS

DUCHY OF
Dijon
BURGUNDY

COUNTY
OF
BURGUNDY

The Low Countries and Burgundy in the later fourteenth century

Calais •St Omer

PICARDY

Cherbourg
•Amiens
•Harfleur
Laon•
Rouen
•Reims
St Malo *NORMANDY* Paris •
Brest• *CHAMPAGNE*
MAINE Chartres •Troyes
BRITTANY Orléans
Nantes *ANJOU*
•Avallon
BERRY •Dijon
La Roche-sur-Yon• *POITOU* Moulins *BURGUNDY*
Poitiers•
Niort *BOURBONNAIS*
La Rochelle *MARCHE*
Limoges
Saintes *LIMOUSIN* Lyons•
Tulle *AUVERGNE*
Perigueux
Bergerac
Bordeaux
GASCONY
•Agen
Avignon *PROVENCE*
Dax
Bayonne Orthez
BEARN Lourdes •Toulouse
FOIX

France in the later fourteenth century

xv

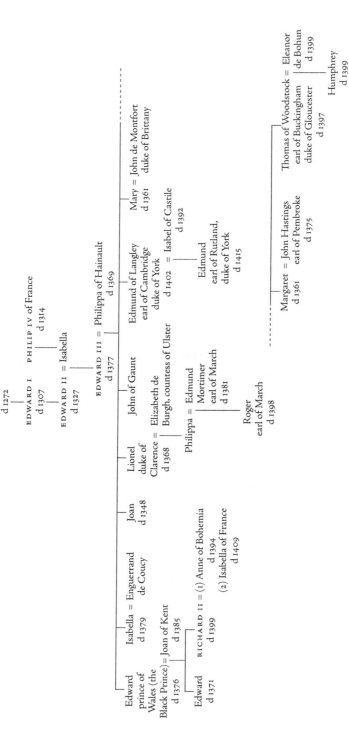

The descent and family of Edward III

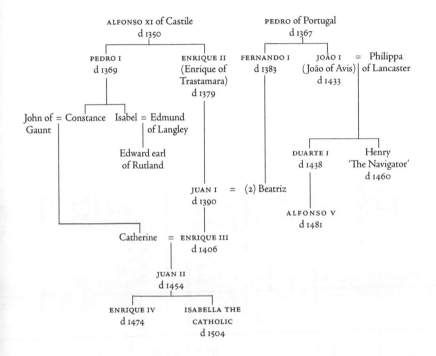

The Royal houses of Castile and Portugal

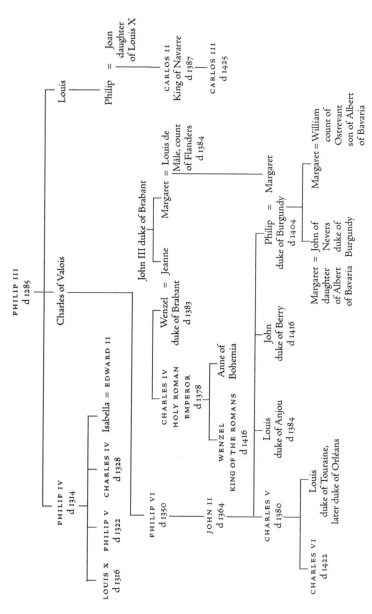

French Kings and some of their connections

Loosened Bonds

JOAN PLANTAGENET, widely acclaimed as the 'Fair Maid' for her great beauty, was born in a century marred by domestic and foreign upheavals and by dynastic struggles. It was moreover a time of persistent, deeply entrenched attitudes towards women, their natures and their roles. Yet there were also some green shoots of change which were to produce significant and more diverse attitudes. Joan's life clearly reflects these changing attitudes.

In the fourteenth century, there were deeply embedded beliefs that, although male and female souls were equal, Man was superior in physique, intellect and purpose because he was made in God's image – and Woman was not. This tenet, and the hierarchical deductions which flowed from it, were upheld by formidable cohorts of authorities. These were passages from the Old and New Testaments and the works of the Church Fathers, ancient works on philosophy and medicine, and the formulations of modern theologians and experts in canon law. Let us consider the medical imperatives, as laid down by classical Greek writers, whose influence survived into the nineteenth century. Food, it was thought, was converted in humans into four sets of intermingling fluids, known as 'humours', whose particular mixture determined character.[1]

Men's predominant humours were characterised as hot and dry, inclining them to be strong and courageous, whereas women's typically cold and wet humours made them weak, timorous and devious. Women were programmed to cling to men, distracting them from their naturally brave and lofty purposes. This view of gender relations was to be encapsulated by Shakespeare in *King Henry IV, Part One* (Act 2 scene 3). Hotspur, desperate to be at the head of an imminent rebellion, is trying to conceal his intentions from his wife. She is suspicious, prying, wheedling. She threatens feebly. Hotspur (Henry Percy), exasperated, makes a show of repudiating her love, and of despising her charms. He cruelly distrusts her discretion:

> Constant you are
> But yet a woman; and for secrecy
> No lady closer, for I well believe
> Thou wilt not utter what thou dost not know.
> And so far will I trust thee

However, Hotspur is portrayed as a swaggering braggadocio, conspicuously lacking his wife's good sense. Shakespeare is here playing with and subverting traditional stereotypes. That was, indeed, a medieval topos; its great English creative exemplar was Joan of Kent's contemporary and probable acquaintance, Geoffrey Chaucer.

Nevertheless, in Joan's time male superiority was sustained by feudal customs, the common law, and in some fundamental respects by modern developments in theology and canon law. In common law, husbands had control of any property that wives brought to the marriage – and of the movable goods they possessed. Elizabeth de Bohun, countess of Northampton, in her will of 1356 made many valuable bequests, but was careful to note that the will had been made with her husband's consent. Any authority which a wife exercised over the marital household or her separate establishment was dependent on her husband's delegation.

Nobly born widows were entitled to hold at least one-third of the property their husband had owned, for life. But, traditionally, they faced strong pressure from kinsfolk to remarry speedily, or from the king, who, as direct feudal overlord of the higher noble families, had the right to license the remarriage of heiresses. A new husband was considered inherently more likely to uphold the king's and kinsfolk's interest by having the property well managed, and by holding royal offices and commissions, for which women were ineligible.

However, from the twelfth century onwards, as we shall see, changes in religious sensibilities, together with aspects of the theologians' and canonists' remodelling of the rules for Christian life, encouraged reverence for female potentialities, and the bestowal of greater respect on children, wives and widows. These trends we see coming to fruition particularly in the fourteenth century. The life of Joan of Kent provides a prime example of circumstances in which a spirited and talented noblewoman could assert an independence of action, and become a respected power in the land.

Joan's life, besides, provides an often distinctive (though sometimes opaque) perspective on the experiences of a noblewoman at the centre of affairs in Plantagenet England, in a century in which the Crown and polity, besides enjoying some striking triumphs, plunged to nadirs which shook conventional expectations and hopes. The dramatic peaks and troughs of Joan's life often mirror these events as well as contemporary divergencies over gender roles. Some of her dramatic experiences could not have been anticipated – her imprisonment twice before she was of age, her three scandalous marriages, the courtly sway she was to hold over much of France, her involvement in the decline of English rule there and, in her later years, the key interventions she made in English politics. Furthermore, she held landed power in large parts of England and Wales, and dabbled in encouraging the sort of religious reform which one day would empower the English Reformation. However, she did not enjoy a quiet old age. She was to suffer degradation at the hands of the rebellious commons during the Peasants' Revolt of 1381. Then the tranquillity to which she aspired was clouded by the tensions between her son Richard II and his magnates. Her death, in the view of some contemporaries, resulted from grief at the apparently unpardonable offence committed by another of her sons, Sir John Holand, in slaying an earl's son.

We do not know the exact year Joan was born: it may have been 1328. What prospects were in store for the infant? They rapidly changed from glittering to tarnished, and speedily back again. She was a granddaughter of England's remarkable warrior king, Edward I (d. 1307), and a younger child of his son Edmund of Woodstock, earl of Kent. In 1328 the English polity was in disarray, its nobility at odds with one another. That stemmed from the rule of Joan's uncle, the incompetent Edward II, and from his deposition the year before, and replacement by her cousin, his son Edward III, aged only fourteen at his accession. The young king was treated as a minor, and the real rule of England, it soon became clear, was not in the hands of his formally appointed and weightily composed council. Instead, it was exercised by the king's mother, Isabella of France, and her lover, a baron from the

Welsh Marches, Roger Mortimer, lord of Wigmore. The earl of Kent's hare-brained plotting to remedy this degrading situation resulted in his execution, and in disaster for his wife and Joan's family, in 1330. However, soon afterwards Edward III overthrew the rule of his mother and her paramour, and restored the fortunes of Joan's mother and her family.

The young Joan was doubtless taught to obey God's will, the king's and her mother's, and to give precedence to her two brothers Edmund and John, successively heirs to the restored earldom of Kent. Her education was conventional. The ladies who schooled her in courtly ways, and the clerics who instructed her in religious duties, would have warned her especially about inherent female frailty, the occasion for sin for herself and for the young men who clustered in large numbers at court and in the households of the higher nobility. Her expectations would have been that she would be betrothed by her early teens in accordance with the wishes of the king and her family. Her eminent status dictated that her prospective husband would likely be an earl or a foreigner of at least equivalent rank. Edward III had a skein of family and diplomatic entanglements in the Low Countries, being married to the courtly and cultivated Philippa, daughter of William the Good, count of Hainault. Edward chose an English option for Joan – the son of one of his leading supporters and closest friends. When she was probably still in her early teens (c. 1341), she was married to William Montague, teenage son and heir of the earl of Salisbury.

What Joan omitted to tell anyone when she made her marriage vow was that she had apparently already secretly married someone else – someone absolutely unsuitable both in status and in background. Her husband was a young knight, Thomas Holand: outstanding in gallantry, but impecunious, and with a dark family background. For perhaps as long as seven years after her bigamous marriage to Montague (possibly unconsummated), Joan and Thomas kept quiet about their consummated union.

Thomas was focussed on making a military name for himself, especially in the king's service on campaigns in France. These were the early phases of the conflicts (commencing in 1337) known in modern times as the Hundred Years War. Edward III was determined to resist Philip VI of France's decision to confiscate from him his valuable duchy of Gascony, for which Philip was his feudal overlord. It was a relationship which the French Crown had long been inclined to exploit as a means of subordinating English kings. Edward, in order to lure some of Philip's other leading vassals to his side, from 1340 onwards asserted his own claim to the throne of France, through his mother's direct descent from Philip IV.

Thomas Holand flourished in warfare, and in 1347 was emboldened to reclaim his wife at law. Joan, for her part, stoutly resisted harsh pressure, allegedly from both the Montagues and her mother, to declare that she had not made a precontract with him. In 1349, on her testimony, the validity of her marriage to Thomas was recognised by the pope Clement VI, and she was reunited with him.

The couple remained married for about eleven years, till Thomas's death in 1360. We do not know whether they had more children than the two boys and two girls who survived into adulthood. That does not seem a large total, at a time when it was not uncommon for women to give birth frequently. For instance, Margery Kempe, the famous mystic and author of *The Boke of Margery Kempe*, tells us that she had fourteen children between her marriage in c. 1393 and c. 1413. However, it may be that, in Joan's case, cohabitation was occasional because Thomas was often absent on the king's business, campaigning and governing in Brittany and Normandy. He did not live to see the fruits of English victory fully realised. In 1360, the year of Thomas's death, Edward III and Philip VI's son and successor, John II, agreed terms of peace, in which Edward undertook to stop styling himself king of France, and received, in full sovereignty, the long-defunct duchy of Aquitaine, covering south-west France, and including Gascony.

Joan remained a widow for less than a year. She was an excellent catch, because of her royal birth and tenure of the earldom of Kent, which she had inherited as a result of the youthful deaths of her brothers. According to our sole full account, she boldly engineered her own, highly controversial choice of husband. This was no less than her kinsman Edward Prince of Wales (known to posterity as the Black Prince), England's great military hero. Without royal permission, and in defiance of the king's current marriage diplomacy, a woman best known for her dubious marital past wedded the heir to the throne in her second clandestine marriage. Knowing the headstrong character of the couple, the king swallowed his pride and chagrin, and bent to their will. He hastened to take the measures needed to ensure the marriage's legality and its fitting public celebration.

For the remaining twenty-four years of her life, Joan the princess did not cause renewed scandal of the kind which had made her notorious. She projected a suitably iconic profile. Both courtly and monastic writers inclined on the whole to be complimentary about the ways in which she fulfilled her public roles. Criticisms and allusions to her earlier peccadillos were muted. She did not sully the immense prestige which accrued to her as the wife and then the widow of the Black Prince, and as the mother of Richard II. Unlike Edward III's disgraced mother, Isabella of France, she was not banished by her son to live in rustic obscurity, away from the royal court. After the Black Prince's death in 1376, it was thought appropriate that Joan should remain for the time being in charge of nine-year-old Richard. Afterwards, she was given as her principal residence Wallingford Castle, one of the Crown's most imposing and luxurious fortresses, within easy reach of the court's usual haunts.

But these were dire times. As far as the fortunes of the English Crown and realm were concerned, the wheel had turned again. There were widespread rising tensions between elites and commoners over wages, and customary rents and services. French, Spanish and Scottish opponents threatened war. Joan, one of the few English ladies who had experienced closely and intimately the English debacle in France in 1369–70, when she was princess of Aquitaine, was given, as principal elements of her dower, vulnerable areas of Britain – South Wales (a claimant to whose Principality was given countenance by England's enemies) and parts of the West Country.

One notable feature of Joan's second widowhood is that, though she had previously shown eagerness to marry, this time she remained single. Yet, when widowed, she was probably not yet aged fifty. There were surely lords around who would have revelled in the position of being the king's stepfather, and would have eagerly exploited it. But Joan now appears to have had a settled determination to command and order her own affairs as a dowager. More importantly, her devotion to her son as a king who had succeeded hazardously under age probably made her fear that remarriage would cause her to be marginalised in her role as the king's respected mother. For it is likely that Richard's three closest mature male relatives, his uncles – Edward III's sons, John of Gaunt, Edmund of Langley and Thomas of Woodstock – would not have tolerated the intrusive influence at court of another of the Fair Maid's fancies. She was determined to be mistress of her fate, in a period when the times were once more out of joint, and when she now had the experience and prestige to exert female power in novel as well as conventional ways, for the good, as she conceived it, of the king and community of the realm.

Let us then consider Joan of Kent as an example of how far a woman in times of strong – but challenged – female subjection was able to exert her individuality and exercise power.

·: 2 :·

Tragic Beginnings

nothing in his life
Became him like the leaving it.
(*Macbeth*, Act I scene 4)

JOAN OF KENT'S FATHER Edmund was a victim – due mainly to
his lack of political adroitness – of the chronic political instability
characterising his half-brother Edward II's reign, which was
increased by his deposition and murder in 1327. Though he had been
a prime supporter of Edward's overthrow, Edmund soon chafed
under the tight control of government exercised by the king's callous
widow Queen Isabella and her lover Roger Mortimer during her
son Edward III's minority. The couple's sense of the precariousness
of their scandalous rule, and their awareness of Edmund's habitual
unreliability and current disaffection, made him a potential danger.
He was arrested during the parliament held at Winchester in 1330,
and accused of treason. Mortimer played a leading role in producing
evidence against him, and informed the young king, then 'at his meat',
of his uncle's conviction. Fearing that Edward would grant Edmund his
life, Mortimer and Isabella, without consulting any royal councillors,
sent orders in haste to the bailiffs of Winchester to have him executed.[1]
Hence the specially degrading circumstances of his execution, as the
doubtless alarmed citizens scrambled to fulfil their deadly remit.

At first light on a March morning in 1330, it is likely that an
expectant crowd gathered outside Winchester Castle. A platform had
been erected at its gate for an unprecedented event – the execution
for treason of a king's son, of the royal blood of both the Plantagenet
kings of England and of the Capetian kings of France. Edmund was
the sixth (and third surviving) son of Edward I, by his second wife
Margaret, a daughter of Philip III of France and Marie of Brabant.
Edward and Margaret already had one son, Thomas of Brotherton.

Edmund was born on 5 August 1301, in the royal palace of Woodstock (Oxfordshire).[2]

Accounts of his execution describe especially pitiful circumstances. When he was led out by the bailiffs of Winchester, he was, it was said, clad wretchedly (especially for the time of year) only in his shirt. Both victim and onlookers were for long kept waiting, as an executioner could not be found, perhaps because men shrank from killing a king's son. A messenger was allegedly sent to London in search of one. The twenty-eight-year-old earl remained on the platform all day until a candidate arrived; Edmund was apparently not beheaded until nine o'clock in the evening. One chronicler, Geoffrey le Baker, wrote that the executioner was a 'gonge fermer' – a carter who collected ordure to fertilise fields. According to Thomas Burton (who became abbot of Meaux Abbey in Yorkshire in 1396), the executioner was a 'ribald' from the Marshalsea prison in London. These stories alleging Kent's ignominious end may have been spread around to blacken the reputation of his enemies, and to suggest that he had died a martyr.[3]

By contrast, in his youth, Edmund of Woodstock had had shining prospects. Edward II made substantial grants of land to him in 1315 and 1319, when he was still under age. In 1321 he bestowed on Edmund the earldom of Kent. Soon after his elevation, Edmund was involved in the recurrent violent factionalism – as a staunch supporter of the king. In 1322, Edward moved against a coalition of rebellious lords from the Marches of Wales, including Roger Mortimer, who resented the aggrandisement, especially in those regions, of the king's favourites, Hugh Despenser and his father Hugh. The new earl of Kent was in the force with which the king advanced through the Marches, enforcing submissions on Mortimer and his allies. Some of them fled to join the potentially formidable leader of revolt – the king's cousin Thomas earl of Lancaster, Edward's inveterate opponent.[4]

However, Lancaster failed to disrupt the king's advance northwards. On 11 March, the king issued a writ of aid at Tutbury in Staffordshire (where he had occupied Lancaster's castle) to the earl of Kent and to an experienced commander, John de Warenne, earl of Surrey. They were commanded to arrest Lancaster and his leading confederates, and to lay siege to his great castle at Pontefract (Yorkshire). However, a siege proved unnecessary, for five days later Lancaster was defeated and captured by other converging royal forces at Boroughbridge. Soon afterwards, Kent was among the magnates who condemned Lancaster to death for treason in the king's presence in Pontefract Castle. He was executed on a hill outside the town and buried in a local priory. Kent was well rewarded for his support of Edward, receiving a royal grant of some of the castles and estates in the Marches of Wales forfeited by Roger Mortimer.[5]

The king, hardly a shrewd judge of character, seems now to have regarded his half-brother as a valuable supporter, and as an up-and-coming military man. That summer, Edmund took part in his fruitless invasion of Scotland, and was subsequently with the king when he was ambushed by a Scottish raiding force as far south as near Byland Abbey (Yorkshire), and fled with him from the rampaging Scots, via Rievaulx Abbey and Bridlington Priory.[6]

Edmund's role in this dismal campaign, whatever it was, seems to have increased the king's reliance on him and trust in his martial abilities. In November, Edmund was specially commissioned to arrest disturbers of the peace throughout the realm. The following February, he was appointed royal lieutenant to defend the northern Marches against the Scots, a crucial post in view of their military dominance in those regions. He was one of the judges in the trial for treason of Andrew de Harcla, earl of Carlisle and sheriff of Cumberland, who, despairing of Edward's failures against the Scots, had made his own treaty with their king, Robert I. In March, Edmund was ordered to serve against the Scots in person.[7]

Edward soon afterwards switched his brother to fill the main role in a crisis on another frontier. The recurrent Anglo-French problems over the English king's tenure of the duchy of Gascony came to focus on the exercise of the competing royal jurisdictions, the counties of Agenais and Saintonge. In 1323 Edward's officials committed an outrage against his brother-in-law Charles IV of France's officials at Saint-Sardos in Agenais. A mission, which included Edmund, was unable to settle the issue. As aggrieved overlord, Charles formally confiscated the duchy of Gascony from Edward. Edmund was appointed king's lieutenant to defend it (July 1324). Aged only twenty-two, he faced a challenging task. Gascony largely lacked rugged natural boundaries which might facilitate defence. The resources he received in men and money from

England were probably inadequate in face of Charles IV's large invasion force. It overran nearly all of Agenais and Saintonge. Edmund was besieged for five weeks in La Réole in Agenais, then capitulated (September 1324). The terms on which he did so were favourable to Charles: a truce for six months was concluded, leaving the French in possession of parts of the duchy, including La Réole. However, most of the Gascons held firm in allegiance to their duke. Edmund's brief defence of La Réole, though a signal defeat, may have bought sufficient time to blunt further prospects of invasion.[8]

Edward II was furious about the truce, concluded without his authority. He now needed to make strenuous diplomatic or military efforts in order to regain control of the whole of his duchy, or, at least, to prevent further losses there. In seeking diplomatic leverage, he committed blunders from which his own dire fate was to flow. In March 1325 his queen, Isabella, arrived in Paris, to act as his intermediary with her brother Charles IV. She was followed in September across the Channel by her son Edward, heir to the English throne – with Edmund in his company. The king had sent the boy to join her as a means of circumventing an impasse to the making of peace. For Charles had at first insisted that Edward II should perform his long-delayed homage for the duchy of Gascony in person, as part of a settlement. Edward's favourites, the Despensers, were worried that there might be revolt if he left England. Charles was prepared to accept the compromise that the young Edward should be invested by his father with the duchy, and come to perform homage for it.[9]

Diplomacy thus regained most of Gascony for the Plantagenets, but, incidentally, the process created conditions in which Edward's kingship unravelled. He had failed to grasp the depth of the queen's alienation from him, and her determination to destroy the Despensers – and, if later events are anything to go by, to destroy him, too. She refused either to return from France to England, or to send her son back there. Instead, she formed her own court over the water, composed of exiles who had fled after rebelling in 1322, and others who were discontented with Despenser rule. The most influential of them was Roger Mortimer, who had escaped from imprisonment in the Tower of London. In Paris, he became her lover, to the scandal of the French court.

Among the nobles who threw in their lot with the queen in exile was Edmund of Woodstock. It is hard to know why. Edward had demonstrated anew his confidence in him by entrusting his son and heir to his care on the mission to France. Perhaps Edmund had had enough of the predominance at court of the Despensers, notwithstanding that the younger one was married to his niece Eleanor de Clare, a granddaughter of Edward I. In Gascony he had been in the company of the younger Despenser's men, and had corresponded a good deal with him, ostensibly in amicable vein, on business affairs. But maybe, as an embattled royal lieutenant, he felt that Despenser had been insufficiently supportive, and had come to resent dependence on his favour.[10]

It was after Edmund arrived in France that a papal dispensation was issued for him to marry his kinswoman Margaret, widow of John Comyn, lord of Badenoch in Scotland. He had been killed at the battle of Bannockburn (1314), fighting for Edward II against Robert I. It is surprising that Edmund, aged twenty-four, had apparently not yet been betrothed: perhaps he was aggrieved that the king had not provided him with a suitably endowed heiress. Margaret brought him good aristocratic connections, but only distant prospects of wealth. A reversal of English fortunes in Scotland (such as Edward II seemed incapable of achieving) might provide her with a substantial Comyn dower forfeited to the Scottish Crown. Moreover, she was the sister and also prospective heir of Thomas Lord Wake, who was a few years older than Edmund, and, as far as we know, childless since his marriage, which had taken place as long ago as 1316, or before then.[11]

The Wakes were an old-established and distinguished baronial family who had estates in Lincolnshire, notably Bourne Castle. They had acquired the fine manor of Cottingham, near Hull, and the barony of Liddell in Cumberland, its great motte situated vulnerably on the frontier with Scotland. There were notable family estates in Scotland – the lordship of Liddesdale and the barony of Kirkandrews (Dumfriesshire) – which had been confiscated by Robert I, and which Thomas Wake for long made strenuous efforts to recover, like some other lords disinherited because of their adherence to the English allegiance.[12]

Like many nobles, Wake had had mixed relations with Edward

II. In his teens, he had offended the king by marrying without his permission. Edward had planned to marry him to the daughter of his disgraced and murdered favourite, Piers Gaveston. Instead, Wake made a far more exalted marriage, which put him into the orbit of the king's kin, but also that of his chief opponent, Thomas earl of Lancaster: his bride Blanche was the earl's niece, his brother Henry's daughter. Blanche of Lancaster long outlived her husband, and was apparently vigorous and active into the early years of Richard II's reign. She is likely to have become a close confidante of her niece, Joan, the Fair Maid of Kent. Joan's probable closeness to the forceful Blanche echoed her father's alliances with Blanche's husband – though the latter seems to have been a dominant and perhaps baleful influence on the rudderless Edmund.

In the years 1318–23 Thomas Wake was busy campaigning against the Scots, establishing his reputation then as a fine soldier. He cannily refrained from taking up arms in support of Thomas of Lancaster in 1322, despite his marriage into his family. Two years later, he was ordered to go to Gascony to support Earl Edmund. He was among the nobles who joined Isabella and Mortimer in Paris. It seems likely that Edmund admired his prowess and prudence, and was willing to share his dream of recovering estates in Scotland, an outcome which could also be to Edmund's benefit. Edmund's marriage also connected him with Thomas of Lancaster's brother Henry (earl of Leicester, 1324), providing him with a potentially powerful ally.

Other than shaky landed prospects and good connections, Edmund's bride can have brought him no other additional worldly benefits. She was, indeed, to show herself to be a forceful and determined character, especially in adversity. But we know hardly anything about Edmund's marriage, except that it was prolific; the first child was born in 1326, and christened Edmund. Joan may have been born in 1328. There are hints that Margaret was especially close to her husband in matters of policy and piety. A chronicler noted that, exceptionally among the nobles, the earl was accompanied by his wife in the force which hunted down Edward II in 1327.[13] In October 1329 (perhaps within a year of Joan of Kent's birth) the pope commuted vows which the couple had made to go on pilgrimage to Santiago de Compostela in Spain. Edmund had made his vow to do so in fulfilment of one made by his mother Queen Margaret shortly before her death in 1318.[14]

Countess Margaret was soon to be implicated in Edmund's treason. That may have been why Isabella and Mortimer intended to have her treated harshly when he was accused. After Edmund's arrest, arrangements were made for her and her children to be kept in the royal castle at Old Sarum (Wiltshire), a bleak old county gaol, despite her advanced state of pregnancy. Edmund had appointed her as one of his executors. He had laid down that Margaret should choose his place of burial, a task she carried out with alacrity, in a manner which did him appropriate honour, in the Franciscan church at Winchester. It seems likely that the friars were willing to receive his remains because his mother had been a conspicuous patron of their Order, donating large sums to the construction of their London house.[15] As regards Joan of Kent's parents, we can therefore tentatively conclude that they had a compatible, even affectionate relationship. Perhaps – considering there were so few tangible material gains in their alliance for Edmund – theirs had been a love match, as the first and third of their daughter Joan's three controversial marriages were to be.

Let us return to the period when Edmund married. Queen Isabella had eventually been induced by her brother Charles IV to leave Paris in 1326, together with her son Edward, Mortimer and her supporters, including Edmund. His lands in England had been confiscated because of his failure to comply with the king's orders to return thither. The exiles went northwards to the county of Hainault (now in Belgium). Edmund was among the witnesses to his nephew Prince Edward's marriage to Philippa, daughter of its count, who provided the main support for an invasion of England. When Isabella landed with a small force in the estuary of the Orwell (Suffolk) in 1326, Edmund was the only English noble of an equal status to her. As she advanced across England, opposition melted away, and the king and the Despensers fled westwards. Henry earl of Leicester (now styled earl of Lancaster) was one of the first nobles who joined her standard. Edmund's brother-in-law Lord Wake joined too. Success was complete: the Despensers and then the king were captured without a fight. Wake read out the charges against the elder Despenser at his trial, and, along with Edmund and the latter's elder brother Thomas of Brotherton (earl of

Norfolk), Lancaster and Mortimer, was among those who sentenced him to death. Edmund was a member of the council which decided on the deposition and imprisonment of the king; Wake was a vociferous advocate of deposition.[16] In these dire circumstances for the monarchy, the deposed king's son was recognised as King Edward III.

Like Wake, Edmund was lavishly rewarded with forfeited lands for his part in the destruction of Edward II's rule. A grant to him of the castle, town and honour of Arundel (Sussex) was dated the day after the start of Edward III's reign. This estate was a main part of the forfeited inheritance of Edmund Fitzalan earl of Arundel, who had remained faithful to Edward II, and consequently was executed without trial in 1326.[17] Both Kent and Wake were appointed on the council which was ostensibly intended to rule during the new king's minority.

In the summer, a major Scottish incursion in the North-East had to be countered. Kent had been appointed as joint commander of the forces in the Marches, together with Lancaster. In fact, Kent speedily demitted this command.[18] If he took part in the campaign, it is likely to have been a dispiriting experience. The youthful Edward III felt humiliated by the boldness of the Scots, and his inability to bring them to battle when encamped on his soil. As a sequel to the failure of the campaign, peace was made between the English and Scottish Crowns in 1328 – a peace widely regarded as humiliating by the English. The claims of most of the English lords who had forfeited lands in Scotland were neglected: they included Wake's claims. The failure to recover Edmund's wife's dower in Scotland in the settlement affected his prospects too. He was prominent in support of the subsequent armed protests against Isabella's and Mortimer's control and exercise of government, protests headed by Henry earl of Lancaster. Also to the fore in these demonstrations, as the Scottish historian Ranald Nicholson pointed out, were the 'disinherited' lords, including Wake. However, Edmund and his brother Thomas of Brotherton withdrew their support for Lancaster in the face of Mortimer's resolute stance. Wake was among those not pardoned after these tentative risings collapsed: he fled into exile.[19]

In 1330 Isabella and Mortimer may well have considered bitterly that they had sustained Edmund in adversity. They were probably outraged and apprehensive at what appeared to them as his unreliable and threatening behaviour. Moreover, if the confession which he allegedly made at his trial in 1330 is to be believed, he had become vehement in the conviction that Edward II was still alive, and determined to rescue and restore him. This was despite the fact that he had been present at his supposed interment in Gloucester Abbey (later Gloucester Cathedral). When visiting the papal court at Avignon in 1329, Edmund said that he had solicited and received the support of Pope John XXII to restore his brother to the throne. It would appear from the confession that Isabella and Mortimer, through their proxies, had used Dominican friars as *agents provocateurs*. They encouraged Edmund in his belief in Edward's survival, and in his plotting – one of the friars did so with the aid of a demon summoned up across the Thames from London at Kennington. Edmund tried to visit the phantom king in his supposed prison, Corfe Castle in the Isle of Purbeck (Dorset), and wrote to him there. During the Winchester parliament, Edmund's fate was sealed when he broke down and confessed all, after Mortimer had publicly read out incriminating correspondence. It is easy, on the partisan evidence we have, to condemn Edmund's last machinations as foolish in the extreme. But he does seem to have won significant support, especially among high-placed clerics, for his conviction that Edward II had survived, and for his plans to restore him.[20]

Furthermore, contemporary chronicles record expressions of outrage at Edmund's execution. However, his abrupt changes of political allegiance in the years 1326–30 seem at times to have been cynical and time-serving. Yet, other nobles perforce performed such contortions, in a period of faction run riot and of abrupt changes of royal fortunes. On the other hand, complaints suggest that Edmund was prone to weak governance, and failed to curb oppressions that his men committed. According to French sources, he had aroused resentment as lieutenant in Gascony because of the imposition of heavy levies, and the abduction of a girl from Agen. On the advance of Isabella's army across England in 1326, his and his brother Thomas of Brotherton's contingents were said to be the worst plunderers. The chronicler Geoffrey le Baker alleged that he had an 'evil' household, from the oppressions of whose partisans people had suffered much.[21]

Edmund's belated reconversion to Edward's cause may suggest that, in politics, he could exhibit some shards of decency, but, as presented by his enemies, he acted in this case with credulity and folly. Overall, his lack of good judgement appears largely unredeemed by qualities of character, or by any worthwhile achievements. Perhaps an indication of how he was generally regarded was that no cult apparently developed at his tomb, though cults did at those of some other political martyrs, such as the unpleasant Thomas of Lancaster, who came to be widely revered as a saint. Perhaps Edmund's one worthwhile achievement was to father Joan, who was to be a star in the courtly firmament, and who was in her maturity to shine as a beacon of good political sense and reformatory zeal.

However, there were some who remembered Edmund with favour. Jean le Bel, canon of Saint-Lambert in Liège, describing Edmund's downfall in his chronicle, said that he was 'very upright and good-natured' (*moult præudomme et debonaire*). Since le Bel had visited Edward III's court in Edmund's lifetime, and had as his patron Queen Philippa's uncle John of Hainault, he may have been echoing opinion in royal circles and among Edmund's Netherlandish kinsfolk.[22] In one prominent clerical circle Edmund was recalled prayerfully. A shield of his coat of arms appears prominently in a central light of a window in the south aisle of the nave of York Minster. The window was donated by Robert de Ripplingham, Fellow of Merton College, Oxford from 1285 to 1297, and Chancellor of York Minster from then until his death in 1332. The window depicts scenes from the life of St John the Divine, and one of the donor teaching boys from the text of St John's Gospel. To the left of Edmund's arms are those of two leading landowners in Richmondshire in the West Riding – Brian Lord FitzAlan of Bedale (d. 1306) and Henry Lord FitzHugh of Ravensworth (d. 1305), or his son and heir Hugh (d. 1352); to the right, those of John of Eltham, and the family of Holand. John was the short-lived brother of Edward III (1316–36); Holand may represent either the powerful northern landowner Sir Robert Holand (d. 1328) or his son Robert. The Richmondshire lords may have been among Ripplingham's early patrons; Edmund and John of Eltham were, perhaps, among his pupils. It seems likely that his commemoration of Edmund reflected a sympathy in some York clerical circles with the latter's fate. According to the earl's confession, Archbishop William Melton of York had sent a chaplain with money to support Edmund's aim to rescue Edward II. The year after his execution, Melton appointed Ripplingham as his vicar general in spirituals.[23]

The fall of Edmund entailed disaster and disgrace for his wife and their children. The birth of their son Edmund in 1326 had been speedily followed by that of two daughters, Margaret and Joan. Perhaps after Edmund's execution, Countess Margaret, due to another pregnancy, was excused from imprisonment at Old Sarum, and allowed to go with her children to Arundel Castle, his recent acquisition, in which he had granted her a joint interest with himself. There she gave birth to another son. On 7 April 1330, less than a month after his father's execution, he was christened John, in the priory next to the castle. The disgrace which the family endured, and the way in which they were being shunned by aristocratic society, are starkly suggested by the lack of exalted godparents available to sponsor the infant at the font. Instead, John de Grenstede, prior of Arundel, was one godparent. The others, quite extraordinarily, were the baby's tiny siblings, Edmund and Joan.[24] Joan's first public duty, precocious and bewildering, was to undertake a grave family responsibility in the midst of mourning for her father.

In that October, indeed, events occurred which once again transformed the family's fortunes. The young Edward III, showing astuteness beyond his years, plotted that summer with a trustworthy group of friends to overthrow the rule of Mortimer and Isabella. The coup was well organised. When the pair thought themselves safely ensconced in Nottingham Castle, the king with a small band crept at night into the castle up a subterranean tunnel, surprised the guards and arrested Mortimer. He was accused in parliament and convicted of notorious crimes, including having procured the death of the earl of Kent. He was duly executed.

Countess Margaret acted with alacrity to procure the rehabilitation of her husband and the restoration of his earldom. In the parliament which met in November 1330, petitions were submitted in her son Edmund's and her names asking for the conviction to be reconsidered, in the light of Mortimer's public confession on the scaffold that it had been wrongful. The Lords responded by recognising the truth of Mortimer's confession, and Edward, with the assent of parliament, granted that all the lands held by Earl Edmund at the time of his arrest were to be restored to his son and heir. Normally, the wardship of the lands of a leading tenant-in-chief would have been either retained by the Crown or granted in wardship to another lord. It was a mark of the strong feelings of Edward and the Lords about the wrongs done to Edmund and his family that it was agreed that Margaret should have the heir's wardship until he came of age. Unusually, too, the circumstances in which Edmund had been led to believe that Edward II had survived were outlined on the Parliament Roll. He was declared to have been 'wholly good and loyal', and those who were to be impeached for deceiving his 'innocence' were named.[25]

Margaret was determined that Earl Edmund should receive every due honour. She wished his remains to be translated to Westminster Abbey, where those of his royal father and grandfather lay. A papal mandate to this effect (13 April 1331) was issued in response to a petition from herself and her little son Edmund.[26] By then, tragedy had struck the family again. Young Edmund may have been ailing by January 1331: he was dead before 15 February. The heir was his brother John, less than a year old. Edward III's recent feelings of generosity towards Margaret now seem to have become overshadowed by other concerns, for he kept the lands of the Kent inheritance (apart from her dower) in his own hands, to be granted out piecemeal during the heir John's minority to nobles and royal officials. Edward granted some parts of the earldom in 1335 to the boy's uncle, Edmund's elder brother Thomas of Brotherton, whom he needed more urgently to conciliate than the infant John. The king retained control of John's marriage in order to use it for diplomatic purposes: in 1334 he appointed commissioners to find the infant a French bride, but nothing seems to have come of this.[27]

It is likely that Edward's concern for the Kent family encompassed Joan, who had had early lessons in vicissitudes. Perhaps his sympathy for them coloured his apparent tolerance towards her floutings of his authority by making clandestine marriages, both as a teenager and as a mature woman. Joan may therefore have been placed for her education in the royal nursery, under the control of Queen Philippa (see Plate II), probably only about fourteen years her senior, to whom she became personally attached, apparently adopting her emblem of the hind. The queen was munificent and tactful, and favoured the sophisticated tastes of her native court of Hainault. She shared with her husband a love of magnificence and chivalrous entertainments, which was to make the English court one of the most admired of its day internationally. Philippa enjoyed romance literature and music. The queen's household thus currently provided the best education for young English girls – but also dangerous ideas about love, which could have beguiled the young Joan.[28]

Can one discern any traits of her unfortunate father in Joan's behaviour? In the major decisions in her life, Joan was to exhibit a similar recklessness, but it was allied with a stubborn determination to stick to her decisions and fulfil her obligations under pressure. She was not, it appears, easily deceived; there was nothing 'innocent' about her. One wonders what she knew of her father's life, and how what she knew influenced her conduct. She became a faithful patron of the Franciscan Order. That may in part have reflected her feelings about the kindness that the Franciscans of Winchester had shown to her father in dire adversity. By contrast, she failed to exhibit warmth for the Dominicans – members of whose Order had apparently helped to ensnare him.

It seems likely that there was one person to whom Joan became close in later years, and who remained for decades a firm friend, who must have had a wealth of information that she could impart to Joan about her father and about events in Edward II's later years and Edward III's minority. That was her aunt, Blanche of Lancaster, Lady Wake, whose forceful husband had so often been associated with the earl of Kent in the changeable and lethal politics of that period. It would have been hard for Lady Wake or any other well-informed confidante of Joan to have realistically categorised her father as a paragon of contemporary secular virtues, despite the parliament's encomium on his virtuous qualities.

Is it entirely fanciful to surmise that, partly as a consequence of her father's wavering image, Joan from her early years was drawn to impressive, decisive men, of striking military bearing and attainment, and high chivalrous repute? His resounding rehabilitation from treason meant that she could hold her head high, but she may have concluded at a tender age that serpentine worldly wisdom was in practical terms preferable to 'innocence'. Perhaps she inherited her steely qualities, especially in adversity, from her mother.

However, there may have been a family myth, to which Joan subscribed, which enshrined Edmund's supposed virtues of goodness, loyalty and innocence. The facts that Joan was a steadfast patron of the Franciscan Order, and that her younger brother Earl John was buried in the Order's Winchester house (which had given a resting-place to their father's remains), strongly suggest the existence of family reverence for Edmund's memory. Moreover, a sense that he had died in a righteous cause may have been enhanced by the development of a cult of martyrdom centring on Edward II's tomb in Gloucester Abbey. This was a cult to which Richard II was to subscribe, hoping to secure Edward's canonisation.

This is one background therefore which may have helped to determine the selection of one of the three saints depicted in the altarpiece now known as The Wilton Diptych (see Plate VI), presumably commissioned for Richard about ten years after his mother Joan's death. The saint was St Edmund, the Anglo-Saxon king martyred by the Danes whose shrine in his imposing Suffolk abbey Richard had visited in 1383. The saint's figure in the painting surely recalled the fate of Richard's maternal grandfather. The king's promotion of Edward II's cult had indirectly honoured Edmund. If the king had succeeded in getting his ancestor canonised, what would that have done for Earl Edmund's reputation as his would-be saviour? It is not clear as to what first inspired Richard's devotion to Edward. One wonders whether Joan encouraged it when he was a boy in order to enhance the somewhat indifferent reputation of her father. His memory could not compete in chivalry with the stellar reputations of any of her three husbands, especially that of Richard's father, but in the higher sphere of devoutness he had a claim which might yet shine more brightly.

The surprising thing about the young Joan, as we shall see, is the marriage which she made secretly, of her own volition. For in doing so, she knew she was grossly disobeying both her mother and the king. We can only speculate that her family tragedies had darkened her childhood, and that, as a vivacious young teenager, she ardently wished to escape the past in the arms of Thomas Holand, a kindred spirit in family suffering.

·: 3 :·

Bigamy

JOAN'S PROSPECTS in her early teens were bright. She was a close kinswoman of the king. There coursed through her veins the blood of the Emperor Charlemagne and of St Louis (Louis IX of France), as well as that of William the Conqueror. She was hailed as exceptionally beautiful. She was her brother John's prospective heir. It was, however, to be anticipated that, if he survived into adulthood and fathered an heir, she would not bring the great prize of the earldom of Kent to a suitor. Nevertheless, she would still receive a dowry commensurate with her high birth. Since John was under age, his wardship was in the king's gift, and it was therefore the king's right either to arrange her marriage, or to bestow the right to arrange it on whomever he wished.

However, Joan's first marriage did not by any means conform to the king's or her kinsfolk's likely plans. When she was in her early teens, or even younger, she married a certain Sir Thomas Holand, in about 1339 or 1340 according to later testimony. Then probably in his early to mid twenties (born c. 1315), he was a promising young man. We can infer from his subsequent career that he had shown exceptional youthful fighting skills. In 1338 Thomas had been appointed as a knight of the king's household. How had he gained a knighthood? Possibly he had given good service in the king's wars in Scotland, perhaps serving there under his elder brother Sir Robert.[1]

According to the findings of a later ecclesiastical tribunal, which were to be universally accepted, Thomas and Joan were married privately, before witnesses, but without the calling of banns or a public ceremony of blessing. In such cases, the marriage was perfectly valid in ecclesiastical law. Moreover, the tribunal accepted too that the couple had consummated their union. This marriage was a secret one, contracted without the knowledge of Joan's family or the king or queen.

It remained secret.[2] From the prevailing point of view in society, this manner of marriage showed Joan to be a disobedient and undutiful girl, whose headstrong and devious behaviour marked her out as being prey to the weaknesses considered as natural to her sex. On the other hand, it is possible that some giddy contemporaries, whose heads were turned by romances, would have seen her as an exemplar of *amour courtois* – and that is how this passionate young teenager may have seen herself.

Moreover, to compound her undutiful conduct, Joan had chosen a bridegroom whom her kinsfolk would have denigrated as of inferior status and of bad blood – besides being landless and lacking in assured prospects. Thomas was merely one of the younger sons of Sir Robert Holand of Upholland in Lancashire (1270–1328), of knightly ancestry. Thomas's mother Maud was, indeed, of old baronial stock: she was the daughter of Alan Lord Zouche of Ashby (Leicestershire) whose death in 1314 left Maud and her two sisters as coheirs of his extensive properties.[3]

Sir Robert earned himself a lasting reputation for villainy. He had blighted the family honour during the troubles of Edward II's reign. His name was to live on in infamy as the betrayer of a saint. Holand had been one of Thomas earl of Lancaster's most favoured retainers. In 1322 he had been expected to reinforce the earl's army, in rebellion against Edward II, with a contingent of 500 men. He failed to join the earl, round whom the net of the king's forces fatally converged at Boroughbridge. His treachery, however, did not save him from having his estates confiscated by the Crown, nor from arrest and imprisonment in Dover Castle. The episode was related in the chronicle known as *The Brut*, continuations of whose accounts of the national history were to be the most popular writings on the subjects in later medieval England. *The Brut* has the betrayed earl exclaiming: 'He [Holand] hath full evil yielded to my goodness, and the worship that I to him have done, and through my kindness have him advanced, and made him high from low, and he maketh me go from high to low; but yet shall he die a cruel death.' This was an accurate appraisal of the earl's lavish treatment of him, and its outcome.[4]

The supposed prophecy (token of the earl's imminent 'martyrdom') was fulfilled. At first, after Edward III's accession in 1327, things went well for Sir Robert Holand. His lands were restored to him, despite the objections made by Earl Thomas's brother, Henry earl of Lancaster. Yet, not long afterwards, Sir Robert shared the fate of Joan's father: he was beheaded, possibly at Earl Henry's instigation, or by allies and supporters of the House of Lancaster. Earl Thomas's contrasting reputation as a saint burgeoned soon after his death. That must have been galling for the Holands. Henry Knighton (d. c. 1396), canon of Leicester Abbey (a house in Lancastrian patronage), writing his chronicle later in the century, described Sir Robert as 'hateful to all for having deceived his lord, who had loved him exceedingly and raised him from nothing to be a great man'.[5]

It may betoken mixed feelings on Thomas Holand's part about his father that, when he attained baronial rank, after his marriage to Joan was publicly recognised, he appears to have ceased using a version of his father's coat of arms (azure, florette and a lyon rampant and gardant argent). He had used this blazon, undifferenced, on a seal, between 1341 and 1343. But a seal he used in 1354 simply had a blank shield on it, and so did one he used in 1357, together with a shield of the Wake arms (reflecting Joan's position as heir prospective of the Wakes). A roll of arms also shows the shield he adopted as black. Why, one wonders, did he switch to this mournful blazon? Did it betoken shame at his father's actions? His son and heir Thomas used the three lions, derived from the coat of arms of the royal house, and so did his younger son John.[6]

The dire fate and evil repute of Sir Robert surely weighed heavily on his widow Maud, his son and heir Robert, and the latter's siblings, Thomas, Alan, Otes, Isabella, Margaret and Maud. The shared legacy of an unfortunate past perhaps helped to induce an evident family solidarity. Thomas's mother and Robert both generously supported Thomas's ambitions by granting him a life interest in manors. Both Alan and Otes, like Thomas, pursued military careers. Alan may have died young: he disappears from the record. Thomas and Otes were to have a lifelong association. In the 1350s Thomas was to use Otes – like himself, an outstanding soldier – as his deputy in military commands, and helped him to receive a landed income.[7]

Since Joan of Kent's uncle Lord Wake (her mother Margaret's brother) was married to Thomas of Lancaster's niece Blanche, her mother had a good family reason for disliking Joan's secret bridegroom.

Edward III, however (as the advancement of Thomas Holand illustrates), was prepared to patronise the sons of those who had been disfavoured by his father. The wars which he was pursuing in Scotland and France in the 1330s and 1340s made him eager to engage the services of young men of address and ability, like the Holand brothers, however murky in his eyes their families' conduct may have once been.

In 1337 Philip VI of France declared that Edward was a contumacious vassal, and that his duchy of Gascony was consequently forfeit. Edward's initial strategy in the Hundred Years War was only in part to defend his distant duchy against French occupation. He also threatened the more accessible heartlands of the French monarchy, basing his threats on alliances with principalities to the north-east of France, which were mostly in the neighbouring parts of the Holy Roman Empire. Thomas Holand was slated in 1337 to serve on an expedition to reinforce Gascony. He was also appointed to go to the Low Countries, to Valenciennes, on a diplomatic mission from the king to his brother-in-law the count of Hainault. In 1338–39 Edward conducted diplomatic and military operations against the French Crown whilst staying in the lands of his ally the duke of Brabant. Thomas Holand was in the royal retinue. In September 1339 the allies invaded Philip VI of France's lands, conducting a brief but fruitless campaign of destruction.[8]

Edward, back in England after these frustrations, now favoured an alliance with the ruling clique in Bruges (England's leading trading partners), who were in revolt against the authority of their ruler, Philip VI's loyal vassal the count of Flanders. Edward revived his claim to the succession to the French Crown and began in 1340 to style himself as king of France, so strengthening his stance, and giving his adherents a cloak of legitimacy. Holand was in the army which he assembled at Ipswich (Suffolk) to invade Flanders.[9] Sailing to the port of Sluis, the English encountered, at anchor there, the navy which Philip was assembling for the invasion of England. The English won an overwhelming victory.

Edward, with his Flemish allies, went on to invest Philip VI's city of Tournai. Neighbouring villages were pitilessly burnt. However, Edward failed either to capture the city or bring the cautious Philip to battle. A stalemate had been reached: in September 1340 an Anglo-French truce was concluded, and Edward, his finances exhausted, returned to England. For Holand, the campaigning of 1337–40 provided varied, invaluable military experience. We may infer, from the subsequent regard as a soldier in which he was held, that he acquitted himself well.

For much of this period, Edward's queen, Philippa of Hainault, stayed in the Low Countries, where she was very much at home. She had sailed to Brabant in 1338, and gave birth in Antwerp to her second son Lionel, later duke of Clarence. In 1340 she gave birth in Ghent to another son, John, who was to be known as 'John of Gaunt'. It is not clear whether the queen took Joan with her on her visits to the Low Countries, though the likelihood is, if Joan was attached to her household, that she did so. Experience of francophone princely courts there would have aided an aristocratic girl's polite education, and have facilitated her being trailed as a possible bride for some of the ruling families. However, it does seem feasible that, because of the upheavals in the queen's household consequent on its unusual patterns of itineracy in these years, and her pregnancies in quick succession, if Joan was there, the queen and her ladies would have been less vigilant in their supervision of the 'Fair Maid'. In such circumstances, Thomas would have had particular opportunities to woo and marry her.

After his marriage, Thomas, in the cold light of realities, was surely a very worried man. He had flouted convention by marrying a lady of the blood royal without the permission and the blessing of her family. His action was in contempt of his sovereign's rights. His one hope of keeping royal favour, and claiming his bride, when the truth came out, was the hazardous one of gaining a great military reputation, and so making himself indispensable to the king in warfare. He absorbed himself in campaigning. Opportunities for him even to see or give a greeting to his bride must have been occasional and fleeting. There was no question of them setting up house together, or even probably of being alone together.

In addition to his strenuous engagement on expeditions in the king's wars in France, Thomas fitted in participation in crusading. He went to Prussia, probably taking advantage of the brief Anglo-French truce in the summer of 1340. According to his testimony, he went there soon after his marriage. The principal bases of the crusading Order of Teutonic Knights were there, having been transferred from the

Middle East in the thirteenth century, when Muslim advances swept westerners from the remaining enclaves they ruled in the Holy Land. In Prussia, the Teutonic Knights waged frontier warfare, gruelling and savage, against the pagan Lithuanians. In addition, the Knights now faced a new, formidable threat originating in the Asian steppes – the invasion of a horde of Tartar nomads.[10]

What were Thomas's likely motives for choosing to campaign on crusade? It was an expensive as well as an extremely hazardous undertaking, and unlikely, in Prussia, to bring material rewards which soldiers craved – none more so than Thomas. A crucial motive for crusading was to gain plenary remission for one's sins: among these was marriage without the Church's blessing, a venial sin, which might nevertheless be punished by excommunication. Those who courted martyrdom by going on crusade acquired an exalted reputation by fulfilling their vow. That might have aided Thomas's position when his marriage became generally known. In particular, crusading with the Teutonic Knights, involving such harsh terrain and ferocious opponents, was highly regarded in England, as is shown in Geoffrey Chaucer's later sketch of his ideal knight, who had been honoured in Prussia on his crusade, as recounted in the Prologue to *The Canterbury Tales*. However, Thomas had also a less worthy motive than many crusaders – the need to make himself scarce, in case Joan, under pressure or through impulsiveness, revealed their secret, probably thus blighting his career, and bringing the accusation on his head that he was treacherous like his father.

Joan kept her counsel, though the crisis over her future that she and her secret husband must have anticipated came to a head presumably whilst he was in Prussia: she was confronted with a new prospective bridegroom. She felt compelled to acquiesce in a bigamous marriage to conform to the wishes of her mother and kinsfolk. In February 1341 William Montague, first earl of Salisbury, granted a joint life interest in his manor of Mold (Flintshire) to his son and heir William, aged thirteen, and to Joan. This was clearly part of a marriage settlement. In 1343, John Grandisson, bishop of Exeter, wrote to a correspondent that his nephew (William) had married the niece of Thomas Wake, that is, Joan.[11]

In terms of lineage, she was a splendid catch for the ambitious

Montague family, bringing them into the circle of royal kin. It was not a wildly exalted match for Joan: above all, it was a reflection of the high royal favour in which the earl basked. He and his wife Catherine (Grandisson) came of worthy families of gentlefolk of only local importance. In 1321, still under age, he had succeeded to part of his inheritance which then consisted mainly of manors in Somerset, taking full possession in 1323. He then became a confidant of Edward III in the fraught early years of his reign, and in June 1330 Montague stood as godfather to Edward's firstborn Edward – the future Prince of Wales. Soon afterwards as we have seen, he masterminded the coup which overthrew the rule of the queen mother and her lover Roger Mortimer, and which enabled the king to establish his personal authority.[12]

Edward III never lost his sense of gratitude to Montague, who, for the rest of his life, continued to give him sterling service. After the coup, Montague was well rewarded with royal grants of estates, including forfeited Mortimer ones. He worthily fulfilled leading military and diplomatic roles in the years 1333–35 in the renewed Scottish wars, in which Edward now supported the claim of Edward Balliol as king of Scots against that of Robert I's son David II. Besides receiving notable land grants on both sides of the Border, Montague had the singular favours of a grant of the Isle of Man with regal powers from Edward III, and the right to display the king's own crest of the eagle. Edward had no more qualms than his father about offending old nobility by elevating favourites to its higher ranks. In 1337 he created Montague earl of Salisbury. A scheme to ally the Montagues by marriage to the inner circle of royal kinsfolk had already been considered. In 1331 Joan's future 'husband', William Montague (then aged three), was contracted to marry Alice, daughter of the king's and Joan's uncle Thomas of Brotherton, earl of Norfolk. This fell through – as, indeed, did many contracts of marriage made for infants. Edward and Salisbury cast about for another suitable bride for young William. Since in 1341 Joan's brother John, heir to the earldom of Kent was still under the age to inherit, and in royal wardship, the king is likely to have proposed or promoted her marriage. If he or Queen Philippa had had the remotest idea that Joan was already married, it is inconceivable that they would have treated their old friend the earl so shabbily as not to inform him that there might be the problem of a precontract of marriage. In recent years, Salisbury had been zealous in the king's service on the continent. In 1339 he had remained there, when the king returned to England, as a hostage for his debts, and in 1340 he had the misfortune to be captured by the French in a skirmish outside Lille.[13]

Several years later, Joan's mother, Countess Margaret, asserted her belief that Joan had not married Holand. If, before her marriage to William, Joan had revealed to anyone that she was already a wife, she could have been intimidated by her family into keeping quiet about it. It seems likely that she decided to remain silent because she believed she had been widowed. Perhaps Thomas was seriously injured on active service abroad, and rumour had it that he was dead or dying at the time when young William Montague's suit was being pressed on Joan. At the siege of Caen in 1346, French knights recognised Thomas from meeting him on campaign in Prussia and Spain, since he had only one eye. This may have been a birth defect, but it is unlikely in that case that when a youth he would have been earmarked for military training rather than for a career in the Church. It is more likely that his disability dated from his recent campaigning.[14]

Thomas returned from Prussia between the summer of 1341 and spring 1342, and only then, according to his later petition to the pope, did he discover that Joan was remarried (presumably, quite recently). He asserted to the pope that Montague refused to consider his claim on Joan, and was aided and abetted by her mother.[15] Considering the high favour in which the earl of Salisbury stood with the king, Thomas must have concluded that it would be pointless, and, perhaps, disastrous for his career prospects and his finances, to launch an appeal to ecclesiastical authority in order to reclaim his wife. Though he had doubtless enhanced his reputation for prowess, he remained a landless younger son, whose income and advancement depended on patronage, especially the Crown's. Rather, his marriage strategy was to seize on the new opportunities which arose in the 1340s to serve the king in France. Edward, hitherto stalemated there, was able to strike anew at Philip VI's authority in another part of his realm. After the death of John III, duke of Brittany in April 1341, the succession to the duchy was disputed between Jeanne de Penthièvre, who was married to Philip's nephew Charles of Blois, and the rival John de Montfort. The latter, anticipating that Philip, as overlord of the duchy, would recognise his nephew's claim to it, attempted to seize control. He soon enlisted Edward III's aid in securing the duchy, in return for his acceptance of Edward's title as king of France and his suzerainty over the duchy. Not surprisingly, Charles of Blois' claim was recognised and supported by Philip. In 1342 Edward dispatched expeditions to Brittany in aid of Montfort, leading the biggest one there himself in the autumn. Thomas Holand and his brothers Sir Alan and Sir Otes all took part in the Breton campaign. They led insignificant companies: Thomas and Alan had a joint company with three squires, and Otes had his own company with two squires. Thomas was one of the captains whom Edward left to besiege Nantes after his return to England, and he took part in the assault on Vannes. This was to be the start of Thomas's distinguished involvement in the civil war in Brittany, where for several decades English garrisons were to uphold the Montfort cause against Blois partisans.[16]

General truces ensued in 1344. These possibly enabled Thomas to rekindle his passion for crusading. As we have seen, at some point he certainly went on crusade to Granada, which was the last remaining Muslim kingdom in Spain. The most powerful kingdom in the Peninsula, Castile, which had frequently been at war with the Moors of Granada, had St James as its patron and protector against them. As a crusader in Granada, Thomas may have been in part inspired by devotion to a cult dear to his mother's family, as well as Joan's. In 1308 his maternal grandfather, Alan Lord Zouche, had been intending to go on pilgrimage to the saint's shrine at Santiago de Compostela, and his mother Maud was intending to go there in 1336. Thomas's elder brother Sir Robert was to be buried in the church dedicated to St James (and St John) at Brackley (Northamptonshire).[17]

In 1342–43 Alfonso XI of Castile was besieging the port of Algeçiras in Granada. As soon as the Breton campaign ended, Henry of Grosmont earl of Derby (son and heir of Henry earl of Leicester and Lancaster), together with the earl of Salisbury, set out to join the siege of Algeçiras, where their contingents distinguished themselves in Spanish eyes. Their mission was undertaken very much in Edward III's interest. He was the grandson of Eleanor of Castile, Edward I's first queen, and he hoped to revive the old Anglo-Castilian alliance. Derby and Salisbury were empowered to negotiate a marriage between Joan, one of the king's daughters, and Alfonso's son and heir.[18] This was the major English crusading expedition to Spain in the period – it is likely that Thomas served on it. It would have been piquant if he served under Salisbury's command. Derby was an up-and-coming young commander, close friend as well as cousin of the king, and someone whose goodwill (especially in view of their families' past hostility) would have been important for Thomas to gain.

Fortune was to smile in the next few years on Thomas's ambition to recover his right to Joan as his wife. In January 1344 the earl of Salisbury died unexpectedly, as a result of an accident in a tournament. That may not have seemed at first to benefit Thomas's ambition, since the earl's son William, being still under age, came into royal wardship. It may have been anticipated that Edward would be strenuous in defence of his late friend's family interest. But in the long run, as we shall see, Salisbury's death worked to Thomas's advantage. Meanwhile, the expiry of the Anglo-French truce in 1345 opened up new opportunities for Thomas to win fame and fortune in war, which must have seemed to him the only likely chance he had of advancing his cause, a means especially hazardous for a man who was visually impaired.

Edward III was determined to make a major military effort against Philip VI. This time he tried his luck by invading a different province of France – Normandy, rich and untouched by recent warfare. He relied especially on a Norman landowner banished by Philip – Geoffrey de Harcourt. In July 1346 the English army landed at Saint-Vaast-la-Hougue, in the Cotentin Peninsula, where Harcourt had estates. Joan's supposed spouse William Montague was one of the young men who participated: he was now among those knighted.[19] Joan's true husband was with the army, too, and so were two of his brothers. Sir Thomas had in his company four esquires, five men-at-arms and four mounted archers. Sir Otes also served with three esquires. The eldest brother, Sir Robert, had contracted to serve in Thomas Beauchamp, earl of Warwick's retinue.[20]

The English, plundering as they went, did not face any strong opposition until they reached Caen. A defence force drew up outside its walls, but lost its cohesion and retreated in disorder, hotly pursued by the English. They forced their way into the town, and commenced pillaging and slaughtering. Raoul de Brienne, count of Eu and constable of France, and Jean de Melun, count of Tancarville, marshal of France, took refuge with some knights in a gatehouse of the town walls, overlooking the River Orne: they were fortunate to be allowed to surrender. In a letter written in the heat of victory, Bartholomew Lord Burghersh described to John Stratford, archbishop of Canterbury the crucial episode in the capture of Caen. He said that the constable of France surrendered to Sir Thomas Holand with many knights and esquires and that Tancarville was captured by one of the Prince of Wales's knights, and was the Prince's prisoner. The capture of the constable made Holand's name, and brought him lasting chivalrous fame. His achievement, merely mentioned by the chronicler Jean le Bel, canon of Liège, was expanded by Jean Froissart in his chronicle into one of his stirring set pieces. He vividly – and perhaps fancifully – described what turned out to be a key episode in the fortunes of Thomas and Joan:

> Looking out from the gate tower ... and seeing the truly horrible carnage which was taking place in the street, the Constable and the Count began to fear that they themselves might be drawn into it and fall into the hands of the archers who did not know who they were. While they were watching the massacre in dismay, they caught sight of a valiant English knight with one eye, called Sir Thomas Holand, and five or six other knights with him. They recognised him because they had campaigned together in Granada and Prussia and on other expeditions, in the way in which knights do meet each other. They were much relieved when they saw him and called out to him as he passed: 'Sir Thomas, come and speak to us.' On hearing his own name the knight stopped dead and asked: 'Who are you, sirs, who seem to know me?' They gave their name, saying, 'We are so-and-so. Come to us in the gate tower and make us your prisoners.' When he heard this Sir Thomas was delighted, not only because he could save their lives but also because their capture meant an excellent day's work and a fine haul of prisoners, enough to bring in a thousand gold *moutons*. So he brought the whole of his troop to the spot as quickly as possible and went up with

sixteen men-at-arms into the gate tower, where he found the lords who had called him and at least twenty-five knights with them, all looking very uneasy at the slaughter they could see in the town. They surrendered immediately and pledged themselves to be Sir Thomas's prisoners. Leaving sufficient men to guard them, the knight rode through the streets. He was able to prevent many cruel and horrible acts which would otherwise have been committed, thus giving proof of his kind and noble heart. Several gallant English knights who were with him also prevented a number of evil deeds and rescued many a pretty townswoman and many a nun from rape.[21]

This account gives a sympathetic view of Sir Thomas as a quick-witted and efficient officer, and a merciful man. In the turmoil of battle, valuable prisoners were sometimes seized serially, leading to bitter and prolonged disputes as to who had captured them. Yet he is not depicted as sticking like glue to his haul, as stupendous a one as the cargo of a Spanish galleon was to Elizabethan sea captains. Instead, he showed complete confidence in the ability of his small retinue of soldiers to safeguard his prisoner, and going on into the town in order to help to restore order – and presumably to participate in quelling the desultory resistance. In this prioritising, he showed an exemplary sense of duty, one not always displayed by predatory and nervous captors. He and his companions must have been the envy of the army. This young veteran's years of service in the field had paid off, not least due to the fact that he could rely on a small, devoted group who had melded together in years of combat. Le Bel merely stated that 'the knight who had only one eye' had with him five or six bachelors who had served together in Prussia, Granada and elsewhere.[22]

Froissart's account clearly did not derive its detail and eulogizing of Holand from le Bel's terse notice. How did he get it? Perhaps from Burghersh or his son (another Bartholomew) – both of them friends of the king and the Black Prince, and of Thomas Holand and Joan. Joan herself, whom he came to know in the 1360s, might have given him this version to record – the new Holand family legend, eclipsing the old black one, and an episode which ultimately facilitated their marriage. For the capture of a 'capital' enemy of the king was the key to a fortune for the principal captor. Froissart says that the king bought the ransom of the two counts from Thomas and his companions for twenty thousand nobles in cash. In fact, Edward, by letters patent, dated June 1347 (when he was besieging Calais), granted Sir Thomas 80,000 florins for delivering the count of Eu to him, and for good service. Arrangements were made for the grant to be paid in instalments over several years.[23] Probably, Thomas and his companions gave up their prisoners in accordance with the usual terms of captains' contracts with the Crown for service on campaign. It was standard practice for the captains of retinues to stipulate in their contracts that they would hand over to the king any eminent prisoner who had surrendered to them or their soldiers. One or more of Thomas's soldiers may have received compensation from him for their part in the capture, in accordance with prior private agreements between the two parties to split the gains of war. Such agreements were sometimes also made between two gentlemen who were personally close in the pursuit of arms, bound together as 'brothers-in-arms'. One wonders whether Thomas was bound in this way to his brother Otes – or perhaps to a certain Sir Richard de la Marche, with whom he now engaged in a hazardous escapade which some contemporaries may have considered madcap. Thomas, frustrated by his still unresolved marital status, behaved like a driven man.

After the capture of Caen, the king contemplated advancing on the capital of Normandy, Rouen. Sir Thomas and Sir Richard de la Marche slipped away from the army on their own, fully armed, and made their way to the banks of the Seine opposite Rouen. In front of the 'Port-Romput' they shouted, 'St George for Edward'. They slew two men and harried others, and successfully beat off pursuit, returning unscathed to camp. The chronicler from Valenciennes who recounted the adventure regarded it as a daring and brave enterprise (*oultrageuse, come preux et hardi*). But Edward was frosty: he roundly condemned their behaviour.[24] It was, indeed, the kind of adventure that he would have revelled in accomplishing himself when younger, but he was now likely to have been reluctant to lose as valuable a servant as Thomas on such a juvenile quest.

However, the pair may have reconnoitred usefully for him, testing the defences of Rouen. In fact, the well-fortified city had been occupied and garrisoned by Philip: Edward decided against undertaking a siege, and in favour of advancing further up the Seine, instead. Moreover, he reckoned that Thomas was not only a daring soldier, but, potentially, a competent divisional commander, who in future would be able to afford to finance a large retinue. Despite Thomas's relatively low status and small military company, Edward apparently gave him joint command of the rearguard for the advance through Normandy into the Île-de-France.[25]

Thomas was in the thick of skirmishing as the army progressed. At Poissy, not far off from Paris, Edward managed to get the army across the Seine: Sir Thomas was wounded in the assault on the castle there, as was Sir Richard Talbot. This was Lord Talbot, a leading landowner in Herefordshire, adjacent to the Welsh Marches; perhaps he was identical with the elusive Richard de la Marche.[26] Edward was now retreating towards the Channel ports. He spent a night at Poix, an important junction on the road going north from Beauvais, leading to the Somme. It was agreed that the inhabitants of Poix should pay a ransom, and some soldiers were left behind to collect it. But, once the army had moved on, they refused to pay anything. The soldiers there sent messengers who caught up with the rearguard. Its commanders, Sir Reginald Cobham and Thomas, retraced their steps to Poix, where they found their fellow soldiers fighting the inhabitants. The English then overwhelmed them, burnt the castle and the town, and killed most of the inhabitants.[27]

Once the English army had managed, with difficulty, to cross the Somme, Philip at last outmanœuvred Edward, and showed a new confidence in committing his army to battle with the inferior English force. When the battle lines were drawn up at Crécy, Edward switched Sir Thomas to serve in the most honourable place, the vanguard, nominally commanded by the Black Prince, aged sixteen. The earls of Warwick and Oxford were in the van too, and so were knights who were to earn great military fame – Lord Burghersh's son and heir Sir Bartholomew, and John Chandos. Thomas's elder brother Sir Robert may have fought in Warwick's retinue. Famously, the Prince's division had hard fighting on its hands. In likely recognition of his detailed knowledge of the French nobility, Thomas was one of those commanded to accompany the heralds and assist in naming the dead.[28]

After the great English victory, Edward headed for the Channel coast and besieged Calais (1346–47). Thomas and Otes took part in the siege. Since Philip failed to come to the relief of the port, Edward punctiliously secured an orderly surrender. It was a token that Edward valued Thomas's diplomatic as well as military gifts that he was one of a delegation of four, headed by the earl of Northampton and including two other well-known knights, who were sent to parley with the garrison commander.[29] Edward occupied the town, and transformed it into a bastion of the Crown's strategic and economic strength, turning it into an English town, which even briefly elected members of parliament in Tudor times, before being surrendered to the French in 1558.

Nobles typically used their profits of war to purchase estates, to improve and furnish their residences, and to extend their influence through patronage in their shires. Sometimes a captor had to wait years for his prisoner to pay off the contracted ransom, but Edward's purchase from Thomas of the count of Eu's gave him a more assured prospect of instalments. His priority was his marriage. He could now well afford to institute legal process to claim Joan as his wife. His love for her may have been his principal motive, but he certainly had a pressing, more practical one. He could not seek a bride and attempt to set up his own dynastic line until the issue of whether or not he was married was definitively settled. It was, indeed, on the face of it, a risky strategy to challenge the marital status of the heir to an earldom, who had been publicly joined in marriage to a close kinswoman of the king. However, Thomas presumably reckoned that he had made himself so useful to Edward on his great campaign, and had so notably established his chivalrous fame, that he could embark on such an outrageous challenge without loss of royal favour, and without the king trying to interfere in the Montagues' favour in the lawsuit. He seems to have been right. After he started proceedings, he was appointed as one of the founder members of Edward's new, exclusive chivalrous chapter of knights, the Order of the Garter, instituted at Windsor Castle in April 1348. Sir Otes Holand had also so distinguished himself in the king's eyes that he was appointed too – and so was Sir William Montague.[30]

Perhaps Thomas was supported in his resolve to reclaim his bride by his family's elderly and distinguished patron, John de Warenne, earl of Surrey. He had vast estates, in Yorkshire, Sussex and the Marches of Wales. He had undertaken military service in Edward II's reign in Scotland as well as Gascony, and had played canny roles in the king's struggles with his opponents. Edward III, whom he also served in war in Scotland, appointed him guardian of the realm (together with the infant Prince Edward) for the duration of his absence abroad in 1338. He was, indeed, a personal friend of Edward III and his family, as is witnessed by the valuable gifts he bequeathed to the king, Queen Philippa, and their sons the Prince and Edmund of Langley, in his will of 1347.[31]

It was as a consequence of Warenne's marital problem that he came into a close relationship with the Holand family. He had been married since as far back as Edward I's reign, in 1306, to that king's granddaughter Joan of Bar. The marriage was a failure, and there were no surviving offspring. Warenne took a mistress, Maud de Nerford, by whom he had a son. Apparently desperate for a legitimised son and heir, in the 1340s he bombarded the pope with petitions for the annulment of his marriage, on a variety of grounds, including the assertion that, before his marriage, he had had carnal knowledge of his wife's aunt Mary, a daughter of Edward I. Pope Clement VI's response was to insist that he was legally married, and to order that he treat his wife with marital affection. Edward III and his family seem to have been unsympathetic: Queen Philippa had joined with the queen of France in 1344 in petitioning the pope against his attempt to gain a divorce.[32]

However, the lady that Warenne was treating with affection in 1347 was Sir Thomas Holand's sister Isabella, to whom he referred in his will as 'ma compaigne'. In it he showered her with gifts – gold rings, including the one with the good ruby, chapel furnishings, plate, half his farm stock and, after his debts had been paid, the residue of his goods.

Warenne also remembered and relied on other members of the Holand family. The siblings' mother Maud was bequeathed four cattle, and Sir Robert and Sir Otes were to receive harness and armour worn by Warenne's warhorse. Among his executors were Sir Thomas Holand and his mother. Why did the Holands condone Isabella's shame? The most obvious explanation is that they felt the need of a leading magnate, well liked by the king, as patron. Maybe they hoped that

Warenne would procure an annulment of his marriage, or that his wife would die (she lived till 1361) – enabling Warenne to marry Isabella, and, hopefully, father legitimate children.

Considering the closeness between Sir Thomas and Warenne, it may have been with the latter's encouragement, and at his prompting, that Sir Thomas tried to reclaim his bride. It was doubtless to Sir Thomas's chagrin that Warenne died in 1347, before he succeeded. The course of the legal battle over Joan's marital status has been thoroughly analysed by K. P. Wentersdorf.[33] In 1347 Thomas petitioned the papal court at Avignon, alleging that he and Joan had been lawfully married, and had consummated their marriage. Subsequently, the petition alleged, Joan, 'not daring to contradict the wishes of her relatives and friends', submitted to marriage to Montague. Pope Clement VI delegated his kinsman Cardinal Adhémar Robert to try the case, empowering him to summon for examination Montague, Joan, her mother and other material witnesses. The cardinal summoned Montague, Joan and Thomas. Montague was defiant. He did not appear. Nor, presumably, did Joan, since Thomas, in a second petition to the pope, probably made early in 1348, alleged that Montague was holding Joan in solitary confinement under strong guard. In view of Sir Thomas's prowess, his opponents may have feared that he would attempt to abduct her. The Montagues had acquired three castles which may have been fit for the purpose. In Dorset there was the old-fashioned castle at Christchurch, and the more impressive modern one, with its great tower, at Sherborne. In the far north there was the formidable fortress of Wark-upon-Tweed (Northumberland), on the remote and disturbed border with Scotland – despite its strength, not the most secure place for imprisonment.

A papal brief, dated 5 May 1348, addressed to the archbishop of Canterbury (John Stratford) and the bishop of London (Ralph Stratford), asserted that the cardinal's tribunal had been halted because Joan had not appeared before it, nor had any attorney acting on her behalf. The brief ordered them to ensure that she could appoint an attorney. This was done, but the tribunal was unable to reach a decision because her attorney did not submit anything on her behalf. William Montague continued to maintain the façade of his marriage. A royal licence dated 15 October was based on a petition whose terms suggested that she was a free woman and his legitimate wife: jointly with her husband she granted a rent from a property in Somerset.[34]

Pope Clement was dissatisfied at the failure of the tribunal to resolve the issue of the legitimacy of either of Joan's marriages. He appointed Cardinal Pectin de Montesquieu, archbishop of Albi, to make further enquiry. The latter demanded that a new attorney be appointed for Joan. This was done: someone was found who was prepared to act faithfully on her behalf. He apparently submitted a document in which she asserted that her marriage to Thomas Holand was valid, and that she had been coerced into the union with Montague. However, his family continued to try to obstruct proceedings: Montague's attorney was absent when they were held. The cardinal called the family's bluff: he announced that the case was closed, and set a date when he would pronounce his decision. His verdict was to be that the contract between Thomas and Joan was valid. He ordered that Joan be restored to her rightful husband forthwith. Their union, he decreed, was to be solemnised publicly. Her *de facto* marriage to William was declared null and void. A bull (dated 13 November 1349) addressed to the papal legate in England, to Bishop Stratford of London and the bishop of Norwich (William Bateman) enjoined them to enforce the tribunal's findings.[35]

The ways in which Joan's evidence was obstructed, even to the extent of imprisonment, show that the Montague party feared that she would give it convincingly against them. Her tenacity is a tribute to her mental strength, and to her covert devotion and steadfastness to Thomas, maintained for the best part of a decade. What is surprising is the, at least ultimate, failure of Edward III to use his influence to sway papal proceedings which might adversely affect one of his leading wards. Despite his love for William's father, he seems to have shown his young son no particular material favours. Though magnates' heirs were sometimes granted their inheritances before they attained their majority, as was the case with John earl of Kent, William Montague had to wait for his minority to run full-term (until July 1349) – before he was granted possession of his inheritance by the Crown.[36]

As William's guardian, Edward had had a duty to protect his ward's interests. Presumably, in pursuit of these, he was ultimately responsible for Joan's harsh treatment. Yet, if he received reports of her continued defiance, they would have raised concerns in his mind that, even if she could be silenced, a permanent question mark had been raised about the legitimacy of any future offspring she might have by William. The same point may have influenced the Montague family. Their resolution in defying papal pressure and coercing her may have consequently ebbed. We may wonder, too, about William's reactions. For an adolescent, it would surely have been disconcerting to hear that the fair maid he had married claimed not to have been a maid. The marriages of the higher nobility were not necessarily all about dynastic gain. Compatibility and affection were highly prized, too, as the unfortunate predicament of Warenne and his wife demonstrates. Its absence might negate the purposes of marriage. Perhaps Joan, smitten with her mature and battered warrior, did not show warmth to her young husband. That may have sapped his resolution. Illness and death may have deprived Montague of key supporters. In 1349 England was in the grip of the first, and most severe, plague pandemic. Montague's mother Catherine died in April, Joan's uncle Lord Wake in May, and the death of Joan's mother in September was attributed to pestilence.

Moreover, Montague may have given up his cause in despair, overawed by the feats of the valorous Sir Thomas. It is curious that a fifteenth-century chronicler, John Hardyng, wrote that William 'had wed [Joan] of maiden newe / And hir forsoke, after repudiate / Whom his styward sir Thomas Holand wed'.[37] It would be easy to dismiss this as a belated piece of evidence – but Hardyng mixed from his boyhood in aristocratic circles where the family histories of the Montagues and Holands may well have been recalled. In 1390, at the age of twelve, he was a member of the household of Sir Henry Percy ('Hotspur'), the eldest son of the first earl of Northumberland. It would, surely, have been in Sir Thomas's interests to seek office in William's household, so that he could keep more easily in contact with Joan. Henry Knighton, canon of Leicester Abbey, recording the Black Prince's marriage to Joan in 1361, said that she had been guilty of infidelity to the earl of Salisbury. This remark is most likely to have been just muddled, but could it have reflected a belief that Joan had cohabited on occasion with Sir Thomas during her Montague 'marriage'?[38]

Knighton's assertions suggest that the suit of 1347–49 and its dramatic outcome long cast a shadow over the reputations of Thomas and Joan. It may well be that, in that terrible year in which they were reunited, there were many in high places who looked askance on them. But we cannot be sure that William Montague was foremost among them. Seemingly a mild-tempered man, deeply imbued with his father's loyalty to the Plantagenets, he was to emerge as one of Edward III's finest commanders in the wars in France. Though much preoccupied with disputes over his inheritance, he pursued them peaceably. After his union with Joan was nullified, a new marriage was speedily arranged for him – a much less exalted one, to Elizabeth, daughter of a Somerset landowner, John Lord Mohun. There were surer hopes that his bride would be more reliable and malleable than the wayward Joan: she was aged only six. Their marriage ended only with William's death some forty-eight years later. In public affairs, over the years, William's path crossed on occasion with Joan's, but there is no hint that he ever did anything to embarrass her, or that mutual enmity was handed down to their respective children.[39]

Sir Thomas Holand's campaign to reclaim his wife is a testimony to his restraint as well as his tenacity. The king and the 'community of the realm' had been much preoccupied in recent decades with curbing violence in the shires, notably that perpetrated by gentlefolk against one another, often over property disputes. Attacks on manor houses and abductions of ladies occurred. Sir Thomas, with his knowledge of war and siege craft, and his likely closeness to old military comrades, would, one surmises, have been perfectly capable of attempting to rescue Joan from her predicament. That would have been a sure way of alienating king and nobility. In that terrible time, when he and his wife might easily succumb to plague, without ever being reunited, he behaved with propriety and prudence.

·: 4 :·

Married Bliss

FOR THE TEN OR SO YEARS of her publicly acknowledged marriage to Thomas, Joan, like most other medieval wives, left little mark in the surviving records. She no longer attracted the interest of curious and prurient chroniclers, and was doubtless relieved that her marital status ceased to be a hot topic for widespread gossip and innuendo. She became the dutiful wife. Their eldest child, Thomas, was born in 1350 or soon after – within a year or so of the couple being reunited in matrimony. There was one other son, John, and two daughters, Joan and Maud.[1]

It is not clear whether the couple lived on one of the manors in which Thomas had a life interest– Broughton (Buckinghamshire) or Yoxall (Staffordshire). Perhaps Joan was for a while unwelcome at court because of the scandal she had caused, and lived a retired life in the country. However, the Black Prince stood godfather to her firstborn son, and possibly to her second. In 1353 a gift from the Prince of two expensive silver basins to a son of Sir Thomas was recorded – perhaps a gift to the younger son, John.[2] The links which Thomas maintained and cultivated with leading nobles and with some of the Prince's companions may have been social in character, as well as concerned with business and war.

One bleak prospect for Joan's marriage may have been plain to her from the start: that her husband was likely to be abroad a good deal pursuing his military and administrative career. That, rather than adjusting to the bucolic pleasures of a country gentleman's life, may have accorded with his martial temperament, a restless campaigning mindset and talents for governing. However, Joan may have approved strongly of his choice to pursue a career in royal service overseas, for he needed to go on making hazardous farewells to her in order to enhance his honour and profit, and to maintain and embellish a lifestyle appropriate to her high birth. It does not seem probable that Joan accompanied him to France, considering the disturbed state of the provinces where he operated. Even after fortune smiled, and he gained control of a good deal of inherited property in her name, he presumably devoted much of its profits to financing his career. He hoped that the king might be more relenting in rewarding and elevating a high-achieving knight whose actions had surely caused grave offence. Somewhat tardily, in August 1352 Edward granted the couple an annuity of 100 marks, 'in aid of her sustenance'. It was to cease if her brother the earl of Kent died childless, and she thereby inherited the earldom from him.[3] It was to be quite a few years after this happened before the king raised Thomas to an earldom.

During their first years together as acknowledged man and wife, the married life of the Holands was eased (as the birth of their children bears witness) by the making of a series of Anglo-French truces and the concomitant peace negotiations – though Holand continued to have high responsibilities in command in France. As one of Edward's principal captains, he had to be prepared to lead a military retinue on new campaigns at short notice if the peace talks broke down and if truces were not renewed. Philip VI of France had died in 1350, and was succeeded by his son John II. The new king, in Édouard Perroy's judgement, was 'not an incapable man', but 'a mediocrity'.[4] He was courtly, chivalrous and pleasure-loving, but a poor military commander. His preference for negotiating with the English showed his recognition of the weakness of the Crown's position, but he lacked the boldness to make unpalatable concessions which would facilitate eventual recovery.

When Anglo-French negotiations broke down in 1355, the Black Prince, appointed lieutenant in Gascony, launched a devastating raid in France. He did so again the following year; this raid culminated in his hard-won victory at the battle of Poitiers, in which John II was captured. That ultimately led to the peace of 1360, but only after Edward's new invasion of France the previous year.

With the needs of warfare in mind, Edward habitually sought to encourage the martial spirits of young nobles. He had been concerned to boost the military experience of Holand's brother-in-law John, the young earl of Kent, of whom he fleetingly maintained high hopes. The king may have felt especially benevolent towards him because he had been unable to save his father from execution. Besides, John was apparently more amenable than his headstrong sister. The king wanted him to gain military experience, and to focus the resources from his prospective earldom on service in the French wars. Edward had already made clear his intention to raise young John's profile. Before setting out for the Crécy campaign the king had named John as one of those appointed by him to safeguard the queen. In 1347, Edward summoned him, then aged seventeen, to take part in the siege of Calais. Perhaps he displayed military aptitude, for about three weeks after the surrender of the town, order was made for him to receive his father's lands, well before he attained his majority. The young man showed his readiness to do the king's will by relinquishing a prospective part of his inheritance. The reversion of the barony of Liddell, on the Anglo-Scottish border, then in the hands of his aunt, Blanche Wake, as part of her dower, was granted by him to the king and his heirs, and bestowed by Edward on his son, John of Gaunt.[5]

An exalted marriage was arranged for the earl of Kent to a niece of Queen Philippa. It was a politically advantageous marriage for the king, intended to strengthen his Netherlandish ties and influence. In 1347 a papal dispensation was granted for John to wed Elizabeth, a daughter of William margrave of Juliers. The justification for the dispensation was that the marriage was intended as a means of ending the strife between the margrave and John's kinsman Raymond duke of Guelders.[6] However, John died two days after Christmas 1352, probably at the old royal palace of Woking in Surrey, one of his residences. It was there, only a few days before his death, that he had dated a grant of Ryhall manor (Rutland) for life to Bartholomew, Lord Burghersh. The latter was a mature councillor of Edward III, and an outstanding soldier, who had been the master in charge of the Black Prince's education, and had fought alongside him in the vanguard at Crécy. It could be that Burghersh was the young Kent's master, too, and that the grant of Ryhall was an expression of the young man's undying respect and affection for a veteran who had schooled him in chivalry. John died childless: his wife Elizabeth may not have reached the age of safe child-bearing – for she died only in 1411.[7]

In the Holand household, Christmas revels must have abruptly given way to mourning, and the New Year celebrated in low key. It is likely that the couple attended the earl's funeral at Winchester. John was buried in the city where his father had been humiliated and executed, in the friary where his corpse had been laid. The son's exequies were thus not only an occasion for mourning, but a public spectacle which recalled both the nadir of the family's fortunes and their reversal.[8] The choice of the young man's burial place suggests that his father's sad fate weighed heavily on him – and, in that case, is likely to have weighed on Joan, too.

The widowed Countess Elizabeth of Kent took a vow of chastity; the ceremony where she took the oath and received the ring was held at prestigious Waverley Abbey in Surrey, the first Cistercian house founded in England, which had attracted a good deal of royal and noble patronage. It was within easy reach of Woking, which formed part of her dower – she received many of the earldom's properties in southern England.[9] Perhaps she feared the likelihood that she might be pressured into making another diplomatic marriage. Joan and Thomas Holand may have encouraged her pious resolution because of apprehension that, if she remarried, parts of the earldom (to which Joan was now heir) would, as Elizabeth's dower, come into the hands of a new husband who might waste them.

If these were the Holands' fears, as it is likely that they were, they turned out to be prescient. Here let us digress to consider Countess Elizabeth's transgressory search for love, a parallel to Joan's, whose happy outcome she may have envied, and longed to emulate. Eight years after taking the vow of chastity, Elizabeth broke it by remarrying. She chose a dashing soldier, clearly for love. On 29 September 1360, at Wingham (Kent), she wed Sir Eustache d'Auberichecourt, a fellow Netherlander in origins. He was probably a son of the Sir Nicholas d'Auberichecourt whose castle had been near Bouchain in the county of Ostrevant, not far from Valenciennes – the chronicler Froissart's birthplace. Edward II's queen, Isabella, had stayed at the castle on her way to invade England in 1326. Sir Nicholas joined her force, apparently by doing so establishing his family in English royal service.[10]

By 1352, Eustache was in the service of the Black Prince: he conveyed 36s 8d to the Prince for gambling with his mother, Queen Philippa. By May 1355, Eustache was knighted. The chronicler Jean Froissart benevolently highlighted his exploits under the Prince's command in

1356 at the battle of Poitiers. Froissart, as his fellow countryman, was to remain interested in following his notable, if chequered, military career.[11]

In pursuit of profits of war, Sir Eustache was to strike out on his own. He established himself with a military company, as did other captains, in the disordered county of Champagne, and distinguished himself in leading plundering raids on whose brutality Froissart was moved to remark (as had the chronicler le Bel).[12] Ostensibly, he carried these out in the name of Charles II, king of Navarre, and, subsequently, of Edward III. Charles was a descendant of the Capetian kings of France, who, besides ruling his little kingdom stretching down from the Pyrenees into Spain, was the principal lord in the Cotentin Peninsula in Normandy. He tried to maintain his standing, and to punch above his territorial weight, by switching between the French and English causes, as well as between those of the powerful kings of Castile and Aragon.

In 1359 Eustache, in Champagne, set out for Nogent-sur-Seine to confront a French royal force. He had with him a warhorse and a hackney which Countess Elizabeth of Kent had sent him out of affection. Presumably their courtship had started when he was in England in the Prince's entourage. In his speech to his soldiers at Nogent, drawn up on a hillock amidst vineyards, Eustache boasted that he might perform such service to Edward III that he would have an earldom conferred on him. Perhaps he was fantasising about this as a consequence of his possible marriage to the countess of Kent.

However, he underestimated the size of the opposing force and was captured, fighting valiantly, having received a heavy blow to the visor which broke three front teeth. Yet his luck was to turn again. He was apparently soon released from captivity, and had Elizabeth's warhorse and hackney restored to him. Other captains of companies in Champagne valued his leadership so highly that they were prepared to subscribe to his ransom.[13]

In October 1359, a few months after the battle of Nogent, Edward III landed with his army at Calais (with the Prince prominent among his captains). Frustrated in his efforts to make peace with the French Crown, Edward was determined to confront the regent of France, captive John II's son, the dauphin Charles. Eustache seems not to have joined the English army, but to have operated once more in the service of Charles of Navarre. The ending of hostilities by the Anglo-French peace was a mixed blessing for Eustache. It would restrict the opportunities for semi-independent mercenary companies which devoured the land. In his case, defiance risked the loss of Edward III's and the Prince's good grace. In fact it was to be part of Sir Thomas Holand's remit to clear parts of northern France of companies such as Eustache's.[14] It was such a prospect that propelled the gap-toothed veteran to Wingham into the arms of the amorous Countess Elizabeth.

The countess, closely related to the king's family, seems to have been emulating Joan's youthful, romantic marriage to a chivalrous, battered knight of minor noble origins. There was one big difference: Joan's marriage to Thomas was ultimately recognised as legitimate, whereas Elizabeth's marriage was undoubtedly sinful. In 1361 Archbishop Simon Islip of Canterbury censured the couple's behaviour in breaking Elizabeth's vow of chastity, and imposed a regime of penances on them to last for the duration of their marriage. After 'carnal copulation', they were to provide charity to six poor people, and abstain from the dish of flesh or fish they most wanted to eat. Once a year Elizabeth was to go on foot to the shrine of St Thomas of Canterbury. Once a week she was to take no food except bread and a mess of potage, whilst wearing no smock. This she was enjoined to do especially in the absence of her husband.[15] One wonders how Joan and Thomas felt about Elizabeth's clandestine marriage. Perhaps the couple's sinfulness repelled them, and they may have been anxious that Eustache might dissipate his wife's dower. But, had Thomas not died soon after the marriage, Eustache might have proved a useful contact for him, since he had been part of the Prince's select band of military brothers, as well as having close contacts at the court of Navarre and with the mercenary companies.

It is doubtful whether Eustache settled down to domestic bliss in relatively peaceable English courtly and county society. He may have longed for action: the penitential restrictions on his marriage may have damaged connubial bliss and his pride. Tantalisingly, a document of 1365 referred to him as 'of Surrey', which suggests that he had lived for a time at Elizabeth's house in Woking.[16] He probably remained *persona grata* with the king and his family. He had proved his military worth, and the king of Navarre was a rival for his service. In the month before his marriage, Edward had granted him the substantial annuity of forty marks, for good service in war.[17] The commitment of his military service and resources could be expected by the Crown, since he was vassal for the parts of the earldom of Kent which he controlled. In 1364 reference was made to the considerable amount of stock from the manors of Woking and Sutton which the Prince had bought from him.[18]

However, Eustache remained heavily committed to his overseas interests. By May 1364, Charles of Navarre had appointed him guardian of his lands in Normandy, Burgundy and elsewhere in France. On the other hand, that year he performed signal service for Edward III and the Prince in Brittany. The Prince sent his peerless companion Sir John Chandos to command Jean de Montfort's forces against the rival claimant to the duchy, Charles of Blois. Battle was joined at Auray: Eustache was commander of one of Chandos' divisions. Their victory was complete: Charles of Blois was killed in the battle. Consequently de Montfort was able to establish himself more firmly in the duchy.[19]

In the later 1360s renewed conflicts gave more scope for Eustache's military bent. In 1366 he was a captain in Navarre to aid its defence against incursions of the 'Great Companies' of mercenaries which invaded Spain, and he was in the Prince's army in 1367, when the Prince won his last victory, over the Castilians at Nájera.[20] Two years later, after the Anglo-French war resumed, he answered the Prince's summons to help defend Aquitaine, and fought vigorously in sieges and skirmishes, often together with Chandos. In 1371/72 he was captured and, on release, retired to Carentan in Normandy, a town given him by Charles of Navarre. There he was soon to die. He had a son, François – but it is not clear who the mother was.[21] It looks as though his marriage had become a formality. In the will which his widow made many years after his death, she decorously omitted to mention her second husband (her great, and perhaps soured, self-indulgence). She enjoined her burial in the tomb of her first husband, the earl of Kent, at Winchester. In status-conscious mode, she specified him, but not Eustache, in the prayers she provided for souls.[22] As far as we know, she had not attempted a third marriage in the four decades after Eustache's death. In the long run, she found celibacy preferable to marriage to a ruthless soldier on the make.

There are some parallels between Elizabeth's and Joan's marriages to their paragons of chivalry – but important differences, too. Both husbands spent a good deal of their marriages overseas. They used control of parts of the earldom of Kent to further their careers abroad, and died there. But Thomas and Joan established their line and posterity with a clutch of children. Joan, we know, had her husband's remains brought to England, and willed to be buried with them. Eustache, it appears, did not put down roots in England, and is unlikely to have been buried there.

Let us now revert to the Holands, and consider first what their landed prospects were like. In February and July 1353, writs had been sent to county escheators ordering them to give Thomas and Joan seisin of her brother's inheritance, apart from the dower previously assigned to Countess Elizabeth.[23] The proportion of the earldom they received was further reduced because Blanche Wake had been awarded dower from it after the death of her husband Thomas in 1349, when this extensive baronial holding was inherited by Joan's mother Margaret, Thomas's sister. As we shall see, Thomas Holand and Joan also faced the dismal prospect of reduced incomes from many of the properties they did receive, resulting from the first plague pandemic of 1348–49.

The estates of the earldom of Kent in 1352 comprised about fifty properties – mostly manors, some of which were farmed out to tenants. There were also rents from urban and rural properties, and the profits of a few 'hundred' courts – the courts of the ancient administrative units into which typical shires were divided. The estates were widely spread over fifteen shires, mostly in southern England, with some notable properties further north too. In Kent itself, John, besides his annual fee of £30 as its earl, charged on the issues of the shire, had held only one manor, Wickhambreaux (a few miles from Canterbury), and the profits from two hundreds.[24] So the earls were not a dominant landed force in the shire of their title; the shire had other, more influential landowners.

The earldom was originally cobbled together for Joan's father, but shorn of some of the plum forfeitures which he had garnered all too briefly in the hectic politicking of the 1320s. It lacked thick clusters of estates – apart from the recent acquisition of well-established elements of the Wake baronial inheritance. These were in Lincolnshire and Yorkshire. In the more southern parts of the realm, Thomas and Joan received only a scatter of estates. In the south-east there were, besides the Kentish properties, annual farms of £36 from Chichester and £8 from the tenants of Iden (Sussex); Talworth manor (Surrey), Bushey (Hertfordshire) and a farm of £11 12d from two manors of the abbot of Stratford in Essex. Joan later stayed on occasion at Bushey, and so did the Black Prince when he was her husband, which suggests that it had a comfortable manor house for use on journeys. It was within easy reach of London, and conveniently placed too for pilgrimages to the great shrine of St Alban, the first martyr of Britain, in his imposing abbey.[25] In Suffolk, Joan and Thomas received two manors, Kersey and Layham, and in Norfolk a rent of £16 from Ormesby.

In the Midlands and further north there were Torpell, Upton and Easton on the Hill (Northamptonshire), Donington (Leicestershire), Ryhall (Rutland), a large rent, £100, from Droitwich (Worcestershire), Ollerton in Sherwood (Nottinghamshire), and in Derbyshire, Chesterfield and Ashford in the Water (in Bakewell). At Donington (south-west of Nottingham) was one of the earldom's few castles, together with a park, a fishery on the River Trent and a ferry across the river. In Lincolnshire, the couple received the manors of Beesby, Brattleby and Greetham, a rent of £50 from the men of the port of Grimsby and the same from the men of the soke of Caistor.

In Yorkshire there were in the North Riding the manors of Kirby Moorside, which had a market and fair, Buttercrambe in the Derwent valley, and Great Ayton in Cleveland, Cropton and Middelton, Compton, Collingham, Bardesey (farmed at £90) and Hemlington. In the East Riding were Cottingham and, conjoined to it, Wyverton. Cottingham, near Hull, was potentially a particularly valuable manor, which had a saltery, a deer park and two ferries, one of them across the Humber at Hessle, a link in an important route to and from the North through Lincolnshire. The manor had a weekly market and an annual fair.

However, Cottingham's accessibility and its proximity to a leading port made it susceptible to epidemics. It was hit badly by the Black

Death. In 1349, its manor was described as ruinous, and the value of the estate was said to be at most £8 6s 8d, on account of the pestilence.[26] In 1352 the manor's poor state was again attributed to the mortality, the scarcity of tenants and, as well, to inundations of the Humber. Rents totalled at most £106 10s 6d – a respectable return, however, with profits too from other appurtenances. The lord's residence there (so vulnerable to seaborne incursions) was fortified: Thomas Wake received a royal licence to crenellate in 1327. Few traces of the castle survive; the antiquary John Leland in the 1540s wrote that nothing remained of it. But it seems to have been maintained to some extent in Joan's time, for in 1362 she granted Ralph de la Garderobe the keeping of its gate. In return, he was to receive a quarter of wheat every ten weeks, the use of the sheepfold and a robe or 10s yearly.[27]

The effects on estate incomes of drastic falls in population as a result of the plague pandemic had been reflected in the extents of some of the other properties in 1352. The value of Kirby Moorside was lessened as a result of the pestilence. Ollerton was left with few inhabitants, and its dwelling houses were then broken down. No one would lease them. At Ashford, a lead mine, formerly worth £20 p.a., had ceased to be worked because of a shortage of miners. It may be an indication of the desperation of Joan and Thomas to enhance profitability in adverse conditions that in 1353 they procured a licence to hold markets and a fair at Buttercrambe. This does not seem to have taken off. For what it is worth, the extents made of Thomas's properties in 1361 record the customary farms found in the 1352 extents, but do not cite instances of decay of rent like these.[28]

Yet conditions may not have improved on some manors by the early 1360s, when they were in the Black Prince's hands – though the problems experienced then may not have stemmed entirely from the Holands' time of tenure, but from the effects of the plague pandemic of 1361–62, and of the devastating storm which caused widespread serious damage in England for several days in January 1362. Not long after, buildings were being repaired in Cottingham, and so was the bridge at Ashford. The tenants of Brattleby (Lincolnshire) were said to be experiencing hard times in 1363. In Kersey (Suffolk) order was made in February 1362 for the demesne lands to be leased to the tenants, and in July for the sale of the houses which had fallen down in 'the last storm'. At Easton (Northamptonshire) the parker was ordered in April to deliver timber to the poor tenants to repair their houses, and in 1365 the reeve was ordered to have the granges repaired.[29]

However inadequate the propertied basis at the couple's disposal was in order to sustain their aspirations, and whatever declines in income there were from particular estates, Thomas and Joan were determined to reward favoured servants as lavishly as the greatest noble might, as well as retaining in similar mode knights and esquires important for Thomas's career. Let us instance some of the grants they made to servants. They jointly granted £20 p.a. for life from Torpell manor in Northamptonshire to John de la Salle and Hawise his wife. John was eventually to be the Black Prince's yeoman and falconer, so it is likely that he had fulfilled the same office for the Holands. Even taking into account that the grant may have been in part for Hawise's possible services in the household to Joan, such a large grant to a falconer, and one made as a jointure, was remarkably generous. By contrast, in 1383 John of Gaunt retained Arnold Fauconer to serve him for life in peace and war as a falconer, and to go with him whenever he wished, for an annuity of £10. He was to receive wages and food at court as well, and to have the rank of esquire. Gaunt was a keen falconer, but the Holands' grant to de la Salle suggests that one or both of them may have been fanatical about the sport too.[30]

Thomas Duncalf, likewise a yeoman, received a life annuity of £10 from the Holands on the profits of Ashford. We do not know what the couple gave Sir Henry de la Hay: the Black Prince was to bestow an annuity of £20 on him, partly because he had 'held a great place' with them. He may have been their chamberlain or steward of their household, or a key figure in their estate administration. At the other end of the scale, Sir Thomas made a grant of annual produce from Bushey manor to a certain Robert le Fol. Perhaps he was their jester.[31]

Despite Joan's upbringing in southern England, and inheritance of the earldom of Kent, it looks as though in 1353 the couple were thinking of founding a dynasty based on the Wake family's old centres of influence in Yorkshire and, possibly, Lincolnshire, where Thomas was to be buried. They received a good deal of former Wake property in Yorkshire; from 1354 onwards, Thomas was summoned to parliaments as Lord Wake. Joan's aunt Blanche Wake held much of this important inheritance in Lincolnshire in dower, including Bourne (where the Wakes had held land since the twelfth century) and its castle, and Market Deeping.

Blanche may have had more influence at court and in Lincolnshire and elsewhere than Joan and her husband could muster. She was a formidable person to cross. She was responsible for the downfall of a bishop, Thomas de Lisle, a Dominican friar who received the see of Ely by papal provision in 1345. Indictments against him in the 1350s indicate that he protected his servants who terrorised neighbourhoods like criminal gangs. But it was his condoning of violence against a household servant of Blanche, and attacks on her property in 1354–55, which brought about his nemesis. Her valet William Holm was murdered in 1355 as a result of his quarrel with the bishop's chamberlain. The bishop was convicted of instigating grave offences against her. He was deprived by Edward of the temporalities of his bishopric. He went to the papal court at Avignon to plead with Pope Innocent VI to support their restoration, and died there in 1361.[32]

Blanche's influence among the Lincolnshire gentry is reflected in arrangements for a wedding to be held under her auspices, uniting two leading local families. A licence was granted in 1363 for the solemnisation of the marriage of Sir Andrew Luttrell of Irnham (near Bourne) and Hawise Despenser of Goxhill. It was to be held in the chapel of Blanche's castle at Bourne. Officiating were the abbot and the vicar of Bourne. The abbey, whose Augustinian canons were of the French Arroasian Order, had been founded in 1138 by Baldwin FitzGilbert, who married a daughter of Hugh Wake. It continued to be in patronage descended from the Wakes in 1363. The wedding party had a Lancastrian flavour. Sir Andrew had served Blanche's brother, Henry of Grosmont, duke of Lancaster, and his family had long had Lancastrian connections. The Luttrell Psalter, made for Sir Andrew's father Geoffrey, depicts the 'martyrdom' of Thomas of Lancaster.[33]

Blanche was widely respected, too, in her exalted family circle. Her brother Duke Henry made her an executor of his will. When bound for Aquitaine in 1362–63, the Black Prince (then married to Joan) did favours to Blanche in return. He granted Elizabeth de Halton, damsel of her chamber, wardship of land at Riby (Lincolnshire). He ordered the parker of Joan's manor of Torpell to deliver three oaks for the repair of Blanche's drawbridge at her moated manor house at Deeping.[34]

Blanche's household had a reputation for propriety and educational excellence. John and Thomas, the two sons of John Mowbray, lord of Axholme (Lincolnshire) were entrusted by the Crown to her care in 1372. They were descended from Joan's uncle Thomas of Brotherton; their father had been killed in 1368 by Muslims whilst he was on pilgrimage.[35] Also, John of Gaunt (then Joan's brother-in-law), continuing the Lancastrian connection, placed his young children Philippa, Elizabeth and Henry of Bolingbroke in Blanche's household. In 1371 a carter took their belongings from her place at Ware (Hertfordshire) to Deeping, in anticipation that she was going to move her household thither. But this removal was cancelled, on news that the infants' father had returned to England. He had sailed from Aquitaine with his new Spanish bride, Constance. Presumably Blanche and the children were eager to greet the couple. In a mandate of 1373, Gaunt was to describe Blanche as 'nostre très cher et très ame tante'.[36]

There are only a few indications that either Thomas or Joan was involved in Lincolnshire affairs, or those of more northerly shires where they had property. These are not enough to suggest that Joan customarily resided on her estates in those parts, or that her husband did when on furlough from his duties abroad. It is dangerous to argue from silence, but the meagre information we have suggests that Thomas was not heavily engaged in building up local connections in order to enhance his standing and influence in regional affairs. He does not seem to have been in the business, at least for the time being, of creating an extensive 'affinity' composed of numerous annuitants and 'well-willers', primarily in order to enhance his domestic power. As long as he was heavily engaged in governing and defending the king's interests in France, he could ill afford the money and time needed to carve out positions in the shires. Rather, his priorities were to extend his influence in Brittany, then Normandy. He and Joan were perhaps anticipating that they would inherit and elaborate on Lady Wake's connections, not expecting that she would outlive Sir Thomas by twenty years.

However, here are a few instances of his involvement in northern gentry's affairs. In 1351 he was witness to a grant of land in Mirfield,

Yorkshire.[37] In 1359, styled 'lord of Wake', he witnessed a grant of lands in Lancashire by Sir William le Botiller of Warrington to John de Winwick, treasurer of York Minster. The latter was one of the attorneys whom Thomas had appointed when he was intending to go to Brittany in 1354. We can assume that this powerful cleric was in the Holands' affinity and that he was one of their councillors.[38] At some point Thomas and Joan jointly granted their Yorkshire manor of Great Ayton to Sir Donald Hazelrigg (d. 1385) and his wife Joan de Bredon for their lives. The Hazelriggs were a Northumberland family, and in 1362 Sir Donald was purchasing property in the shire. That was a hazardous investment, which suggests that he was a military man, prepared to defend his acquisitions against Scottish incursions. Military prowess may have been why his services were valued by Sir Thomas. Sir Donald's wife had been a damsel of Queen Philippa. That must have been when she was young, since the queen died in 1369, and she survived till 1400. It seems likely that Joan of Kent befriended the young woman at court, and later had her serving in her own household.[39]

Joan, if in England during her husband's absences abroad, might well have been expected to exercise governing roles in the running of their household and estates. So, in her mid twenties, she may well have learned and honed the skills in management which she was to display conspicuously in later life. She was involved when younger with the disposition of some of the ecclesiastical patronage of the earldom of Kent. This included patronage of the Benedictine nunnery of Wothorpe, near Stamford (Lincolnshire), a house which was almost moribund in 1354, perhaps as a result of the plague: there was only one nun left there. Joan took a personal interest in the problem, making a significant intervention in local ecclesiastical affairs. At her request, the house was dissolved. Its endowments and the solitary nun were transferred to another convent just outside Stamford – St Michael's, a cell of Peterborough Abbey.[40]

In 1361 (soon after Sir Thomas's death) a close spiritual connection was formed between Joan and a Yorkshire house of Augustinian canons, Haltemprice Priory, near Cottingham. It had originally been founded on another site, in Cottingham itself, by her uncle, Blanche Wake's husband Thomas. He was buried in the priory. A prominent local landowner, Sir John de Meaux of Bewick, now granted the canons an important addition to their endowments – the manor of Willerby, attached to Cottingham. Sir John, like Joan, had a devotion to the Franciscans. He willed to be buried in the parish church of Aldborough in a habit of the Order; his brother was a Franciscan friar. His tomb remains there, with a knightly effigy over it, in worldly contrast to his humbly swathed burial.[41]

A condition for the grant was that daily prayers were to be said in perpetuity for Sir John and members of his family, and for 'Lady Joan Countess of Kent'. Apparently, news had not yet arrived in those parts that the widowed Lady Joan had wed the Black Prince six days before then! The reason for her inclusion in the prayers for the Meaux family was that she was patron of the house, as representative of its founder. Perhaps she had visited her manor at Cottingham, and the neighbouring priory, and had come to share a reverence for the priory with local gentry. There may have been other reasons for her to esteem it. By the time of the Reformation, miracles were thought to be wrought at Thomas Wake's tomb. He specialised in cures for fever. Perhaps, too, in her time, the priory already possessed their 'girdle of Our Lady', one of many such in religious houses, which were lent to ladies to wear during pregnancy or delivery. That would have been of practical use for Joan.[42]

The Holands cultivated a more far-flung network of relationships with nobles and gentlefolk, some of which doubtless related to Thomas's need for alliances and support in his international career. He and his brother Otes sought friendly contacts at two royal courts – the king's and the Prince's. Some of their connections were continued from those which Joan's late brother had inherited or formed. The couple confirmed his grant of Ryhall in Rutland to Lord Burghersh. He died in 1355, and they subsequently granted Ryhall to his son and heir Bartholomew, as his fee during pleasure. He had similar qualities, talents and interests to his father. Highly esteemed from his youth by Edward III, he was a notable soldier as well as diplomat. Like Thomas, he had fought in Brittany in 1342–43. He was in the Black Prince's retinue at Crécy, and took part in the siege of Calais. In warfare Bartholomew the younger became particularly associated with the Prince, in whose campaigns in Aquitaine in 1355 and 1356 he took part.[43]

Another associate of Joan's brother Earl John with whom Thomas developed ties was Sir Gerard Braybrooke of Colmworth (Bedfordshire). He was related to Joan and her brother through the Wake family. Braybrooke was one of Earl John's executors, and witnessed his grant in 1352 to the elder Burghersh. Earlier in the year, Braybrooke had been one of the attorneys whom Holand had appointed in England for the duration of his impending tour of duty in France.[44] Joan cultivated her Braybrooke kin. She was to have a long and, certainly in her later years, close relationship with Sir Gerard's son, the cleric Robert Braybrooke (1336/37–1404). He received papal preferment at her petition in 1363, and was secretary to her son Richard II in the early years of his reign, until he was provided in 1381 at the king's request to the bishopric of London.[45]

Thomas specially needed to cultivate friends in princely courts and among the military elite. The Burghershs were important ones, as the coats of arms of a galaxy of exalted families on the elder one's tomb in Lincoln Cathedral exemplify.[46] Another such friend was Sir John Chandos, to whom Thomas granted a life annuity of £20 from Chesterfield manor.[47] He was one of the most famous soldiers of his generation. He was a Derbyshire man, who deservedly became a favourite of both Edward III and the Black Prince. They valued him too as an emollient councillor and diplomat, and as an accomplished and delightful companion. An anecdote told by Froissart has Edward and Chandos anticipating Sir Francis Drake in a display of martial insouciance. In 1350 they were standing on shipboard together in the English Channel, off Winchelsea. The fleet was at battle stations, ready to confront a formidable Spanish fleet. Edward was in a light-hearted mood. 'He told his minstrels to strike up a dance tune which Sir John Chandos ... had recently brought back from Germany. And out of sheer high spirits, he made Sir John sing with the minstrels, to his own vast amusement. At the same time he kept glancing up at the mast, on which he had posted a look-out to espy the coming of the Spaniards.'[48]

Sir Thomas retained another highly reputed warrior, Sir Richard Pembridge, who seems to have lacked some of Chandos's amenable courtliness. In 1354 he was appointed as one of Thomas's attorneys. Five years later, Thomas granted him for life an annuity of £11 16s, due to the Holands from the abbot of Stratford (Essex). Pembridge, son of a Herefordshire knight, had been a boisterous, troublesome youth. But he fought at Crécy; he received substantial annuities from the Crown in 1352, and fought again at Poitiers. In 1372, laden with honours, and holding high office as one of the king's chamber knights, he earned Edward's undying wrath by refusing the lieutenancy of Ireland.[49] Pembridge's fine armoured effigy can be seen on his tomb in Hereford Cathedral; his great helmet is in the National Museum of Scotland in Edinburgh. Another life annuity which Sir Thomas granted was to a royal retainer of a different stripe: £6 to John Herlyng, usher of the king's chamber.[50] Since Sir Thomas envisaged that he would often be abroad, it was important for him to have an official in the chamber of the royal household who could act as his eyes and ears.

However, it seems to have been magnates to whom Sir Thomas turned to provide cash for his enterprises. In 1353 he acknowledged large financial obligations to nobles who were leading military men. These loans may have been intended to help to finance his projected expedition to Brittany. One of the magnates was Richard earl of Arundel, practised courtier and valued royal councillor. The other was a notable northern warrior, Ralph Lord Neville, who had estates he needed to defend against Scottish incursions, in the bishopric of Durham, as well as estates in Yorkshire. Holand made the lands he held security for the loans.[51]

Let us now turn to consider Thomas's career abroad during his marriage. In the early 1350s, in the period of truces with the French Crown, Edward III needed to consolidate his position in Brittany, and wished to improve it in Normandy. Holand's talents and his deep knowledge of Breton and Norman affairs made him an ideal instrument for the king's purposes. Edward did not need to cajole his support, but could play him along, exacting the services required by exploiting his financial needs, his *amour propre* and his ambitions. He held only parts of the earldom of Kent – as we have seen, Blanche Wake and Countess Elizabeth of Kent had substantial portions of Joan's inheritance in dower. Edward for long kept the title of earl in abeyance, pointedly refraining from investing him.

In 1352 Thomas had been appointed to the key post of captain of Calais, but he was soon to be switched to his old stamping ground, Brittany. For in the following year he was appointed king's lieutenant and captain there, and in the adjacent parts of Poitou, for the duration of the war. In 1354 he was reassigned to the post, and was preparing in March to sail to Brittany.[52] In 1354–55, says Jonathan Sumption, his lieutenancy was a turning-point in English control in Brittany. Within a short time of his arrival he reached a settlement with the independent captains of garrisons in the interior. The castles were taken into the king's hands, and granted out on terms more favourable to the Crown, strengthening its control.[53]

When open war between the English and French Crowns resumed in 1355, northern France remained Thomas's sphere of activity, though Henry of Grosmont, duke of Lancaster now took control as lieutenant in Brittany.[54] Despite Thomas's connections with the Black Prince and some of his leading knights, he did not take part in the Prince's spectacular campaigns south of the Loire in 1355 and 1356, which were based on the Prince's lieutenancy of Gascony. That was in contrast to Joan's erstwhile husband, the earl of Salisbury, who had the distinction of commanding the rearguard at the battle of Poitiers. Salisbury was an able soldier, and he could bring a much bigger military retinue to the Prince's aid than Thomas. Maybe the two of them, because of their past rivalry over Joan, deliberately soldiered in different spheres of operations. However, Edward and the Prince may have straightforwardly judged that it benefited operations in northern France to leave Thomas embedded there.

In 1354 Thomas had been appointed warden of the Channel Islands, an appointment renewed in 1356, for a farm of £200 p.a. He is unlikely to have customarily resided there, though it was anticipated that he would be there in 1358, when his prisoner Jean Viscount de Rohan was granted a safe-conduct to visit him there, in order to negotiate over his ransom.[55] But Thomas had appointed his brother Sir Otes as his deputy in the Channel Islands in 1355, an appointment confirmed by the Crown.[56] Thomas regarded Otes as his right-hand man. He and Joan provided him with landed resources with exceptional generosity, facilitating his tenure of important offices and commands. They gave him a life interest in a wide scattering of manors – but not including any of those they held in Lincolnshire and Yorkshire. In 1356 they received royal licence to grant him the Derbyshire manors of Chesterfield and Ashford in the Water (in Bakewell), and the advowson of the Hospital of St Leonard in Chesterfield. Other manors which Sir Otes held of them for life were Kersey (Suffolk) and Talworth (Surrey). Thomas also made over to him the life interest in Yoxhall (Staffordshire) which he held of their brother Sir Robert.[57]

Sir Otes in his turn appointed a deputy in the Channel Islands – a certain Thomas de Langhurst, a yeoman in his service. French raiders seized Castle Cornet in Guernsey in 1356 – which reflected badly on the Holands' newly installed governance. However, Langhurst recovered the castle. Sir Otes succeeded his brother as warden of the Channel Islands in 1357, on the same financial terms, but he demitted office the following year, probably because Thomas was anxious to secure his military support in Normandy. In 1359 Otes was preparing to go on the king's service to the duchy. He was there in July, and died there later in the year.[58]

Otes had relied on his brother's patronage to further his career, but clearly they had similar military and administrative talents. Otes too had had the great privilege of being a founder member of the Order of the Garter. But he had committed a foolish blunder. He was entrusted with the custody of the king's prisoner, the count of Eu, captured by Thomas at Caen. Otes seems to have been putty in the distinguished Frenchman's hands. He allowed the count to persuade him to escort him across the Channel to Calais, without royal licence.[59] That may have marked him in Edward's eyes as a man who, where high affairs of state were concerned, was not a safe pair of hands. Consequently Otes remained dependent on his brother Thomas's patronage. He died without issue, and may not have married: the eldest brother Robert was his heir. Here we seem to have an example of a well-regarded soldier whose achievements in the wars in France did not enable him to accumulate wealth and found a family fortune back home.

Thomas was focussed on Normandy as his main sphere of activity. Royal backing facilitated the development of his interest there, for which the Channel Islands lacked scope. In 1357 Edward had granted him the fortalice and place of Crocy, near Falaise.[60] Two years later, the situation of English influence in the duchy was critical. For Charles of Navarre made peace with the dauphin. The English were now unable to rely on using Charles's major Channel port, Cherbourg in the Cotentin. Sir Thomas occupied a crucial position there: he was captain of the fortress of Saint-Sauveur-le-Vicomte. To secure communications with England, he took a force to occupy the harbour at Barfleur, and refortified the parish church there.[61] On 30 September 1359, shortly before Edward set sail for France, he also appointed Sir Thomas as his lieutenant in Normandy. He shared command there with Philip of Navarre, count de Longueville, who, though he was the king of Navarre's brother, adhered to Edward. In Thomas's commission, he was styled earl of Kent. Edward had at last relented towards him, investing him with the earldom, presumably in recognition of his sterling service in recent years, and to smooth his co-operation with Philip of Navarre.[62]

After the ratification of the Anglo-French peace (October 1360), Edward was concerned about the problems posed by its territorial implementation. He considered that Thomas had the forcefulness, cunning and personal authority to oversee part of this crucial task, and spoke to him about it. He was appointed lieutenant and captain general in France and Normandy, with power to raise and lead an army against malefactors. His commission was to run – optimistically – for only three months. To his credit, he arranged the surrender to the French of most of the English-held fortresses in Normandy.[63]

Thomas had reached a peak of achievement. He had restored his family's honour and attained chivalrous fame. He had mightily enhanced his status: his children were of the blood royal, and the king had at last made him an earl. He had adorned the earldom of Kent with a military lustre and tradition which it had conspicuously lacked. However, like so many English captains who laboured abroad in the period, worn out by their toils and privations, he never returned to England. He died at Rouen on 28 December 1360. Either he or his servants had come to an arrangement with the Franciscans at Rouen that he should be temporarily buried in their house, and so he was five days after his death. His remains were subsequently taken for interment to the Order's house at Stamford in Lincolnshire. Besides the provision for the good of his soul made with the friars, Joan hired a chaplain to say Masses for him in the chapel of their castle at Donington.[64]

We may surmise that Thomas had willed that he should be buried at Stamford (rather than anywhere associated with his father) because of the Wakes' strong links with Lincolnshire, and presumably because both he and Joan intended to make their principal residence in the shire. Furthermore both of their families had a tradition of patronising the Franciscan Order: Thomas's father was buried in the friary at Preston (Lancashire).[65] The Franciscan house at Stamford was one of their most prestigious friaries in England. It had been among the first to be founded there, in 1230, and had received a good deal of aid from Henry III and from noble families. The buildings were capacious, and had housed as many as between twenty-eight and forty-six brethren before the plague pandemic of 1348–49. Its schools, separately housed, were famous. The suggestion has been made that the convent was actually on the site of what was later identified as the Whitefriars (the house of the Carmelite Order of friars), where a gateway survives, dating from the second quarter of the fourteenth century. However, the exact place of this remarkable earl of Kent's interment appears to be irrevocably lost.[66]

Joan's marriage may well have been blissful, but it was overshadowed by Thomas's need – and perhaps inclination – to serve the king in France, so as to enhance his repute and his standing at court. We can confidently conclude that his absences gave Joan the challenges of supervising the running of a household and estates, and also of nothing less than an earldom. Thomas, like many of Edward's lords, geared the resources of his estates towards maintaining the war in France. Despite the count of Eu's ransom, he never seems to have got to the stage, as some did, of investing the profits of war in purchasing land at home. He thus failed to enhance the landed basis of the earldom of Kent. Nor did he build up (as leading landowners usually tried to do) an impressive regional affinity that would give him influence in the affairs of court and county. As far as we know, he did not arrange marriages for his sons and daughters – it was to be as a consequence of Joan's second marriage that brilliant marital opportunities opened up for them.

Characteristic concomitants of the exercise of domestic landed power were normally rivalries among lords for grants by the Crown of wardships and marriages, and petitions by them for a variety of favours and pardons, often for dependants. Not so, apparently, in Thomas's case: his lobbying was more focussed on gaining offices abroad than on domestic plums. He is, perhaps, a characteristic figure in this unusual period, when falling rents at home made it more attractive to concentrate on gaining the rewards of service to the Crown abroad. That unusual balance of profitability may have made the realm more tranquil and governable, despite economic upheavals. However, as success in war later receded, many lords and knights may have focussed on reviving or enhancing their propertied standing at home, from the 1370s onwards. The last decades of the century were to witness a revival of competitive rivalries in court and country for office and influence in England rather than in France. In the next chapter we shall see how some knights who had remained bachelors returned from war determined to make up for lost dynastic time by finding brides well endowed with land. The most eligible bachelor in search of a bride was the Black Prince. In his case, it seems – eccentrically – that amorous inclinations became paramount.

5

A Whirlwind Romance

IN THE NEW ERA OF PEACE in 1360, nobles and gentlefolk who had vigorously plied the trade of war in France, some for decades, had suddenly to consider alternative spheres of action. Some knights and squires carried on soldiering as captains of mercenaries. They led and served in some of the 'Companies' in their attempts to hold on to the places which they occupied in France. Some companies sought their fortunes in other countries, such as politically fragmented Italy, where Sir John Hawkwood and members of the White Company were to operate with famous success for decades. Some now turned to the true highest path of a Christian knight by crusading. Thomas Beauchamp earl of Warwick did so in late 1364, going to Prussia to campaign with the Order of Teutonic Knights against the Lithuanians. He returned with 'the Kynges son of lettowe' (Lithuania), a pagan whose baptism in London he sponsored.[1] Some, like Sir John Chandos, sought offices in the administration of the territories newly ceded to Edward III in full sovereignty by the French Crown. Others wished to return to England, to review or enhance their family's fortunes, and to beget heirs. This was specially necessary for the many knights who had perforce, through indigence or their absorption in campaigning abroad, remained bachelors, and were eager to marry heiresses and perpetuate or found families well endowed with properties.

What path might Thomas Holand have taken in the new circumstances? His career in royal administration in France had just reached a peak when he died. If he had not wanted to adjust to courtly and country pursuits in England, he might well have been employed for further service in the familiar context of Brittany, where civil war continued. He was well qualified to continue as lieutenant for the king's Norman lordships, or to be appointed as *sénéchal* of one of the acquired territories south of the Loire, such as the counties of Poitou, Saintonge or Quercy. He might have been moved once more to take the Cross, as crusading opportunities opened up in the 1360s.

Now, Joan, clad in her widow's weeds, had the sad task of taking control of her own inheritance. Orders were made to escheators to hold inquisitions post mortem on Thomas's lands, dated 16 January 1361. In the next few months, Joan was granted seisin by the Crown of the estates of the earldom of Kent which Thomas had held in her right. She received little or no dower from his own estate, since all he had had was a life interest in a few of his father's former properties.[2]

There may have been concerns that, with the death of an earl, and with no prospects that an adult male heir would be in charge for up to a decade, some Holand officials would seek more secure and lucrative employment in service elsewhere. In a period of generally shrinking populations, consequent on the sequence of plague pandemics, it must have been easier to move in search of more attractive alternative employment at this level of society, just as it was among artisans and agricultural labourers. In her early widowhood, Joan was diligent and prompt in securing the continued services of existing officials in her household and estate administrations. She extended by her letters patent grants of life annuities which Thomas had made; probably in some cases she bestowed such annuities on officers who had been in receipt only of their wages and fees. She was generous – perhaps even profligate – in her potentially long-term alienation of considerable amounts of rent for the purpose. Her grants reflected her desire to continue living as a great lady in the secular world. She was determined to maintain her estate as a magnate. She was not of a temperament like that of Eleanor de Bohun, duchess of Gloucester (d. 1399), sister-in-law of the Black Prince. In her widowhood, the duchess retired to the house of the Minoresses (Poor Clares) near the Tower of London. On her brass over her tomb in Westminster Abbey she is portrayed in widow's garb (or perhaps that of a nun).[3]

Let us take a sample of Joan's grants during her widowhood. Hannekyn, yeoman of her chamber, received five marks p.a. for life from the profits of Chesterfield.[4] William de Harpele received a grant of £5, as he had done from Joan's late husband. It is probable that this was the William de Harpele whom she described as her 'loving esquire' when appointing him as one of her executors in 1385. If so, he is likely to have been one of the few people constantly around her when she was middle-aged, and nearby when she died, who could remember the time of her marriage to Sir Thomas. And, in that case, it would have been a notable example of devotion between mistress and servant for up to three decades.[5] In some of her grants, Joan replicated the generosity to husbands and their wives characteristic of Thomas's regime. She granted £5 p.a. from Ryhall (Rutland) to William le Kell and his wife Joan. If he died in his mistress's service, his widow was to receive half that sum for the rest of her life.[6]

Yet more cause of gloom for Joan resulted from the second plague pandemic which broke out in 1361. On 31 March, Joan's highly distinguished kinsman Henry duke of Lancaster (Blanche Wake's brother), with whom Thomas Holand had co-operated in diplomacy and war, succumbed to plague. He died in his borough of Leicester, and was buried on 14 April in the fine collegiate church of the Newarke which he had founded there near his castle. In his will, he had requested that the Black Prince and his brothers, among others, should attend the funeral. Perhaps this was one occasion that year when the Prince and Joan met.[7]

Since Joan was a descendant of Edward I, the holder of an earldom, still of child-bearing age and famously beautiful, she became the most desirable English widow available on the marriage market. She does not seem to have been adamantly inclined, like some widowed ladies, to fend off unwelcome suitors and resist pressure to remarry from kinsfolk by taking a public vow of chastity. Presumably, when she received the earldom from the Crown, she made an undertaking not to remarry without royal licence, as Blanche Wake had done when she received her dower.[8] Joan's marriage was now a more useful political asset to the king than it had ever been. However, the one account we have of her dealings with the Black Prince over her marriage makes the assumption that they both behaved as though it was a private matter, and that royal assent was merely a formality.

According to the *Chronique des Quatre Premiers Valois* (the chronicle written in the second half of the fourteenth century in the Franciscan friary at Rouen), Joan was 'one of the most beautiful ladies in the world and the most noble'. The writer said that many knights

A Whirlwind Romance

who had done much service to King Edward and the Prince asked the latter to speak on their behalf to her. After all, they may have reasoned, the hand of the other widowed countess of Kent, her sister-in-law Elizabeth, also of princely ancestry, had been won by a gallant knight of inferior ancestry – as we have seen. A certain 'Monseigneur de Brocas', who had served the Prince with distinction, especially in his wars, persuaded him to act as go-between on his behalf. Brocas has been identified as Sir Bernard Brocas (c. 1330–95), the younger son of a Berkshire landowner. Sir Bernard had fought at Poitiers, and had an outstanding military and diplomatic career. He had been a retainer of Duke Henry of Lancaster. The trouble with this identification is that he had had his existing marriage nullified, and then had remarried, the previous year.[9]

Indeed, it does not seem out of character for the headstrong Prince to have pressed the suit of one of his knightly friends, if not Brocas, for the hand of a countess of the blood royal. Having lived much in military society, he had come to value the company of knights such as John Chandos and Hugh Calveley, whose outstanding prowess and whose courtliness in his eyes compensated for their relatively undistinguished origins and their mediocre status. Moreover, the king himself was prepared to approve such alliances. In 1359 he had handsomely endowed Sir Andrew Luttrell of Chilton, Devon (kinsman of the Lincolnshire Luttrells) and his bride Elizabeth, daughter of Hugh Courtenay, earl of Devon, a kinswoman of the king.[10] If the gist of the Franciscan's story is true, the Prince may have reasoned that Joan would be amenable to such a proposal, since in her first marriage she had shown ardour to wed a lowly, landless knight, even one whose family background was tainted. With future wars in mind, the Prince may have thought it would be useful for him to have the earldom of Kent once more in the hands of a highly reputed knight – and one on whose service he could depend.

However, the mature Joan, now much exalted in status, may well have been disdainful and irritated if her royal kinsman did indeed show enthusiasm to pair her off with one of his campfire companions, however chivalrous and courteous the latter might be. The story of the Prince's surrogate courtship is best told in the words of the Franciscan of Rouen:

67

The prince spoke on behalf of the said knight to the said *dame de Hollande* on several occasions. For he was very keen to go for his own pleasure to see the said lady, who was his cousin, and he often beheld her very great beauty and very gracious mien, which gave him immense pleasure. And when on one occasion the prince spoke to the said countess on behalf of the said knight, the countess replied that she would never have a husband. And she, who was very cunning and clever, said this many times to the prince. 'Ha! A!', said the prince, *'belle cousine*, if you do not wish to marry one of my friends, your great beauty will be the worse for you. And if you and I did not have a common lineage, there is no lady under the skies that I would hold as dear as yourself.' And then the prince was overwhelmed by love for the countess. And then the countess started to weep like a woman who was subtle and full of wiles. And then the prince took to comforting her and kissing her frequently, being very saddened by her tears, and said to her, *'Belle cousine*, I have spoken to you on behalf of one of the most valiant knights in England, who is besides of high lineage.' My lady countess said, amidst tears, to the prince, 'Ha! sire, for God's sake refrain from making me such speeches. For it is my intention not to marry. For I have wholly given myself to the most valiant knight beneath the firmament. And for the love of him, I will never have any spouse but God as long as I live. For it is impossible for me to have him, and for the love of him I wish to avoid the company of men, and it is my intention that I will never marry.' The prince wanted to know very much who was the best knight in the world, and persistently asked the countess to tell him. But the said countess, the more she saw him become heated about it, the more she prayed him to stop trying to find out, and said to him, 'For God's sake, very dear lord, on my knees, for the sake of God and the very dear Virgin mother, I implore you to desist from the matter.' To tell it briefly, the prince said to her that, if she did not tell him who was the most valiant in the world, he would be her mortal enemy. And then the countess said to him. 'Very dear and redoubtable lord, it is you, and for the love of you no knight will ever lie at my side.' The prince, who was then smitten with love for the countess, said to her, 'Lady, I vow to God that I will never, as long as I live, have any other woman than you.' Then he pledged himself to her and soon afterwards he married her.[11]

This was a form of private, clandestine marriage, lacking the calling of banns and a public ceremony in which a priest blessed the couple, of which the Church disapproved, but recognised as valid. The writer who penned this filmic scene appears to be following the conventions of courtly romance, but his moral is a typical clerical one: to point up the frail but cunning nature of women, and the physical and verbal wiles they use to entrap weak-minded men. To the mind of a cleric (in this case, probably a Frenchman), the great English hero and the flower of English courtliness were reprehensible. Their kind of love radiated idolatry, and was an emanation of the sin of lust.

How was the supposed episode known about in the friary at Rouen? It may well be that it took some time to provide a fitting setting for Thomas Holand's reburial, and to arrange the transfer of his remains to Stamford. Friars and perhaps laymen from Rouen may have formed part of the cortège which crossed the Channel and wended its way to Lincolnshire. They may have picked up sensational gossip about the countess's speedy remarriage on the journey, or at the reburial, which was surely attended by Joan, and probably by the Prince. The account, however fictionalised, does have a ring of authenticity. For the marriage seems to have been an impulsive one, at least on the Prince's part. It is credible that Joan, in view of her past marital entanglements, might have emphasized her readiness to live chastely unwed, and that the exasperated Prince, in somewhat discourteous allusion to her dubious past, suggested that her beauty might get her into trouble if she did not marry according to his will.

The documentation about their marriage complements the Franciscan's account. For the second time, Joan married privately and wilfully. She and the Prince acted heedlessly and outrageously, casting aside doubts and obligations. Froissart says that they were married without the king's knowledge.[12] They ignored the fact that their marriage was sinful and invalid, since they were within forbidden degrees of kinship. By remarrying at the advanced age of about thirty-three, Joan put herself at higher danger from child-bearing. The Prince was throwing away his father's and his own great international prize of his marriage. Instead, he was marrying a lady whose chequered marital past might cast doubts on the legitimacy of any children they might have.

The Prince does not seem to have had a reputation for amorous dalliance, such as was to be acquired by his brother John of Gaunt, though he did acknowledge an illegitimate son, Roger de Clarendon, whose mother, Edith de Willerford, was one of Queen Philippa's ladies-in-waiting. Perhaps he had been fixed on strong emotional ties with knights with whom he had campaigned – a man of action whose happiest hours had been spent arduously with them, sharing the challenges and dangers.[13] At the age of thirty, he was an ageing bachelor: the marriages of princes and nobles were usually arranged for them in their more amenable childhood or youth. Now, being used to a high degree of independence, he was perhaps irked by the prospect of a diplomatic marriage, a lottery where love or affection was concerned. He had the dreadful example of the long-lasting unhappiness of the earl of Surrey and Joan of Bar in their marriage. He may have long had affection for Joan of Kent, and feelings of admiration and envy for the romance of her steadfast and heroic love for Holand. At least we can say for certain that his behaviour was an amazing testimony to her magnetism.

Where did their courtship and clandestine marriage take place? It could have been at court: it would have been considered proper and natural for the Prince to console her privately in her widowhood, as her kinsman and godfather to at least one of her children. Mandates in *The Black Prince's Register* give indications – but not fool-proof ones – of his whereabouts. In 1361 he does seem to have been in London and Westminster quite frequently, and on occasion across the river from Westminster in his house at Kennington. For much of June and July he appears to have stayed in his manor of Byfleet (Surrey). The manor house there had been a favourite residence of his grandfather Edward II, and the Prince had added a new kitchen to it.[14] It was within easy reach of Woking, then in the hands of Joan's former sister-in-law, the recklessly romantic Lady Elizabeth d'Auberichecourt, *alias* the dowager countess of Kent. In the summer time, princes and nobles often took off with a small 'riding' retinue to enjoy country sports in relative privacy with close friends, away from the prying eyes of their great household. Edward IV, on progress in Northamptonshire in 1464, was able to get married without the knowledge of his companions. Could it be that the Prince rode over to Woking to convey his explosive surrogate proposal of marriage?

The couple knew that their conduct would provoke dismay and even outrage. The Rouen chronicler asserted that Edward III's immediate reaction to the news was to want to have Joan put to death – which sounds highly unlikely. The chronicler may have been echoing and magnifying fears expressed by Joan, or members of her household, about the king's wrath at the loss of his principal remaining diplomatic card, the marriage of his son and heir. Edward may well have imprudently exclaimed that he wished his troublesome kinswoman were dead – though he was far too honourable to instigate or encourage such a foul act. Now a mature and supposedly responsible lady, she had behaved towards him as impudently as she had done when she was a slip of a girl.

The royal anger is likely to have been redoubled because the king was currently trying to negotiate a marriage alliance between the Prince and Margaret, the daughter and prospective heir of Louis de Mâle, count of Flanders. Control of Flanders would enhance the English triumph over the French Crown, and also give hopes of a long-term strengthening of the terms of England's all-important trade with Flemish cities. Such a marriage would have made the Prince prospective ruler of one of the most prosperous principalities in Christendom. Edward now had to substitute one of his younger sons, Edmund of Langley, as prospective bridegroom. English diplomatic efforts were to end in failure. John II of France's fourth and youngest son, Philip duke of Burgundy, won Margaret's hand in 1364. The eventual control he gained of Flanders was to pose dire threats to Richard II and his realm in the mid 1380s. But Edward seems to have speedily forgiven his son and Joan. All the evidence suggests that he loved the mettlesome, impulsive and widely admired Prince – and tried to manage him without falling out. The king's wedding gift to the couple of over £1,500 worth of jewels certainly reinforced his support for the match. The post-wedding celebratory tournament in Cheapside was provocatively based on the theme of the Seven Deadly Sins.[15]

Edward took urgent measures to retrieve the marital situation. He sent two petitions to Pope Innocent VI (generally inclined to be amenable to the king). One requested that he lift the sentence of excommunication the couple had incurred through marrying within the forbidden degree of kinship, and that he would grant them a dispensation to marry legally. The other petition, to which the pope acceded, asked him to delegate the authority to settle these matters to a commission consisting of the archbishop of Canterbury (Simon Islip), the bishop of Exeter (John Grandisson) and Simon de la Brosse, the abbot of Cluny. Grandisson was the uncle of Joan's second husband, William earl of Salisbury. His inclusion suggests that Edward was in no mood to do Joan any favours. In accordance with their findings, a papal bull was issued on 7 September, freeing the couple from the penalties of excommunication which they had incurred by transgressing canon law, and granting them a dispensation to marry in a public ceremony. As a penance, two chapels were to be founded.[16]

In this case of urgent princely necessity, the wheels of papal and royal administration had turned with uncharacteristic speed. There were worries that a future heir to the throne of England might be conceived – perhaps even born – out of lawful wedlock. Maybe it had been considered prudent by all parties that the couple should ostentatiously demonstrate that they were not cohabiting. A number of the Prince's warrants are dated at Waltham (Essex) late in August, in September and early in October 1361.[17] Waltham was away from his usual haunts. It seems likely that he was staying in the highly respectable precincts of the Benedictine abbey there. It was famed for its miracle-working Holy Cross. Also there was the tomb of King Harold, killed in the battle of Hastings in 1066, who in the traditional view had defied God's will in opposing William the Conqueror's claim to the throne and had been duly punished – an example for a headstrong prince, who might soon be king, to take heed of.[18]

Pope Innocent considered – and so, we may assume, did the king – that any doubts about Joan's previous marital status needed to be urgently reviewed and settled. The pope ordered Islip to enquire as to whether anything had come to light to challenge the papal nullification in 1349 of her marriage to the earl of Salisbury. The investigation by Islip and his colleagues confirmed that earlier papal judgement. On

6 October 1361, the Prince and Joan were espoused in the chapel of Lambeth Manor, the archbishop's residence across the Thames from London. Among those present were the bishop of Winchester (William Edendon), Roger Lord de la Warre, and the knights Edward Courtenay (a son of the earl of Devon), James Audley and Nicholas Lovayne.[19] Lord de la Warre had close family connections with Joan. His mother Margaret was one of the late Thomas Holand's sisters, and his wife Eleanor a sister of Joan's aunt Blanche Wake. De la Warre had served under the Prince on campaign, and he and his family were to be closely connected with the Prince over the next decade. Audley and Lovayne were the Prince's knights: Audley had a reputation for prowess and chivalry rivalling that of Chandos.[20]

Four days later, on 10 October, the Prince and Joan were married in the chapel of Windsor Castle – presumably the magnificent chapel built by the king in honour of St George. The bride wore a scarlet wedding dress, which was donated as an offering to St George's Chapel, and long remained there. This was a bold, even defiant piece of symbolism: the colour signified courage and other princely qualities. There was an impressive tally of witnesses from the episcopal bench, the king's family and the magnates. Among those present were Bishop Edendon of Winchester, John Gynwell, bishop of Lincoln, Robert Wyvil, bishop of Salisbury, and John, bishop elect of Worcester. There were present, too, the king's sons John of Gaunt, Edmund of Langley and Thomas of Woodstock (the last aged six). Also among those present were Thomas Beauchamp, earl of Warwick, Robert Ufford, earl of Suffolk, the king's sister Joan, queen of David II of Scotland, and Maud, countess of Hainault, elder daughter of the recently deceased duke of Lancaster. Joan's previous husband, the earl of Salisbury, was conspicuously absent.[21]

However much merriment there was at Windsor, some of the participants surely had mixed feelings about the marriage. It would, indeed, have been easy for the Prince and Joan to have stepped back from what some must have regarded as their high-handed and irresponsible folly. They could have parted from one another, on the grounds of the invalidity of their original vows. Perhaps they had come under pressure from the king and their close kinsfolk to part. However, apart from their strong feelings for each other, both of them probably considered that it would not have been consonant with their honour to back out. Joan's reputation would have been finally damned, as being a mature woman of high degree whose incorrigible lust had ensnared the highly respected Prince into having an illicit affair.

Indeed, chroniclers were spare in their comments, tellingly silent or reticent about this sudden and sensational event which must have created a stir. Probably – following opinion at court and among the nobility – people were disinclined to cast aspersions on the Prince, since his martial achievements had brought both him and the realm great honour. There were a few pointed comments. Henry Knighton, canon of Leicester Abbey, recalled unhelpfully that Joan had been married to the earl of Salisbury, divorced him and married Holand, 'for whose desire for her it was said the divorce had been made'. The chronicler of Wigmore Abbey (Herefordshire) referred to the somewhat doubtful subject of her former virgin status, saying (perhaps ironically) that she was 'known as the maid of Kent' (*cognomento virginem Cancie*). Froissart stuck to the facts and avoided indiscreet comment, simply writing that the Prince had married Joan 'for love' without his father's permission.[22]

It is most likely that the couple stayed for four weeks or so from soon after their official marriage in the Prince's house at Kennington.[23] It was a favourite residence of the Prince. The manor, in Lambeth parish, had come into his hands as part of the duchy of Cornwall. Its location was attractive. It combined ease of access to Westminster and London by boat across the Thames with a congenial rural environment, a contrast to the fumes of the city and its straggling suburbs.

The Prince spent lavishly on transforming Kennington manor house into a country residence befitting his status: expenditure was especially high during the periods 1340–52 and 1353–63. The house was not rebuilt by the Prince on the popular plan of four ranges enclosing a rectangular courtyard, but as a series of separate buildings, some of them aligned on the same axis. The principal structure was divided into the two main residential components of English medieval houses: hall and chamber. A new great hall was raised over a vaulted undercroft – probably used as a wine cellar. The most fashionable architect of the day, Henry Yevele, was contracted in 1358 to complete two spiral staircases and three chimneys at one end of the hall, and to furnish two buttresses for the hall porch at the opposite end with statues ('images') standing on 'babewyns'. The latter were a type of figures of fun also found in manuscript illuminations. They were often monkeys, but sometimes they were other sorts of grotesque figures. Perhaps the babewyns indicate a playful side to the snappish warrior-prince's character – he wanting an amusingly decorated doorway to greet his guests and put them in the mood for jollity. The stairs up from the hall from the porch presumably led to a Great Chamber behind the dais. In this chamber, the Prince or Princess might hold audience for guests and petitioners. There is likely to have been, too, an adjacent Privy Chamber where the couple could relax with family and friends in private and more intimate surroundings.

At Kennington, the chapel and the domestic and service buildings were housed in a series of separate 'kiosks'. The grounds were pleasantly landscaped. The Privy Garden and Great Garden (including a vineyard) probably stretched south of the main buildings. To the north lay the great pond, the park and the warren. Visitors arriving on horseback are likely to have ridden through the park and clattered over a little wooden bridge which gave access to the precinct outside the great hall. The Prince had been a bachelor when he set in motion the creation of a rural retreat near the capital, one fit to house a princely court. He surely set out too to charm and provide fittingly for a future bride. His son Richard II was to stay there on occasion as a boy and when he was king. Richard, tireless improver of royal palaces, seems (perhaps nostalgically) to have kept Kennington as he remembered it from when young, his father's house intact.[24]

The couple celebrated their first Christmas and New Year's festivities together at the Prince's castle at Berkhamsted in Hertfordshire (see Plate IV). It was, as the surviving earthworks and fragments of stonework display, an old-fashioned 'motte and bailey' castle, with an imposing keep on the great mound. The Prince had restored the castle from a ruinous condition to one fit to entertain royal guests. It was a favourite place for him to spend his Christmas holidays. He and his bride probably removed there in November 1361 and stayed till after Twelfth Night. According to Froissart's differing versions, either Queen Philippa, or she and her husband and children, made a brief visit there before Christmas. Froissart, young, newly arrived in England, and attached to the queen's service, retained vivid memories of the visit. Many years later, he recalled how a knight much respected in royal circles, Sir Bartholomew Burghersh, sat on a bench there and told two of the queen's maids-of-honour from Hainault about prophecies on English history. Froissart was insistent that the purpose of the visit was to take leave before the Prince and Joan left for Aquitaine. However, Richard Barber has shown that this is unlikely, as they did not embark until 1363, and Froissart cannot have mistaken it for the Christmas season of 1362, as the record of the Prince's itinerary does not support his presence at Berkhamsted then.[25]

The Prince took good care to set up the two chantries whose foundation had been ordered as a penance for his sinful marriage, within the stipulated period. They were endowed in Canterbury Cathedral.[26] The Prince and Princess are likely to have shared in the widespread devotion to St Thomas of Canterbury, and were probably eager to please Archbishop Islip, who had sure-footedly and expeditiously helped to negotiate around the obstacles to their marriage.

Marriage to the Prince may have been financially providential for Joan. He provided fittingly for her material and personal needs. She was to receive 2,000 marks (£1,666 13s 4d) annually, in instalments, to be paid into her chamber; £2,000 gross was then considered an income fit for an earl. Other large sums were paid out by the Prince's officials for her clothes and furnishing over the next few years. The huge sum of over £715 was paid for a London embroiderer's provision over nearly two years of decorated fabrics for the Prince, the Princess and her two daughters (Joan and Maud). As much as £200 was spent on sets of fashionable buttons for the Princess's gowns, and £6 13s 4d for mending a corset which Queen Philippa had given to her.[27] Joan's four pregnancies would have made her especially figure-conscious; evidence from later in her life suggests that she may have had a fuller figure and a tendency to put on weight. It must have been a joy for Joan and her daughters to wear bright fabrics and glittery buttons instead of the mourning raiment appropriate to the bereaved. Over £108 was spent on a litter made in London for her: this must have been of awesomely luxurious construction.

The Prince was especially concerned to please Joan by confirming annuities which she had ratified in her brief widowhood. So he strove to ensure that she had some familiar and trusted faces around her, and to faithfully support her obligations to her fee-holders. He shrugged off the consequent long-term diminution of cash resources available to him from the earldom of Kent: in some cases, he augmented existing rewards to Holand's former retainers.[28] The Prince's readiness to take on Joan's officials reflects not only his affection for her, but his trust in her late husband's and her own judgements.

As we have seen, attempts were made by the Prince's officials to improve some of the Holand properties – and in some cases in ways which were beneficial to the tenants. It may be that there were fears that the Prince's regime would be more efficient and perhaps oppressive. But for gentlefolk, and those aspiring to gentility, the lordship of such a great prince offered new opportunities to seek exalted patronage, or at least constituted a tenurial link with a paragon of chivalry, a source of pride. The decorative schemes which were once in Cottingham parish church were a striking memorial to the Prince's possession of the earldom of Kent, especially its lordship of Wake, and to his marriage to Joan. The church was rebuilt in the fourteenth century on an impressive scale. The nave and aisles of the church were ascribed by A. S. Harvey to the second quarter of the fourteenth century: he said that the transepts were started c. 1330, and attributed these works to the patronage of Thomas Lord Wake. The inscription on the brass over the tomb of the rector Nicholas Louth (d. 1383), in the sanctuary, describes him as the chancel's maker and erector. This claim was repeated in the glass formerly in the east window, where it was asserted that he caused the chancel to be made in 1374. Louth was a clerk in the royal Exchequer, and was presented to the living of Cottingham by the Prince. He was a canon in two cathedrals, but his unusual elaboration of his devotion to the Works of Mercy in the inscription on his tomb suggests that he may have had a conscientious care for his parishioners. His magnificent rebuilding certainly suggests his devotion to the parish.[29]

However, the most remarkable features of Louth's chancel, for which he may too have been responsible, in honour of his royal patrons and especially the Prince, have long since disappeared. These were seventy-four emblazoned shields in the east and side windows, and shields carved on the misericords of the stalls, identifications for which were suggested by Harvey. In the east window, Edward III's arms were in the central light, and the others blazoned were those of his sons, and of Joan. The north and south windows had coats of arms of nobles and knights prominent in Edward III's reign, many of them closely associated with the Prince.

We have no evidence that the Prince or Joan subscribed to the costs of these schemes, or ever viewed them. Perhaps Louth was encouraged and supported in the project by lords in the region who wished to commemorate their associations with the Prince and magnates with whom they had multiple bonds, especially ones forged in the wars in France. Harvey identified – often tentatively – many of the thirty-two coats of arms displayed on the misericords as those of Yorkshire lords and knights. Maybe, as he suggests, they were donors to the costs of the chancel. Perhaps the stalls were places some of them might expect to occupy if they were passing through Cottingham. The heraldic schemes there suggest parallels with other notable religious commemorations of chivalrous groups in the period. The Knights of the Garter had plates with their blazons affixed to the back of their stalls in St George's Chapel, Windsor Castle. The great east window of Gloucester Abbey (now the Cathedral) is filled with the coats of arms of nobles and knights of Edward III's reign.[30]

Joan probably spent periods of the year 1362 at Kennington, where some of the Prince's warrants were dated. In May 1362 he was present at (and presumably participated in) jousts held in Smithfield, the horse market just outside the walls of London. That day he had alms given to the four Orders of friars and to two anchorites. Joan (presumably also present) bought lengths of cloth.[31]

The Prince's mandates suggest that he may have been at Peterborough on 12 April and on 24–5 June 1362.[32] He may have prayed at the abbey's statue of Our Lady, and at the shrine containing St Oswald's incorrupt arm, which had a long miracle-working tradition. The cult of a king whose death in battle was considered martyrdom for the Faith would have had a particular appeal for the Prince. Moreover, Peterborough was within easy reach of Thomas Holand's burial place at Stamford, and Blanche Wake's residences at Deeping and Bourne.

1 Portrait of Joan of Kent (c. 1380) from the St Albans Abbey *Liber Benefactorum* (Book of Benefactors).

11   Queen Philippa of Hainault at her coronation in February 1330. Joan and
her brothers were placed under the queen's care in the royal household a few
months later.

III   Edward the Black Prince receives the grant of the Principality of Aquitaine from his father Edward III.

IV Berkhamsted Castle, Hertfordshire. One of Edward the Black Prince's favourite residences. The prince restored the castle before his marriage to Joan and the newly wedded couple spent Christmas here in 1361.

v Prince Edward's tomb in Canterbury Cathedral. Joan was a regular visitor to Canterbury, where she offered prayers at the Shrine of St Thomas and for the soul of her husband.

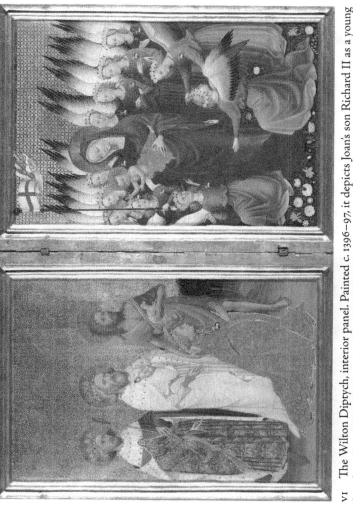

VI   The Wilton Diptych, interior panel. Painted c. 1396–97, it depicts Joan's son Richard II as a young boy, kneeling and praying to the Virgin and Child. Behind him stand (from left to right) St Edmund the Martyr, St Edward the Confessor and St John the Baptist.

VII   Richard II confers with the rebels from a barge outside London during the Peasants' Revolt, 1381.

VIII   Wallingford Castle, Oxfordshire. The castle was Joan's principal residence after the death of her husband Prince Edward. She died here in August 1385.

It is likely that the Prince, together with the Princess, was visiting thereabouts, and he was being received as lord on some of her estates. One would have expected the pair to have been visiting shrines in order to pray that their anticipated voyage to France would be blessed – and for the birth of an heir, which would manifest divine approval of their marriage. The Prince certainly made offerings of wax candles before an altar at Peterborough Abbey and one at St Albans Abbey.[33] It is surprising that Joan apparently did not conceive for over two years after their union, a matter surely of adverse comment among detractors, and of some distress to the couple. In her previous marriage, Joan had been fertile: one wonders whether the Prince was not.

On 19 July 1362, at Westminster, in the presence of a galaxy of nobles, Edward III invested the Prince as ruler of the newly created Principality of Aquitaine (see Plate III).[34] Edward had decided that a unitary authority was needed to combine the rule of the duchy of Gascony with that of the adjacent territories ceded to him by the French Crown, and that the Prince, used to ruling and leading the Gascons as royal lieutenant, and well acquainted with southern France, was the man for the job. He above all others appeared to have the ability and prestige to make this resurrected Aquitaine a viable and flourishing entity, ruling it with the aid of his experienced cadre of officers, and hopefully attracting to court regional nobilities with no recent tradition of homage to a Plantagenet. Edward's elevation of his recently out-of-control son was typical of his generosity towards his offspring and his recognition of their talents. He may have considered, too, that his habitually good relations with the Prince might be damaged if the latter, headstrong, restless for action and authority, was now to reside permanently in England. It could be anticipated that he would hold an alternative court to his father's, one likely to be a cynosure of chivalry and lavishness, presided over by a beguiling lady, so recently the focus of ambitious men's desires and aspirations. Anyway, in view of Joan's outrageous entrapment of his heir, it is unlikely that Edward contemplated the prospect of her absence with sorrow.

Plymouth was to be the couple's embarkation port. In the autumn and winter of 1362–63, some of the Prince's mandates were dated at nearby Plympton, and some at his castle of Restormel, near Lostwithiel.

He (and Joan) may have stayed in the rich Augustinian priory at Plympton, where he convalesced on his return to England in 1371.[35] Alternatively, the princely household may have stayed in Plympton Castle, imposing, but now long vanished. It belonged to the earl of Devon, whose grandson and heir, Hugh Courtney, was to be betrothed to Joan's daughter Maud. Restormel Castle's main feature is its keep, within which were a circle of well-appointed residential apartments. Another attractive feature was the surrounding deer park.[36]

According to the dating of the Prince's warrants, he seems to have been in London and Windsor on occasion in the early months of 1363. He dated warrants at Reading (Berkshire) on 24 and 25 April. He is likely to have visited the imposing abbey there, and prayed at the shrine it housed, containing the principal relic of St James in England – one of his hands.[37] In May the Prince was back at Plympton – and Joan was presumably there too. Doubtless they wondered if and when they would see England again. They rented out the useful and valuable manor of Bushey for as long as twelve years.[38] On 8 June the Prince was on shipboard in Plymouth Haven, preparing for the arduous voyage down the Channel and round the coasts of Brittany, heading for the port of La Rochelle in south-west France. The voyage ushered in the crucial chapter in their married life, in which they were to experience courtly triumphs and crushing tragedies.

6

Princess of Wales and of Aquitaine

A NOVEL ENVIRONMENT

THE NEWLY CREATED PRINCIPALITY of Aquitaine comprised those territories which had been granted to Edward III and his heirs in south-west France in full sovereignty by John II in 1360. At its governmental core was Gascony, ruled by the kings of England as its dukes since Eleanor of Aquitaine's husband became Henry II in 1154. Besides Gascony, John II had ceded to Edward other substantial parts of the historical duchy of Aquitaine: to the north of Gascony, Saintonge, Angoulême, Limousin and Poitou; to the east, Périgord, Agenais, Cahorsin, Quercy, and to the south, Armagnac, Condom, Bigorre and Rouergue.[1] In January 1361, Sir John Chandos had been appointed 'lieutenant and captain general ... and special conservator' of the peace and truce in France. He was one of those who had the tasks of negotiating the return of the places ceded by Edward to the allegiance of the French Crown which still housed supposedly 'pro-English' garrisons, and of receiving homages to Edward III in those places conceded to him. In many parts of Aquitaine there was reluctance to embrace a long-dormant Plantagenet allegiance. Chandos was tactful but firm, confirming with alacrity the privileges about whose security under an imposed alien rule nobles and communes were anxious. He had completed the task by the spring of 1362.[2]

According to a monk-chronicler at Canterbury Cathedral Priory, the Prince arrived in Gascony on 29 June 1363. He stayed for a while at the castle of Lormont, three miles outside Bordeaux.[3] It was a residence of the archbishops of Bordeaux. The city was the only one in south-west France comparable to London in its size of population (about 30,000 in 1300), in the scope of its trade and in the wealth of its leading merchants. They were dominant in the civic elite, and played important roles in the overseas trade of south-west France, importing foodstuffs and finished goods, and shipping wine produced in the Bordelais and the wider south-west down the River Garonne for export, much of it to England or Flanders. Indeed, the recurrent wars with the French Crown since the 1290s had disrupted the trade of Bordeaux, especially through long-term damage to Aquitainian viticulture. The peace of 1360 gave hope of renewed stability and a recovery of prosperity.

The families of the mercantile elite of Bordeaux were long accustomed to intermarrying with the nobility of the Bordelais. The latter were, typically, petty seigneurs, for whom the infusion of commercial wealth was a welcome boost to family finances.[4] For some of the Gascon nobles and commons, the English connection had given opportunities for direct profit. From Edward I's time onwards, members of the nobility had contracted to give paid military service, with their retinues, for the English Crown's wars. In the 1350s the Prince's employment of Gascons had carried some of them to peaks of military honour and profit, especially on the campaign of 1356, culminating in his victory of Poitiers. However, the advent of peace restricted military opportunities in France. Expectations among seigneurs that the Prince in his new role would have a cornucopia of patronage to lavish on them may have generally been mixed, for the ducal domain in Gascony was small, and throughout Aquitaine lords and communes jealously guarded their patronage of the offices they controlled. Moreover, the Prince had Englishmen and other foreigners in his service to reward – though he was to show some sensitivity to the susceptibilities and ambitions of local elites in his choices for appointments in his gift. Indeed, some strangers may have been welcome as *sénéchaux*, as they were more likely to be neutral in the disputes with which the elites were characteristically riven.

Service to the English Crown had brought recent generations of Gascon nobles within the orbit of English courtly culture, just as the similar service of nobles from some other parts of Aquitaine had brought them within that of the courts of the Capetian and Valois kings – whose cults of courtliness and chivalry were closely interlinked with those practised at Windsor and Westminster. On arriving at Bordeaux, Joan entered a world whose Occitan language is unlikely to have been familiar to English ladies. They conversed politely in

Norman-French, which is likely to have facilitated communication with the higher nobility of the region. The social values which she was to encounter in Gascony and elsewhere in Aquitaine were in many ways akin to her own.

Acculturation occurred in religious devotion as well as in courtly and chivalrous style. In Bordeaux, there was the ancient, imposing and rich collegiate church of Saint-Seurin (Severinus), who had been archbishop of Bordeaux c. 420. If, as is likely, Joan made offerings there, she may well have marvelled at its relics of heroic figures much reverenced by the English nobility. Its necropolis was one of the most hallowed in Christendom. There, Charlemagne was said to have had buried the remains of knights who had fallen with Roland in battle with Muslims at the Pass of Roncevaux. The church housed the heart shrine of Roland himself. Near Saint-Seurin was a chapel dedicated to a saint especially dear to Edward III and his family – St George. It had been founded by a canon of the cathedral in the previous century. A saint widely reverenced in Gascony as well as in England was St James the Greater, the Apostle. Joan's parents had intended to go on pilgrimage to the saint's shrine at Santiago de Compostela in Galicia. The church of Saint-Seurin was a station on one of the pilgrim ways to Santiago, but that was not the way taken by most English pilgrims, who sailed from England direct to La Coruña.[5]

Joan would not only have found that ecclesiastical institutions and religious sentiment in the city resembled those in English cities, but that specifically English pious resonances were prominent there. The revered English Carmelite St Simon Stock (d. 1265) – whose vision of the Blessed Virgin Mary resulted in the Order's adoption of the scapular – was buried in the Carmelite house there. The foundation stone of the Franciscan church recorded that it was founded in 1249 in honour of St Mary, St Francis and St Edward – that is, the English royal saint, Edward the Confessor.[6] The favour Joan and her family circle habitually showed to the Franciscan Order makes it likely that she patronised this house.

Moreover, in Bordeaux's magnificent cathedral of Saint-André there was a poignant reminder of the Plantagenet connection – the tomb in the choir of Joan's namesake, the Prince's little sister, who, aged only fourteen, had died of plague in the city in 1348. She had been on her way to Castile as the prospective bride of Pedro, heir to the throne – with whom, when king of Castile, the Prince and Joan were to become only too well acquainted.[7] The cathedral was the most impressive and dominant building in the city. It had been in the process of being rebuilt from the later thirteenth century onwards. The works had received a boost from the donations of Pope Clement V (d. 1315). He was born Bertrand de Goth, member of a leading noble family from the Bordelais. The striking addition to the church of the north transept, with its elaborately sculpted ceremonial entrance, had been completed a few years before the Prince and Princess arrived. Saint-André was served by Augustinian canons, who controlled a large regional lordship.[8] The cathedral was the spiritual centre of the archdiocese. Local noble families cherished their burial places there, and in that period the number of obits set up there for both clerics and lay folk, especially from in or near the city, was increasing.[9]

It was in the great church of Saint-André that the Prince commenced on 9 July 1363 to receive Gascon and other homages, positioning his first formal assertions of personal lordship in one of the most awesome sacred settings in the Principality. He took more homages there later that month, and some in the nearby archbishop's palace. In that year and the one following, he made his first solemn entries into cities in other provinces of Aquitaine, to gather in allegiances.[10] It is not clear whether Joan accompanied him or not on these visits. Indeed, it is not certain where she spent most of her time during her years in Aquitaine. It may not have been wholly, or even mainly, in Gascony. Chandos Herald, writing his life of the Prince about ten years after his death, reflecting some roseate personal memories, located the Prince's household as residing typically at Angoulême in Angoumois, as well as Bordeaux,[11] as did Froissart.

SPLENDOUR AT COURT

IT MADE GOOD SENSE for the Prince to spend some time in Bordeaux. Through sailings and commercial networks, the city had well-established communications with England. It could readily fulfil the consumption needs of the large and lavish household that he wished to maintain. It was habitually visited by many Gascon nobles.

There, he and his Princess could conveniently attempt to strengthen loyalties by their well-versed practice of courtliness, and by displays of power and chivalry. Chandos Herald claimed that every day eighty knights and 320 squires were fed at the Prince's table. 'There were held jousts and revels in Angoulême and Bordeaux; there dwelt all noble qualities – largesse, gentility (*franchise*) and honour.'[12] Froissart, too, commented (also from personal experience) on the high estate that the Prince and Princess kept at court – though sourly, in the context of the eventual decline of the Prince's rule.[13]

We cannot be certain where the couple held court when they were in Bordeaux. The residence de l'Ombrière, which housed the administrative offices of the duchy of Gascony, is unlikely to have had suitable accommodation. We cannot be certain that they lodged principally within the city walls. Yves Renouard thought that the Prince's household might have stayed outside the city (as, indeed, it had outside London in rural Kennington) – perhaps either in Blanquefort castle or the castle of Lormont – and that indications that their court might have been located in the archiepiscopal palace in Bordeaux are slight. On one occasion the Prince had certainly exercised the ducal right to receive hospitality (*gîte*) in the palace – he had stayed there in 1355.[14] In 1370 he addressed the nobles, according to Froissart, in the chamber of the 'abbey' of Saint-André.[15] Froissart repeatedly refers to the Prince's and Joan's residence in 'l'abbeye de Saint Andrieu' in 1366 – presumably reliably so, since he was at their court in Bordeaux on Twelfth Night 1367.[16] 'Abbeye' would seem an odd way of describing the long-vanished medieval palace situated near the cathedral. However, the cathedral had up to eighteen canons – perhaps the Prince and Princess took over some of their also vanished residences and public spaces. In 1399, according to Froissart, Henry of Bolingbroke told Richard II that it was rumoured that 'your father was a clerk or a canon. At the time when you were conceived and born at Bordeaux on the Gironde there were many young and handsome ones in the Prince's household.'[17] This nasty piece of gossip may have its origins partly in garbled memories of the princely couple living alongside the resident cathedral clergy, socialising with them, perhaps to some extent merging with their households. If there were close and amicable relations between the resident clergy and the princely household, they could have fostered ducal influence, since the canons tended to be drawn from leading families of the Bordelais. But it seems most likely that the palace itself was the couple's normal residence. For it would surely have had fuller accommodation, and a hall, presence chamber and private chambers more fitting for the projection of courtly magnificence than any other buildings associated with the cathedral, or, for that matter, than any nearby rural castle.

As we have seen, Chandos Herald specified Angoulême as the court's other habitual place of residence. There, the castle provided an undoubtedly grand setting for the household, and for the reception and entertainment of notable guests such as Pierre de Lusignan, the king of Cyprus and titular king of Jerusalem, and John count of Armagnac. Over several days in August 1363, the Prince had received the homages of the lords of Angoumois, some in 'la salle' of the chateau.[18] Why, besides the attractions of the princely residence at Angoulême, did the Prince decide to reside there a good deal? One probable reason was that the city was an important centre of communications, especially with northern and western parts of the Principality, as well as with Bordeaux. There was a good road to the port of La Rochelle. The counties of Poitou, Limousin and Périgord were within easy reach. Moreover, as well as being an important strategic centre, Angoulême was highly defensible. On a bluff above the river Charente, it dominates rolling, hilly countryside (reminiscent of some of the more douce English shires), and it then had a formidable enceinte of ramparts and towers. Its fairs attracted the produce of Angoumois.

The princely couple may have considered the place a pleasant change from the bustle of low-lying Bordeaux – less noisome, quieter, airier and healthier. There was good hunting country near Angoulême. In July 1365, the Prince, writing from Bordeaux, exasperatedly summoned Gaston Fébus, count of Foix, to come in September to him at Angoulême or Périgueux in order to perform homage for the county of Béarn. Gaston in his reply tried to lighten the mood. He said that he hoped that Sir John Chandos would bring his pack of hounds, and, as the great expert on the chase, he somewhat condescendingly offered to give his advice on hunting.[19]

The imposing castle of Taillefer at Angoulême, previously belonging to the French Crown, was a more fitting residence for a prince than any in Bordeaux. It had been rebuilt by a queen – Isabella, heiress of the Taillefer counts of Angoulême. She had been married to King John of England, and later brought her inheritance to another husband, Hugh de Lusignan. She had commenced the rebuilding of the castle in 1228.[20] It covered a large area in a small city; its great courtyard was dominated by a fine donjon. The two remaining towers give some idea of its impressive scale.

This was the residence that was prepared for the birth of the child who was, as far as we know, Joan's first offspring by the Prince.[21] The date usually given for the birth is 1365. This is the date found in some independent contemporary English chronicles.[22] It receives some corroboration from the date on which the generous annuity of £40 was granted by Edward III to John Delves, a leading official of the Prince, for bringing him news of the birth: that was 20 November 1365. However, other chroniclers date the birth to 1364. That date, too, is suggested by the boy's age in 1367 as given by Froissart, and by the date of his death given in the Wigmore Abbey Chronicle.[23]

Froissart's mention of the visit to the court at Angoulême of Pierre de Lusignan, king of Cyprus, is relevant. Pierre toured northern European courts in 1363–64 in an effort to drum up support for a crusade in the Middle East. His degree of success in putting the crusade high on western lords' agenda is a testimony to his persuasive character. However, Edward III courteously excused himself from crusading on the grounds of his advanced age. The Prince was also otherwise engaged. Froissart says that, after his wife's delivery, he was planning jousts and entertainments involving forty knights and forty squires, in her honour, when he heard that Pierre (then on his way home) had arrived at Poitiers. The Prince sent Chandos to meet him there and bring him to the festivities at Angoulême.[24] The king's itinerary makes clear that his visit must have been in 1364.[25]

The infant Edward's baptism was carried out in the cathedral of Saint-Pierre in Angoulême in the presence of a large and distinguished company. The celebrations for the churching of Joan after Edward's birth were to be a high point of the Prince's rule. An account of them reached a chronicling Franciscan at Lynn in Norfolk, one perhaps derived from a *confrère* in Joan's household or in the Order's house at Angoulême, or else from one of the Prince's servants, several of whom hailed from Norfolk. The friar says that 706 knights and 154 ladies (*domine*) were present. The festivities lasted ten days and cost 18,000 écus. Joan had twenty-four knights and the same number of ladies in fine array at jousts, dances and 'other transient pleasures', as the friar wrote starchily. He was amazed by the amount spent just on wax – £400, he had heard.[26]

Such lavishness had a practical purpose. It was intended to advertise hopes of perpetuation of a dynasty, one whose ancient royalty was enhanced by a new princeliness. Among others present, such festivities would surely have been attended by the nobility of Angoumois, Saintonge and Poitou. When warfare with the French Crown resumed in 1369, these regions remained remarkably loyal to the Prince, in contrast to others to the west and south of Gascony, and, indeed, in Gascony's southern reaches.

Joan's household doubtless had some Aquitanian servants. A certain Garcius Arnaud may have entered her service there; he later was one of her favourite esquires in England, when he was said to be 'of Aquitaine', but also from Salines, which can be identified as a place south of Besançon in the county of Burgundy (Franche Comté), part of the Holy Roman Empire. However, other individuals whom we can surmise to have been among her household servants in Aquitaine appear to have been English. One Englishwoman who was certainly with her in 1367 was Anne Latimer, whose husband, Sir Thomas of Braybrooke (Northamptonshire), was then in the Prince's retinue, and, as we shall see, later back in England had connections with Joan. Anne was present at the birth of Joan's second son Richard of Bordeaux, and took the news to the Prince.[27] Joan's kinswoman Eleanor de la Warre was probably important among the ladies in Joan's household: in 1366, on her petition, the pope granted Eleanor the privileges of having a portable altar and of receiving plenary remission at the hour of death. Her husband, Roger, and Roger's elder son John served the Prince when he was ruling Aquitaine.[28]

Another of Joan's *domicellae* there was Lady Marion Louches, possibly the wife of one of the Prince's knights, Sir Adam. In 1366 she received similar privileges at Joan's request as those bestowed on Lady de la Warre, and so did Johanneta Peverel (possibly wife of the Prince's knight, Sir Hugh).[29]

Elizabeth Luttrell (the earl of Devon's daughter) was another who may have attended on Joan in Aquitaine. She, with her husband Sir Andrew, who was a knight of the Prince, was named on the roll of petitions which Joan had presented to the pope that year. In response to Joan's petition, the couple received the privileges of having a portable altar, and of choosing their own confessors over several years. By a warrant dated at Plymouth, 10 June 1363, the Prince ordered the delivery of a tun of wine, which he had left there, to Sir Andrew Luttrell and his wife (styled the Princess's kinswoman), for their voyage. But we cannot assume that they sailed in the wake of their patrons to Gascony. For the couple were, it seems, ardent and intrepid pilgrims, who may have been fulfilling postponed earlier vows. In 1360 Andrew had been planning to go to the Holy Land, and in 1361 a Privy Seal letter had been issued ordering the provision of a ship for him and Elizabeth, for their passage with twenty-four men and women, and their mounts, to sail towards Santiago.[30] Joan's connections in this period with ladies whose husbands served the Prince suggest one way in which she was brought into the orbit of his well-established affinity, and also that, as a princess, her household was augmented with more distinguished ladies than hitherto.

Another for whom Joan procured a papal privilege in 1363 was definitely one of her *domicellae*: this was Margery de Mere. She could not digest fish, and wished to be permitted to follow a diet of milk, cheese and eggs in Lent. The pope granted this if it accorded with medical advice, and if potage (soup seasoned mainly with vegetables) was insufficient to compensate for her weakness.[31]

Two laymen can be tentatively identified as members of Joan's household in Aquitaine. They appear as recipients of spiritual benefits at her request. In 1366 Walter Bray was her butler; Roger Foljambe, probably a member of a distinguished Nottinghamshire family, was in receipt of a life annuity of £5 from the Prince in 1362, to be paid by the reeve or bailiff of one of Joan's manors (Ashford).[32]

Family affairs were a preoccupation of Joan in 1365–66. The Prince was concerned to promote the interests of her Holand children. Indeed, their marriages were a means for him to strengthen his domestic and international ties. Circa 1365 Joan's daughter Maud married Hugh Courtenay, grandson and heir of the earl of Devon. In that year,

too, the Prince and Joan made a settlement with Richard third earl
of Arundel (one of the king's closest friends) for the marriage of the
Prince's godson Thomas Holand (then aged about fourteen) to the
earl's daughter Alice. They were to enfeoff Thomas and Alice with
Wake estates in Yorkshire valued at 500 marks, and Arundel was to
give them 400 marks. In October 1366 the Prince petitioned Pope
Urban V for a dispensation for the marriage. This seems to have turned
out to be a successful arranged marriage between two young people,
for over thirty years later Alice was entrusted by Thomas to carry out
(with their son) testamentary intentions, 'for the love and trust that has
been between us'.[33]

Young Thomas had received a royal licence to go to Gascony.[34]
Perhaps it was envisaged that he would accompany his teenage sister
Joan, who was affianced to John de Montfort, claimant to the duchy of
Brittany. Duke John, aged twenty-seven, had spent much of his youth
in exile at Edward III's court, and had married his short-lived daughter,
Mary. As we have also seen, he still had to contend with the rival Blois
claim to the duchy, supported by the French Crown. The Prince took
the young man under his wing, and promoted a favourable settlement
of his claim. He was in the Prince's retinue in the Dominican friary
at Agen on the occasion in January 1364 when Gaston Fébus of Foix
enraged the Prince by declining to perform homage to him for all
his lordships. As we have seen, Montfort gained the ascendancy in
Brittany with the Prince's aid at the battle of Auray. In 1365 the Prince
and Duke John made a formal alliance, and by 26 March 1366 the duke
had married Joan Holand.[35] It made good sense for the Prince to try to
safeguard the north-west flank of the Principality through this alliance.
However, Michael Jones suggests that the marriage took place without
Edward III's licence or even knowledge, though Duke John had legally
obliged himself to consult the king about any such intended union.
If the suggestion is right, it shows the Prince still being cavalier with
regard to his father over high-level matchmaking. Froissart says that
the wedding ceremony was held at Nantes – the principal city in the
duchy, convenient for a journey from Angoulême.[36]

The Princess had another cause for rejoicing – and for
apprehension – in 1366. She became pregnant again, conceiving (if she
went to full term) early in April. At the age of about thirty-eight, the

prospect of childbirth in that period was indeed perilous. Sometime between late March and late April Pope Urban granted her indults to choose her own confessor, to have plenary remission at the hour of death, and to choose a priest to minister the Sacrament to her and four members of her household.[37]

WARFARE AND DECLINE

THERE WERE OTHER CAUSES for apprehension for Joan that year, as the possibility that the Principality might soon be at war turned into a certainty. Since the peace of 1360, bands of the Companies had remained a menace in France. Some still defiantly refused to give up the castles and towns they had originally seized in the name of one or other of the royal protagonists. Others, having evacuated their strongholds, menacingly sought sustenance and employment. Neighbouring rulers, such as Pope Urban V at Avignon, were rightly apprehensive of their intentions. Besides, some of the English and French soldiers who had worked with the Companies in the service of either the Prince or the French Crown were likely, too, to have chafed at the decline in military employment. However, plans to revive crusading were in the air: Pierre de Lusignan's crusade in 1365, on which he captured and briefly occupied the great port of Alexandria in Egypt, was the most striking western success in the Middle East for generations, in which prominent Englishmen participated.[38] But the venture demonstrated the difficulties of making permanent gains in that ephemeral sphere: there were tempting prizes for pious and acquisitive knights nearer at hand.[39]

In the early 1360s plans were afoot, promoted by the pope, for prominent French and English knights, commanding the companies of footloose mercenaries, to go on crusade against the Moors in Spain, and conquer their one remaining kingdom there, Granada. Yet, however tempting that vision was, the situation in Christian Spain was hardly conducive to a revival of traditional Iberian crusading. Since the mid 1350s there had been fierce recurrent hostilities between the two most powerful Spanish kings, Pedro I of Castile and Pere III of Aragon. Pere had offered help to Pedro's dissident illegitimate brother Enrique of Trastamara, but Pedro continued to score military successes in his invasions of Aragon.[40] Soon after a renewal of hostilities in 1362, Edward III allied with Pedro. This encouraged Edward's tricky and powerful southern Gascon vassal, the count of Armagnac, to lead a force in support of the Castilians against Aragon. Pere was obliged to make an unfavourable peace the following year.[41]

However, warfare soon resumed. Charles V of France, who had succeeded his father John II in 1364, was looking for ways to diminish English influence. He made an alliance the following year with Pere, who hoped to counter the Castilian threat, and with Enrique of Trastamara, now Charles's vassal, and a protégé of his vigorous and ambitious brother Louis duke of Anjou. The duke, royal lieutenant in Languedoc (that is, in provinces south of the River Loire still ruled by the French Crown), was to show himself dedicated to the destruction of the Principality of Aquitaine. The French and Aragonese agreed that an army commanded by the leading French soldier Bertrand du Guesclin should invade Castile, remove Pedro in Enrique's favour and then go on to conquer Granada – an ambitious programme indeed, neatly dovetailing quests for enormous wealth and for divine favour. Urban V was prepared to give the expedition the status of a crusade. The Companies were to be at its core. Among those who contracted to go were leading English and Gascon knights who had served the Prince. Astonishingly, he made no objection to their participation, or that of any of his Aquitanian subjects.[42] Why not, since Pedro was his father's ally? Conventionally devout, the Prince naturally approved of crusading. He may have seriously regretted his inability to respond positively to Pierre de Lusignan's earlier exhortation to join him on crusade. The alternative of campaigning against the Muslims of Granada had long had an appeal to the English nobility. The Prince and Joan probably recalled how Thomas Holand and other English knights had won great honour by participating in Alfonso XI of Castile's siege of the Moors in Algeçiras in 1344. They perhaps thought it shameful that Pedro showed no inclination to follow, with St James's spiritual support, in his father's footsteps, and in those of his famous crusading ancestors, from some of whom the Prince was descended, too, through Edward I's first queen, Eleanor of Castile. By contrast, Pedro was a lover of Moorish culture, who had apartments built in the Alcazar of Seville in exquisite Moorish style by Mudejar craftsmen – who decorated them with verses from the Qur'an. The propaganda of his half-brother Enrique's supporters, which projected him as a favourer of both Moors and Jews, had reached England.[43]

The Prince was inclined to see political relations in highly personal terms, and to be carried away in his decision-making by tides of strong emotion. That had been demonstrated most notably by his highly unsuitable marriage. However, in supporting Iberian intervention he may have been motivated, not just by dislike of Pedro, but by a desire to foster the honour and needs of Aquitaine, as he saw them. It would relieve his subjects if the threat of incursions by the Companies was removed, and they would be uplifted by the opportunity to participate in a crusade. Aquitanians had distinguished traditions of crusading in the Holy Land and against the Moors of Spain. As we have seen, the church of Saint-Seurin in Bordeaux was a shrine to Charlemagne's supposed crusading in Spain. There is also another vivid and prominent reminder of glorious mythical deeds on this expedition in Angoulême. News of the capture of Saragossa from the Moors by Alfonso of Aragon, aided by Aquitanian contingents, in 1118, had inspired the bishop of Angoulême to commission a long bas relief for the west front of his cathedral. It celebrates the deeds of Charlemagne against the Moors. Two episodes from the crusading epic *The Song of Roland* were sculpted: the duel of Archbishop Turpin with Abisme, and that of Roland with the Moorish ruler, Marsilion, with the latter's flight and death outside Saragossa.

Edward III, reacting to the plans to invade Castile, showed better sense than his son. In response to a protest brought to him by an envoy from Pedro, he intervened as suzerain of Aquitaine, ordering that his subjects there should desist from plans to attack his ally (5 December 1365). In fact, it was too late: that month the Companies were crossing the Pyrenees, passing through Aragon to prepare for the invasion of Castile.[44] In the month before it commenced, on 5 February 1366, Pope Urban V had written to Joan, asking her to urge the Prince both to mediate between the kings of Castile and Aragon, and to assist his nuncio, the bishop of Chichester (William Lenn), in a mission to foster peace between them.[45] It might have been that the pope – hypocritically – wished to advertise that he deplored the threat of war between two leading Christian princes. Perhaps he was concerned lest the Prince might now attempt to disrupt the expedition. In such case, a proposed papal initiative for peace may have been a tactic to appease the Prince. Why write to Joan? It was, indeed, not unusual for queens and princesses to receive requests to supplicate their husbands: one to prevent the effusion of Christian blood was especially appropriate for the gentle sex. The letter suggests that Urban had an appreciation of Joan's pacific character, political talents and her influence over the Prince. However, he does appear to have been trying to hoodwink her. Joan certainly had the means to be well informed about current Iberian affairs – for instance, through Sir Eustache d'Auberichecourt, husband of her former sister-in-law Elizabeth countess of Kent, who, as we have seen, played a role in these events.[46]

The Prince was now determined to invade Castile himself, in order to reinstate Pedro as its legitimate ruler, if a satisfactorily profitable agreement could be reached with him. The Prince was certain that he could enlist in his enterprise the English and Aquitanian captains who had just helped to depose Pedro. He had already overruled objections to the policy made by some of his English and Gascon councillors. After Pedro's arrival, he lost no time in convening sessions of the Estates of Aquitaine at Bordeaux and Bayonne for the purpose of securing their support and financial aid for the expedition. He gained his father's support, too. When the Estates met at Bayonne, the Prince was present with Pedro and Charles of Navarre. The latter's alliance was now vital to the Prince's plans, as he controlled the Pyrenean passes leading to Castile. The three rulers went north from Bayonne to Libourne, just east of Bordeaux, where the terms of their alliances were formally incorporated into treaties sealed on 23 September 1366.[47]

Joan, well advanced in pregnancy, had probably remained at Saint-André during this period of intense diplomatic activity and military preparation. The intention was that the court should celebrate Christmas and the New Year at Bordeaux. The Prince did not join the muster of the forces in the south. He awaited the anticipated arrival of his brother John of Gaunt, who was sailing with reinforcements from England – as well as the arrival of his own prospective offspring. The festivities of the Twelve Nights must have been laced with stresses.

On the morning of Twelfth Night – Wednesday, 6 January 1367 – Joan was delivered of a son. Froissart (presumably then enjoying hospitality in the princely household) was seated, eating a meal, when the Marshal of Aquitaine, Sir Richard Pontchardon (an Englishman), entered the room and asked him to record the birth of a fine baby boy. Pontchardon's further remarks suggest that the chief excitement in the Prince's entourage centred on the prospects about to unfold for them in Spain. Somewhat fancifully, the Marshal opined that the baby was 'a king's son, for his father (the Black Prince) is King of Galicia. King Peter has given him the kingdom and he will soon be off to conquer it.'[48] Pedro had, indeed, promised to grant the Prince the lordship of Vizcaya, which was on the Atlantic coast, like Galicia. Yet there is nothing in the record evidence to suggest that Pedro was prepared to give up Galicia itself – home to the shrine of Santiago, the lodestar of Castilian kingship. It is understandable that such a wishful-thinking rumour might have spread in the Prince's court in view of the widespread devotion to St James. The Prince's possession of his shrine would have added to his fame and honour, and have been a means to seek the blessing of such a notable crusading saint on any future holy enterprises. Perhaps the suggestion that the Prince should receive this kingdom was touted on his behalf, only to be rejected by the Castilians.

A Benedictine monk of St Augustine's Abbey, Canterbury, William Thorne, enthused in his chronicle that there had been three 'magi' at Bordeaux when the birth of the infant had taken place at Epiphany – the kings of Spain, Navarre and Portugal.[49] The inclusion of the last was highly unlikely as the relevant king of Portugal, Pedro I, actually died in Estremoz in the south of Portugal on 18 January, ten days after the birth in Bordeaux. It should therefore perhaps be regarded as a reflection of how Portugal's importance had come to be appreciated in England. The presence of Charles of Navarre is doubtful too, for early in January he met King Enrique of Castile at Santa Cruz de Campezo, a Castilian town just over the border from Navarre. There he made an alliance with Enrique, reneging on his agreements with Pedro and the Prince. However, the presence at the baptism of Pedro, King of 'Spain', as the English often unofficially described kings of Castile, is plausible. It looks as though Thorne was over-egging a story in order to glorify the Prince, a story for the most part as implausible as Pontchardon's alleged suggestion that the Prince would soon be a Spanish king. However, for the infant's parents, and for Aquitanians, the date of his birth may have had another portentous significance. For at Epiphany St John the Baptist's baptism of Christ was also celebrated. The Benedictine abbey at Saint-Jean-d'Angely, not far from Angoulême, had housed for centuries the notable relic of the head of John the Baptist. The town was familiar to the Prince, and the cult was known to pilgrims who wore its tokens in London. Richard was brought up to reverence St John as his patron saint, as is exemplified by the saint's depiction as his sponsor before the infant Christ on The Wilton Diptych (see Plate VI).

Two days after the birth, according to Froissart, the archbishop of Bordeaux (Elie de Savignac) baptised the infant at his cathedral's font. The godfathers, the chronicler said, were the bishop of Agen (Raimond de Salg) and Jaume, king of Majorca – a king without a kingdom. Its lordships had long since been seized by Pere of Aragon. Jaume's alliance was useful to the Prince and Pedro as a means of putting pressure on Pere. Why was the insignificant – and possibly lunatic – Jaume preferred as godfather to the king of Spain? Maybe there was serious talk of betrothing the infant to one of Pedro's daughters – a union to which his entry into a spiritual relationship with the infant would have presented a canonical impediment.[50]

Why was Joan's baby christened Richard? Richard Barber says that his godfathers were Richard king of Armenia and King Jaume. We have not been able to trace this King Richard. Professor Norman Housley relates how the throne of Cilician Armenia was usurped in 1363 by Constantine VI (d. 1373) – so it may be that there was a footloose rival claimant called Richard trailing around European courts. Why would the Prince and Joan have so honoured such a seemingly obscure refugee?[51] Rather, could the choice of name have had special import for them? It had not been used in Joan's immediate family, nor among the close royal kin since King John had had his younger son named Richard, in honour of his distinguished brother and predecessor, Cœur-de-Lion. John's son Richard (1209–72), earl of Cornwall, crusader and by election king of the Romans (in title ruler of the Holy Roman Empire) was a worthy kinsman for the Prince and Princess to recall. The earldom of Cornwall (elevated to a dukedom for the Black Prince) had been created for this Richard, as the Prince was surely well aware. However, it is likely that in choosing the name, the

Prince and Princess had Cœur-de-Lion in mind too. The mighty ruler of both England and the duchy of Aquitaine, Richard I was a hero of crusading romances, to whom the inhabitants of both principalities could all lay claim as one of themselves. Aquitanians and English were united in their high esteem for him. There was, as we have seen, a contemporary buzz in the air about reviving crusading. Perhaps there was speculation at court in Bordeaux that, one day, a king of England, either Richard of Bordeaux's father, or his elder brother, might grant him the Principality or a lordship in Spain, as befitted a younger son, and that in such case he would be well placed to emulate the crusading exploits of Cœur-de-Lion and of his own Castilian royal ancestors. The Prince, on his deathbed, with the possible intention of inspiring his son Richard, bequeathed him a set of tapestries 'du pas de Saladyn', whose subject was presumably King Richard's struggle with his esteemed Muslim adversary.[52]

The Prince left Bordeaux a few days after the birth of his son, not waiting for Gaunt to arrive, in order to join as soon as possible his army encamped in the foothills of the Pyrenees at Dax.[53] Chandos Herald wrote one of his most lyrical passages about Joan's sorrow, and the couple's farewells:

> according to what I heard, the Prince set out from Bordeaux fifteen days after Christmas. And then the Princess had right bitter grief at heart and she reproached the goddess of love who had brought her to such great majesty, for she had the most puissant Prince in this world. Often she said, 'Alas what should I do, God of Love, if I were to lose the very flower of nobleness, the flower of loftiest grandeur, him who had no peer in the world in valour? Death! You would be at hand. Now have I neither heart nor blood nor vein, but every member fails me when I call to mind his departure, for all the world says this, that never did man risk such a perilous expedition. Oh very sweet and glorious Father, comfort me of your pity.' The Prince listened to his gentle lady's words; he gave her noble comfort and said to her, 'Lady, cease your weeping, be not dismayed, for God has power to do all.' The noble Prince gently comforts the lady, and then sweetly takes leave of her, saying lovingly, 'Lady, we shall meet again in

97

such wise that we shall have joy, we and all our friends, for my heart tells me so.' They embrace very tenderly and take farewell with kisses. Then might you see ladies weep and damsels lament; one bewailing her lover, another her husband. The Princess was so sorrowful that, being then big with child, she through grief delivered and brought forth a very fair son.[54]

Even by his own reckoning, Chandos Herald here seems to have transposed Richard's date of birth and his father's departure. It would be easy to dismiss his account of the couple's farewells as a piece of nostalgic fiction, with its contextualisation of their relationship within the conventions of courtly romance. However, he is likely to have visited the court in Aquitaine frequently, and to have received hospitality there, as befitted a leading servant of Sir John Chandos. He would have been avidly interested in the Prince and Princess, and in gossip about their relationship. He probably concocted this scene in the mode in which the couple would have wished to present themselves, and, indeed, may have seen themselves.

We have little reason to doubt that they were still in love. Furthermore it is credible that the Princess was so distressed at the prospect of the Prince's imminent departure that this hastened her going into labour, and that her turmoil continued after the birth in her weakened condition, compounded by the personal grief of her ladies at the departure for war of their loved ones. During the five years of her marriage, the Prince had not been far distant from her for long, nor had he undertaken any hazardous expedition. He was no longer a dashing young man who could afford to be careless of deprivations and hard campaigning – he was getting on for forty. She had had the bitter experience of losing a beloved husband on service abroad.

Moreover, another reason for anxiety was that her eldest son Thomas Holand, aged about sixteen, was going on the expedition, and so was her equally youthful son-in-law Hugh Courtenay. For Englishmen, campaigning in Spain may have already had a sinister reputation. Its often difficult terrain, unaccustomed food and drink, and summer heat, could combine to cause epidemics among the unwary English, as was to occur in John of Gaunt's army in 1386–87, when many succumbed to dysentery.[55] Despite the Prince's characteristic optimism, Joan's shrewdness may also have led her to doubt whether prospects in Spain were as rosy as they were being painted. Compared with the joyful celebrations after her son Edward's birth, the churching of Joan in 1367 must have been a subdued affair, with many familiar and beloved faces missing.

Soon after the Prince's departure from Bordeaux, John of Gaunt at last arrived there, going to Saint-André, where the Princess lay. She and her ladies greeted him joyfully, but he soon hastened away, joining his brother at Dax on 13 January 1367.[56] Early in the following month, the army was on its way into Navarre, toiling up the Pass of Roncevaux, an environment doubtless recalling invigoratingly to the royal brothers and their companions the supposed crusading exploits of Charlemagne, and especially of his knights Roland and Oliver. The early part of the campaign in Castile was to be grindingly frustrating. Enrique of Trastamara outmanœuvred the Prince and inflicted losses on his army. However, Enrique then rashly committed himself to a pitched battle, and was decisively defeated by the Prince and his allies at Nájera, near Logroño in Castile, just over the border with Navarre, on 3 April 1367. Among those who fought there were the Prince's stepson Sir Thomas Holand, his stepdaughter Maud's husband Sir Hugh Courtenay, and the latter's brothers Philip and Peter.[57]

Two days after the battle, the Prince announced his victory in a formal and terse newsletter addressed to Joan. His mode of address to her contrasted with its general matter-of-fact tone – 'Very dear and very entire heart, well beloved companion'.[58] This was a fulsome way for a husband to address a wife, especially in a missive intended for wide distribution. We have no reason to think that the sentiments (so well attuned to Chandos Herald's later description of the couple's mutual affection) were hollow. In this letter, the Prince publicly placed their relationship within the conventions of courtly love, but also implied (perhaps with Joan's English detractors in mind) that it was a seemly union, characterised by marital fidelity and propriety. At the end of the letter he gave assurance that he, the duke of Lancaster and nearly all the nobles in his army survived in good shape.

With Pedro restored to his throne, the Prince returned to Gascony by the end of August. He hastened from Bayonne to Bordeaux. Chandos Herald described his reception at Bordeaux:

Nobly was he received with crosses and processions, and all the monks came to meet him. Right nobly they welcomed him, praising and thanking God. Then he dismounted at Saint-André. The Princess came to meet him with her first-born son Edward. The ladies and knights came there to welcome him and made great joy. Very sweetly they embraced when they met together. The gentle Prince kissed his wife and son. They went to their lodgings on foot, holding each other by the hand.[59]

There were, however, tensions screened by the public rejoicing. Despite the Prince's military success in Castile, his policy there was in tatters. Pedro had failed either to fulfil his financial obligations to the Prince, or to hand over to him the lordship which he had promised to grant to him. The topsy-turvy Prince was now intriguing with Pere III of Aragon to overthrow the king he had first passively helped to depose, and had just then restored. More desperately, the need to pay debts which he had incurred to finance his expedition led him to take measures which resulted in the unravelling of his rule in Aquitaine. In 1368 he screwed a grant of *fouage* (hearth tax) from the Estates, as he had done in several previous years. The financially strapped Count of Armagnac refused to allow this *fouage* to be levied in his lordships. Defying the terms of the Anglo-French peace of 1360, he appealed against the levy to the *Parlement* of Paris, the French Crown's principal judicial tribunal. The other most powerful southern Gascon lord, Arnaud Amanieu, lord of Albret, followed suit a few months later. In December, Charles V, king of France, publicly proclaimed his right to receive appeals from the Principality, thereby repudiating the peace treaty, and committing himself to war with Edward III and the Prince.[60]

Charles's brother Louis of Anjou encouraged lords and communes in some of the eastern and southern parts of Aquitaine to launch similar appeals. The Prince refused to recognise the jurisdiction of the *Parlement* of Paris. Its judges declared him to be contumacious in May 1369, and the following month Charles announced his intention to make war on him. In November the king had the confiscation of Aquitaine from Edward III proclaimed. By the end of the year, prompted by Anjou's judicious mixture of threats and cajolement, almost all of Rouergue and Quercy had reverted to the French Crown's obedience, as well as southern parts of Gascony under Armagnac's and Albret's lordship or patronage. The Prince's hold on Agenais, Périgord and Limousin was being challenged, too.[61]

Though the French forces involved in the campaigns of 1369–70 in Aquitaine were not overwhelmingly large, the Prince found it difficult to devise an effective strategy to oppose them. His resources were limited by financial constraints, and so was the size of reinforcements from England – for Edward III had to meet French challenges on other fronts as well. Moreover, since south-west France was studded with well-fortified castles and walled towns and villages, to prevent their defection or capture garrisons had to be reinforced. When they fell, sieges needed to be undertaken to regain them, if feasible. So the Prince had to disperse and juggle with his forces. If he had concentrated them in order to constitute the kind of army he was used to leading, it was unlikely that the enemy, now more circumspect, would risk all on a field engagement, and the gains he might make with such an army in one region might leave his forces vulnerably stretched in others.

Doubtless the Prince understood well that he confronted a strategic problem which he had not encountered before, and which could not be solved simply by adhering to the methods of which he was a past master. He did not take an active part in warfare till the autumn of 1370, relying on his trusted captains, above all Chandos, to move around making forays and counter-attacks – a strategy which did bring some successes. On occasion in the years 1368–70 (and perhaps for much of the time), he stayed at Angoulême – as did Joan and, probably, their children. The presence of both boys there is mentioned by Froissart at one point.[62] It may have been in part due to the relative proximity of the Prince's court and military headquarters that allegiances held up remarkably well in Saintonge, Angoumois and Poitou. The vulnerable frontiers of Poitou were vigorously defended.[63]

The Prince's unaccustomed passivity seems to have been caused by symptoms of the disease that was to kill him. The chronicler Thomas Walsingham, commenting on his death in 1376, said that he had suffered from a serious ailment and physical disability for more than five years. During this time he had had, almost every month, a discharge of semen and blood. 'These disabilities rendered him so weak on many occasions that his attendants very often thought he had died.'[64] Dr Chris Cameron suggests that he may have been suffering from a malignant condition such as a tumour of the testes or prostate. Walsingham's remarks take the symptoms back only to 1371, but elsewhere he says that the Prince was poisoned in Spain, and thereafter remained ill for the rest of his life.[65] Another English chronicler, who made additions to a text covering the years 1367 to 1413, wrote under the year 1369 that the Prince 'began to be gravely troubled by dysentery'. Chandos Herald – well placed to recall what happened to the Prince after his return from Spain to Bordeaux – says that soon after addressing the Estates at Libourne, he went to Angoulême: 'there, of a surety, the malady began that thereafter lasted all his life'. The herald was probably right in emphasising that the illness was a key factor in the renewal of war. He said that treason and falsehood were then abroad: 'as soon as it was known that the noble Prince was ill, in peril of death, his enemies were agreed to begin the war anew'.[66]

The news of his debility is likely to have encouraged opponents of the *fouage* and those lukewarm in their allegiance to him. His likely closeness to death was a sore test of often brittle Aquitanian loyalties. He had, indeed, brought relative stability to south-west France and had presided over a magnificent court. However, a high financial price had been paid for his ambitions and failures abroad, and he had not always been sensitive to local privileges. If it was thought that he would soon be succeeded as prince of Aquitaine by his infant son Edward, there was the disturbing prospect of a long minority.

The atmosphere at court must surely have been bleak. According to Chandos Herald, as reported by Froissart, the Prince had few attendants when he visited him, as his knights and squires were away on campaign. Spirits at court were doubtless lifted by the arrival from England, in late April or early May 1369, of reinforcements commanded by the Prince's brother, Edmund of Langley, earl of Cambridge, and John Hastings, earl of Pembroke. These younger men were eager to please him by striking at his enemies. They soon left Angoulême in arms to strengthen loyalties in Périgord, where their long-enduring achievement was the siege and capture of Bourdeilles, not far from Périgueux. In the summer, together with the veterans Chandos and

Audley, they switched their operations northwards to besiege a notable, strategically dominant fortress in the Vendée, in eastern Poitou, which the French Crown had refused to hand over after the peace of 1360 – this was La Roche-sur-Yon. Its garrison now capitulated – an important success for the loyalists, extending the borders of the Principality. However, in the autumn some other aggressive initiatives – raids into Louis of Anjou's own duchy – were less effective, mainly due to friction between the haughty, impulsive Pembroke and a consequently exasperated Chandos.[67]

There were other causes for sorrow at court in Joan's last years in Aquitaine, besides the Prince's incapacity, the treasons committed against him, and military failures and reverses. The princely couple and their now less than lustrous entourage frequently had to don mourning clothes for kinsfolk and outstanding supporters of the Prince. In 1368 the Prince's next younger brother, Lionel duke of Clarence, died in Lombardy. It is not clear whether the brothers were close: the duke's sphere of activities had been far from the Prince's, in Ireland. In April 1369 Bartholomew Lord Burghersh died in London, and in August Sir James Audley died at Fontenay-le-Comte, on his way back from the siege of La Roche-sur-Yon.[68] He was one of the Prince's longest-serving military companions and finest captains. According to Froissart, the Prince and Princess grieved a great deal, and both attended his funeral at Poitiers. These deaths were followed in November by that of a magnate who had been one of the Prince's commanders – Thomas Beauchamp, earl of Warwick.[69] By then, the Prince and Princess had suffered the shock of a very close bereavement: Queen Philippa had died at Windsor a week or more before Audley's death. Christmas revels that year must have been curtailed, or have been swathed in sadness.

Celebrations were to be further subdued by another mortal blow. Sir John Chandos, newly installed *sénéchal* of Poitou, in succession to Audley, determined to deal smartly with a threat posed by the French capture of the abbey of Saint-Savin, to the east of Poitiers. Chandos's foray failed, and without his full complement of troops he was engaged at Lussac by a larger force. He was mortally wounded (1 January 1370). The Prince and Princess, Edmund of Langley and the English knights in Aquitaine were confounded by the news, according to Froissart.

They 'were completely disconcerted, and said that they had now lost everything on both sides of the sea' – referring, presumably, to the queen's death as well.[70]

In 1370 the duke of Anjou and his brother John duke of Berry (commander in the northern parts of Aquitaine) confidently planned to co-ordinate their forces in attacks on parts of the Principality where their opponents were better entrenched. Anjou was to advance through Agenais and Périgord, and Berry through Limousin. One possible aim was to attack the Prince in his lair at Angoulême where, in Chandos Herald's words, 'he stayed, so ill that he kept to his bed ... where he had but scant cheer'.[71] According to Froissart, the Prince's response was that 'his enemies should never find himself shut up in a town or castle, and that he would immediately march and take the field against them'.[72] Perhaps he recalled how Joan's father had been ignominiously trapped in La Réole when trying to defend Gascony against French invasion. Considering the Prince's pitiful state, his resolution was surely alarming to Joan. It shows how far his strategic thinking differed from the successful if debilitating policy to which Charles V adhered in the face of English expeditions. He enjoined his commanders to avoid major field engagements, and to exhaust their opponents by concentrating on the defence of cities and fortresses.

The Prince summoned his loyal vassals, including some from provinces where they were beleaguered or isolated, such as Rouergue, Quercy, Bigorre and Agenais. He removed westwards from Angoulême to less vulnerable Cognac, also in Angoumois, presumably with Joan and his three-year-old son Richard. The castle there belonged to him, in his capacity as regional count; its captaincy had been granted by him to the Captal de Buch. We may surmise that this move was a particular wrench for Joan, who had often stayed in the great regal castle of Angoulême.

At Cognac, the seigneurs of Poitou and Saintonge rallied to the Prince's cause. Another reason for optimism was that his brother John of Gaunt would soon arrive with reinforcements from England. Gaunt had loyally served the Prince on the Spanish expedition, and won distinction on it. He docked at Bordeaux in the summer, and moved northwards to link up with his brother, joining forces on the way with the earl of Pembroke. The Prince, Joan and Edmund of Langley were delighted to see them, though perhaps already in the midst of warlike preparations they endured a new period of mourning with the death of yet another long-time military companion and close friend of the Prince. Roger Lord de la Warre, whose wife Eleanor, as we have seen, was Joan's kinswoman and probable lady-in-waiting, died on 27 August.[73]

The will which Roger had made in England in 1368 suggests an austerity of temperament contrasting with the extravagance and, indeed, frivolity which some had formerly associated with the Prince's court. Roger enjoined that the funeral pomp appropriate to his status should be eschewed – an unusual but not unprecedented provision. The Prince and Joan may have approved of and encouraged a vein of austerity in religious devotions among their companions. Years later, three of the Prince's knights who had served in Aquitaine were to make provision for simple funerals – Sir Guichard d'Angle, Sir Lewis Clifford and Sir Thomas Latimer.[74] D'Angle was a Poitevin nobleman who had fought strenuously against the English, but had accepted Edward III's allegiance when his estates came under the latter's rule in 1360. The king and the Prince had the highest respect for his chivalrous qualities.[75] Clifford married Roger de la Warre's widow Eleanor. Latimer's wife Anne, as we have seen, attended Joan's lying-in in 1367. All three knights were to have close associations with Joan in her widowhood – above all, Clifford.[76]

According to Jonathan Sumption, the Prince had originally intended to confront Anjou, who had advanced to the neighbourhood of the strategically important town of Bergerac, threatening a thrust along the valley of the river Dordogne towards Libourne and Bordeaux. But this advance petered out, whereas to the north forces under Berry's command made a big gain. His leading captain, Bertrand du Guesclin, the finest French soldier of his day, enforced submissions in Périgord and Limousin. A great coup for Du Guesclin was the submission of Limoges, much assisted by the change of allegiance of its bishop, Jean de Cros. The bishop's betrayal put the Prince in a chronic state of fury. He was, Froissart says, godfather to one of his sons – presumably Edward. The desertion of the little boy's spiritual father, at a time when the lad was, apparently, ailing, must have been an especially cruel personal blow.[77]

The Prince's choice of objective – the recapture of Limoges – was reinforced by an error of the duke of Berry. He entered the city late in August, but failed to leave an adequate garrison there. A few weeks later the Prince and his army arrived. He could not ride a horse: one imagines Joan's agony at parting from him when he was carried off in a litter, so different from his eager departure for Spain nearly four years previously. Limoges was speedily captured, and (notoriously in Froissart's eyes) sacked on the Prince's orders.[78] He had, however, made the right strategic decision. For his offensive helped to shore up the defence of the northern provinces of the Principality in the immediate future. Moreover, Aquitanians may have been impressed by the way in which divine favour had shone on the Prince, despite his manifest weakness. He had regained possession of the city where one of their holiest shrines lay – that of St Martial, bishop of Limoges, reputedly one of Christ's apostles, proselytiser of the Aquitanians and founder of the see.

The Prince's last victory was brought at great personal cost: 'he did not feel himself at his ease, as every exertion aggravated his disorder, which was increasing, to the great dismay of his brothers and those around him'.[79] His debilitating participation in the expedition had been completely unnecessary, an expression of his obtuse determination and courage. It had already been agreed with Edward III, before Gaunt arrived, that he should take over the lieutenancy of Aquitaine, for a maximum period of twelve months. Presumably the hope was that the Prince would recover sufficiently to resume personal control after that.

What compounded his misery, and took the lustre from his victory, was that, according to Chandos Herald, when he returned to Angoulême from Limoges, he received the news that his son Edward had died. He was staying at his castle of Cognac when, on 11 October, he made an indenture with Gaunt transferring the lieutenancy to him. At the same place, three days before, he had made separate grants to Gaunt and his heirs in tail male of the lordships of La Roche-sur-Yon and Bergerac, 'for the very great affection and love that we have to our very dear brother'. These grants were untypical of the Prince. They gave Gaunt a potentially hereditary stake in the defence of two of the Principality's strategically crucial centres.[80] Perhaps the Prince was thinking in the long term, envisaging Gaunt as well fitted to be the habitual defender of the Principality in the event of his death or of his succession to the throne in the near future.

Medical advice was given to the Prince to return to England, to try to regain his health. The adverse events of the last few years must have placed an enormous strain on it – a burden surely affecting Joan too. From Angoumois he travelled with her and Richard to Bordeaux. The lords of Aquitaine were summoned to attend on the Prince. In a valedictory address in his 'hall of audience' (presumably in the archiepiscopal palace), he said that, as far as he had been able, he had always maintained them in peace, prosperity and power against their enemies. He asked them to obey his brother. In his presence, they swore oaths to Gaunt, and kissed him. The Prince soon afterwards went on shipboard with Joan and Richard, doubtless a stark sight in their black raiment. They were desperate to leave before the Prince's health deteriorated further, and before the Bay of Biscay became even more unseasonable for sailing. They arrived in England in January 1371. It was left to Gaunt to arrange for the exequies of their son at Bordeaux. These were of great magnificence, attended by the barons of Gascony and Poitou, presumably in the cathedral of Saint-André, where Edward was buried.[81]

Joan had gone to Aquitaine over seven years earlier with clouds of disapproval swirling around her. She returned to England after winning international respect as a Princess who, in good times and bad, had shown herself worthy of her station. She had deferred to and supported her husband, producing an heir for him, and graciously presiding over his court. We have, indeed, only a few indications that she exerted power and influence. In her capacity as Princess, she submitted rolls of petitions to the papacy in 1363 and 1366 on her own behalf and for those in her patronage, requesting spiritual privileges or provision to benefices. The recipients all appear to have been English, and the benefices to which some of them were provided were all in England and Wales.[82] However, in Aquitaine she became a person of authority in right of her character as well as of her status. Joan's tragic experiences in 1369–70 probably drew her closer to gentlemen and ladies in her service and that of the Prince's with whom she had shared the pain of losing old friends, and of enduring the bleak days of the

Prince's convalescence at Angoulême, the upheavals attendant on the Limoges campaign, and the death of her son. The bonds cemented then with knights and ladies may have stood her in good stead in the Prince's declining years in England and in the troubled minority of Richard II. Joan's experiences in Aquitaine prepared and equipped her for the difficult – and, for a time, politically prominent – roles she would be called on to play back in England.

·: 7 :·

Deaths of Princes

THE LAST SEVEN YEARS of Edward III's reign, during which Joan once more lived in England, must have contrasted sadly in some ways with some of her memories of her previous life there. When she had left, the Prince had been at the height of his power and fame. Queen Philippa, such a vibrant influence at court, was now dead. The king's health and political vigour had declined. His house was no longer the exemplar of chivalry and courtliness it once had been. The Prince's chronic debility inhibited his ability to influence and execute his father's policies. If he had the inclination to take the reins of government, as the sick Henry IV's heir Prince Henry was to be determined to do, he lacked the vigour. For the most part, he had perforce to be a spectator of military failures abroad and embezzlement at home. Probably one consolation for him, and for Joan, was that their son Richard grew up (as far as we know) healthy, tall, an apt pupil – and resembling his father in appearance.

The couple and their son made landfall in Plymouth Sound early in 1371: the Prince convalesced at Plympton Priory for about three months.[1] He revived sufficiently to take part in a ceremonial entry into the city of London, whose citizens were eager to secure Joan's as well as his favour. The corporation of London had raised a subsidy from the wards to pay for a present for each of them (perhaps monetary in form) – presents demonstrating the reverence in which they were held, which for Joan may suggest that she had acquired a better reputation in England than the one she had when she left.[2]

In the years immediately after their return, the Prince's health does not seem to have deteriorated further. He was able on occasion to take part in public affairs. In 1372 John of Gaunt also returned from Gascony to England, his lieutenancy expired, with his bride, Constance, eldest daughter of Pedro I of Castile. She had fled to Gascony after her father was once more deposed and replaced as king by his half-brother Enrique of Trastamara – but for the last time, since Enrique himself murdered the captured Pedro in cold blood, publicly stabbing him to death. Gaunt now claimed to be the legitimate king of Castile in right of his wife.

On Constance's first ceremonial entry into London in January 1372, she was accompanied through the city by the Prince, many lords and knights, and a great number of commons, well arrayed and nobly mounted. In Cheapside they were greeted by a large crowd, including especially many ladies and girls who were eager to gaze at the beautiful bride. The procession rode past St Paul's Cathedral, down Ludgate Hill and into The Strand, where Constance entered The Savoy, her husband's magnificent house with its gardens and fine river frontage. The account we have of the episode suggests that the Prince could now sit a horse for at least a limited period, which he had apparently been incapable of doing when he had set out for Limoges.[3]

The Prince was publicly active on some other occasions. He is known to have presided at least twice in the period 1372–74 over meetings of the King's Council.[4] He witnessed a few royal charters, all dated at Westminster (within easy reach of his house at Kennington) – on 8 December 1373, and on 16 April and 2 June 1375. However, he had failed to witness a more important grant in 1372: that of the earldom of Richmond, hitherto held by Gaunt, to John IV duke of Brittany. Gaunt and his other adult brother, Edmund of Langley, though frequently abroad, were more assiduous in witnessing royal charters.[5]

A couple of notices of the Prince's participation in council show him in disgruntled mood, his ire directed not at his father's policies or ministers or courtiers, but at some aspects of the Church's authority and its defence of its privileges and riches, tensions over which rose as the costs of unsuccessful warfare escalated. In April 1371, when the Convocation of the archdiocese of Canterbury was summoned to meet at The Savoy, the Prince forcefully demanded the grant of a subsidy from the assembled clergy. He thought that the wealth of the English Church should be poured forth to support the war and help to turn the tide of the French Crown's gains.[6] Two years later, he was at a Great Council (a meeting of individually summoned magnates and leading royal officials) held at Westminster. Part of its remit was to

consider expert ecclesiastical evidence about the validity of the grounds
on which Pope Gregory XI demanded that the king should raise
a special tax to help to fund his war against the city of Florence. The
chronicle which gives an account of the proceedings represented John
Mardisley, a Franciscan, as leading the anti-papal arguments. Allegedly,
Archbishop William Whittlesey of Canterbury refused to state his
position, until the Prince rudely said to him, 'You ass, reply: it is your
duty to guide us.'[7] If this is indeed an example of the Prince's habitual
choleric mien, he must surely have been difficult on occasion for Joan
to live with, and have raised apprehensions about his future behaviour
as king.

We do not know whether Joan spent much time away from her
sometimes fractious husband. In August 1371, apparently without him,
she attended the obit held for her late mother-in-law, Queen Philippa,
at Marlborough Castle (Wiltshire). The antiquated royal castle there
had been part of the queen's dower, where Joan may on occasion have
attended on her when she was young.[8] On 23 February 1372, Joan was
at the Prince's castle at Berkhamsted. She then wrote to the Mayor
and Aldermen of London, thanking them for their gifts, and asking
for their favour to the goldsmith John de Chichestre and Sir Edward
Chardestoke, both keepers of her Wardrobe in the city (where she is
likely to have had furnishings and other chattels stored).[9]

In 1372 Joan was contemplating making separate journeys from her
husband. This may not have reflected a lack of mobility on his part, but,
rather, an improvement in his health, and his alarming resolution to
campaign abroad again. Joan was considering visits to convents, where
valuable prayers could be solicited. She received a papal privilege in
August, modifying her existing permission to enter them, and to eat
and drink there. Previously, she had been authorised to visit with an
entourage of twenty 'honest' women as much as once a month. Now
the quota of women was reduced to fourteen, and six 'aged' men were
added. The maximum number of visits was reduced to one every
three months. Maybe these terms were altered in anticipation that the
Prince might be absent abroad. Then, she would be preoccupied with
presiding over a perhaps more sedentary household, but preferred to
be accompanied, when more occasionally itinerant, by some of his
more eminent, ageing knights and officials – for her greater 'worship',

and for the easier disposition of business. Besides, advancing age may have made her less inclined to engage in frequent itinerancy. The papal privilege she received the following year to commute vows except those of continence and pilgrimage suggests a wish for a less challenging lifestyle.[10]

It was a remarkable tribute to the improvement in the Prince's health that he could once more plan to go to war. In the early months of 1372 plans were afoot for the king to lead an invasion of France with his principal nobles including the Prince: service was envisaged for a whole year. In July the expedition was rerouted as a naval one sailing into the Bay of Biscay. The plight of the loyalists in Aquitaine, in particular of those who had steadfastly supported the Prince in Poitou, had worsened after the expedition commanded by the earl of Pembroke had been disastrously defeated off La Rochelle by the Castilian fleet, for Enrique of Trastamara had joined forces with Charles V. Froissart says that the Prince had pretty much recovered his health when a delegation arrived in England from the loyal Poitevin defenders of Thouars. They brought the news that the defenders had agreed that, if not relieved from siege by Edward or his sons by 30 September 1372, they would go over to Charles V's allegiance.[11]

Edward III was now sixty years of age. He and the Prince were aware that one or both of them might not return from the expedition. They agreed that Richard of Bordeaux should in due course succeed to the throne of the one who survived. At an assembly at Westminster, the king, his younger sons and the nobles swore to the Prince to abide by this, and submitted attestations under their seals. This unusual measure was taken in case of possible reluctance to accept the succession of a very young Richard, and to forestall any attempts to raise the canard that there were doubts about the validity of his parents' marriage. Moreover, the story that Richard was not the Prince's son may have already been circulating. Certainly doubts about his legitimacy were raised abroad in 1375 or 1376.[12] Calumnies about the legitimacy of princes born out of the realm seem to have sprung readily to English lips, too, when convenient. In 1376 it was to be very publicly proclaimed in London that John of Gaunt was a changeling, the son of a butcher of Ghent.

The expedition assembled at Sandwich (Kent). Froissart says that among its captains were the Prince's brothers Gaunt and Langley, and also a distinguished number of the higher nobility. They were Joan's former husband the earl of Salisbury, the earls of Warwick, Arundel, Suffolk and Stafford, Lords Despenser, Percy, Neville, Roos and de la Warre. The fleet embarked at the end of August and sailed round the coasts of Normandy and Brittany, heading for La Rochelle. But its progress was slowed by bad weather and contrary winds. The expedition had to be abandoned, and the king was back in England in October. The defenders of Thouars, for the most part, went over to the French allegiance, and took most of Poitou with them.[13] As a consequence of this failure – and probably anticipating that he would soon be king – the Prince recognised that it was unrealistic to believe that he would once again rule Aquitaine as its prince in the near future. He formally gave up his title on 5 October. That must surely have been a bitter admission for him and his wife.[14]

After that seafaring ordeal, the Prince – like his father – was too debilitated to participate in a prolonged expedition on land. The lead in war with France now had to be taken by Gaunt and Edmund of Langley. In 1373 Gaunt landed at Calais with a large army which undertook an epic journey to the south of France, ending up in Gascony. Its achievement was disappointing, not least to the king and the Prince. The French, under strict instructions from the prudent Charles V, had avoided occasion to fight a pitched battle, and the English army lacked the resources to besiege and capture a major town.[15]

In 1374 Edmund of Langley led an expedition to Brittany in aid of Joan's son-in-law Duke John. Two years before then, the duke had allied with Edward III, and confirmed his allegiance to him. He had returned to England with the Duchess Joan in 1373, putting her once more within easy reach of her mother. Especially as regards Brittany, English foreign policy was to appear confused in 1374–75, for Langley's expedition was cut short by the making of general truces with the French Crown and its allies at Bruges in June 1375, diplomacy in which Gaunt took a major role. This led to a cessation of hostilities which was to last for nearly two years.[16]

Princess Joan was one of those to whom Pope Gregory XI had

written, pleading in favour of the cause of peace. The pope, apart from his general duty to promote the peace of Christendom, had strong financial and personal motives to do so at this juncture. Joan had sent a certain Master Robert (possibly her kinsman Robert Braybrooke) on a mission to him at Avignon. In his letter to her of May 1375, Pope Gregory said that he was sending the envoy back to her with information about his state and that of the Church. This presupposes that he considered that she might have a well-qualified interest and influence in such weighty affairs which might be useful in moderating the Prince's warlike and anticlerical inclinations. He asked her to use her influence with the Prince in favour of peace, and to procure some amelioration of the captivity of his brother Roger de Beaufort and his nephew Jean de la Roche. Beaufort and Jean's father Hugh had been among the captains at Limoges captured in its siege, whose defiant bravery had been much admired by John of Gaunt.[17]

These were, indeed, trying years for Joan. It is probable that she relied a good deal on Gaunt. After her return to England from Gascony, she was a notable recipient of New Year's gifts from him: he may well have been a particular friend and confidant. In 1372 he gave a white leverer of gold with eight sapphires to 'our very honoured and very beloved sister', the Princess of Aquitaine and Wales. In 1373 he gave the Prince and Princess gold cups. Joan's daughter Maud Courtenay received from him 'a pair of paternosters' (a set of prayer beads), and so did Joan's friend Lady de la Warre, to whom Gaunt also gave a clasp made of gold.[18]

Joan gave Gaunt some splendid presents, too. For New Year's Day 1373 he had a distinctive gift for his father which he had previously received from her – a golden goblet, on whose cover was a white deer, lying down, encircled by a crown. When Gaunt returned to London in 1374 after his gruelling campaign in France, to stay at The Savoy, it seems that Joan promptly sent eight of her minstrels to entertain him (or perhaps had them in her entourage for a reunion with him there). In the summer a papal mediator, Pileo di Prata, archbishop of Ravenna, visited England to discuss preliminaries for Anglo-French negotiations. Gaunt presented him with a big cup and ewer of silver surrorez which he had once received from the Princess.[19]

In the early 1370s notable family events affecting Joan occurred.

Her former brother-in-law Robert Lord Holand died in 1372. Heir to his father's extensive estates, he seems to have lived the life of a well-respected country landowner in Northamptonshire – far from his shamed father's Lancashire origins – after his participation in the Crécy campaign. In the will which he made at Thorpe Waterville in 1372, he stipulated that he was to be buried in the parish church at Brackley. Sir Robert's relations with his brother Thomas had apparently been cordial. As we have seen, he gave Thomas a life interest in manors. He singled out the friary at Stamford where Thomas was buried for a bequest of 100s.[20] With the death of Robert, the senior branch of the Holands came to an end in the male line. Heir to the substantial Holand estates was his granddaughter Maud (d. 1423), who married John Lord Lovell (d. 1408) of Titchmarsh (Northamptonshire).[21]

Sir Robert and Joan had had mutual connections. In 1368 he was first witness to a charter whereby Roger Lord de la Warre granted estates to his son Sir John and the latter's wife Elizabeth.[22] In 1372 Robert appointed John de la Warre as an executor. Robert was also connected with his neighbour Sir Thomas Latimer of Braybrooke, who was a fellow witness to the de la Warre grant of 1368. As we have seen, Latimer was a retainer of the Prince whose wife Anne had attended on Joan in Aquitaine. He was one of the Lollard knights detailed by Richard II to safeguard Joan in 1385, when there were fears of a French invasion.[23]

There was a happy family event for Joan in 1372. She became a grandmother. On 3 April a son was born to her eldest son Thomas Holand and his wife Alice; the infant was named after his father.[24] On the other hand, in February 1374 the husband of Joan's daughter Maud, Hugh Courtenay, died. There were no children. His death dashed hopes that Maud would become countess of Devon. Her husband had only been heir prospective. He had been granted by his grandfather the earl of Devon, jointly with Maud, Sutton Courtenay (Berkshire) and Waddesdon (Buckinghamshire). Hastily, before the inquisitions into her late husband's properties had been held, the earl induced Maud to grant her life interest in them to him and his heirs, for an annual rent of 200 marks.[25] Maud's intentions may have been to live with her mother, rather than as a country widow. Her high birth, however, made her once again an eligible, prospective bride. She, apparently, had no fixed objection to remarrying, but, like her mother, she was high-spirited and independent-minded. She was not to be rushed or coerced into marriage. It was to be six years before she married again, and, as we shall see, she chose her spouse, as many thought, wilfully and imprudently.

Family bereavement was to be followed by occasion for rejoicing. On 2 November 1374, Alice and Thomas Holand had another son, who was christened Richard – perhaps the seven-year-old Prince Richard stood as godfather.[26] Among Joan's continuing main concerns were, doubtless, the state of her husband's health, and how it might affect his ability to cope as 'King Edward IV' (as he was sometimes referred to), if, as seemed quite likely, his father died soon. The current power vacuum facilitated the rising influence of some exceedingly rapacious courtiers, officials and financiers, who were determined to line their pockets.

A key, notorious figure among them was the king's mistress Alice Perrers, who gained such an ascendancy over him, and had such a passion for extortion, that she amassed a fortune fit for an earl. She gave birth to three children, a son, John, and two daughters, both named Joan, who may have all been the King's bastards.[27] It is not clear what the attitudes of the Prince and Joan were to Alice's growing influence over the king. In view of the couple's past sexual peccadillos and the problems they had consequently caused for Edward, it is unlikely that he would have heeded any remonstrations from them of all people. His other adult sons, Gaunt and Langley, had no stomach for challenging their revered father's will, incurring his wrath and risking the loss of his blessing. Gaunt gave Alice fair words at court until after Edward's death, when he furiously denounced the shameful ways in which she had cajoled the ailing king.[28] Joan, too, may have dissembled, tolerating Alice in order not to enrage the king. Could it have been that Joan was godmother to one or both of his putative daughters?

Policy failures, combined with what we might term 'sleaze', produced a crisis in the parliament which met at Westminster in 1376. Contemporaries were to hail it as the 'Good Parliament'.[29] The king, the Prince and the latter's three brothers were present on the opening day (28 April), but the ailing king made Gaunt his lieutenant to preside over the parliament, in the absence of the Prince, who must have also been too ill to attend all its sessions and conduct business. To Gaunt's manifest exasperation, the Commons would not deal with their customary business of negotiating the grant of a subsidy, but insisted – with encouragement from highly respected magnates – on having trials in parliament of prominent royal ministers and their associates, on well-informed charges of derelictions and peculations, which the Commons tabled as a body. They also denounced Alice Perrers. Gaunt's attempts to uphold his father's authority by thwarting their efforts earned him scant sympathy in the Lords and a torrent of popular hatred.

By contrast – according to Thomas Walsingham, chronicler at St Albans Abbey (who had good connections in the Commons and among the London mercantile elite) – it was thought that the Prince sympathised with the Commons' cause. One of Gaunt's esquires, Walsingham reported, had asserted that the Commons had the Prince's support. If this was so, it was muted by the grave state of his health; by 1 June he had to take to his bed at Kennington, suffering from a 'dire malady'. The chronicler had also heard that, when Sir Richard Stury visited the Prince on his sickbed, the latter had upbraided him bitterly for having habitually deceived the king.[30] Stury was one of Edward's most trusted chamber knights, a man in his mid forties who had served in the royal household for twenty-seven years.[31] Joan does not seem to have harboured a harsh opinion of Stury. After the Prince's death, he was closely associated with her, and she granted him the constableship of Llanbadarn (Aberystwyth) Castle in the Principality of Wales.[32]

However, Walsingham's report of this confrontation is not easily dismissed. His account of the dying Prince's exhortations about the disposition of his goods corresponds with the provisions in his will. This suggests that the chronicler had a good source of information about the last days of the Prince – perhaps someone with an office in his household.[33] The Prince was, as we have seen, latterly thought to be inclined to rant. Perhaps, distraught, in physical and mental torment, he overblamed Stury, whereas the Princess came to regard him as less culpable. Stury was an unusually devout man, whose strong if unorthodox beliefs, influenced by John Wycliffe, she is likely to have respected. He had an agreeable personality, too: Jean Froissart, visiting Richard II's court almost twenty years after Stury had served in Edward III's, singled him out as the knight of the royal chamber whom he wanted to meet again, and was made welcome by him.[34]

One of Walsingham's sensational anecdotes about the Good Parliament concerned a former squire of the Prince, Sir John Kentwode. He was one of the two members of parliament sitting for Berkshire. Together with his fellow member, he attempted to assist in the prosecution of Alice Perrers in parliament, though it is not known whether he acted with the Prince's approval. Gaunt had ordered that an aged Dominican friar, a physician, by whose magical devices Alice was thought to have enticed and gained power over the king, should be brought before him. The two Berkshire knights of the shire set out to find and entrap the friar. Disguising themselves, they went to Alice's house at Pallenswick (Fulham, Middlesex). The magician, standing in an upper window, observed that they approached holding urinals. That vividly suggested that they were seeking consultations for bladder problems. Eager to profit by treating their complaints, he went down the stairs to meet them: they promptly arrested him and hauled him off. Brought before the Lords, to their annoyance he gave evasive replies, but was saved from their wrath by the archbishop of Canterbury, Simon Sudbury, who had the friar handed over to the brethren of his Order. Perhaps there were recollections in Joan's circles of how another magical Dominican had deceived her father.[35]

A monastic chronicler independent from Walsingham thought that the Prince approved of the punishment and downfall of one of the leading figures impeached successfully by the Commons for peculations. The well-informed 'Anonimalle' (that is, anonymous) Chronicler of St Mary's Abbey, York told how the London financier, Richard Lyons, had a barrel rowed across the Thames to the Prince at Kennington, ostensibly full of sturgeon, but in fact stuffed with gold. Lyons had been a member of syndicates, including courtiers, which had lent money to the Crown at high rates of interest, and he was an associate of Alice Perrers. The Prince summarily rejected the present, declaring that what was in the barrel was not well and loyally gained. So, he said, he did not wish to receive a present from Lyons, nor show favour to him and his evil doings, but supported the Commons in reforming the state of the realm, and in amending what had been extortionately and evilly done.[36] Even if this story, and the one about Stury, were untrue, their circulation suggests that there were those in the household at Kennington (perhaps Joan herself or retainers close to her) keen to promote the idea that the Prince approved the Commons' unprecedented impeachments of leading royal officials, and of their initiation of reforming measures in government.

Doubts have, indeed, been raised as to whether the Prince actually supported and encouraged the Commons' intrusions on the exercise of royal authority. However, the hapless invalid – and his wife – must have been highly apprehensive about the imminent prospect of either his or their nine-year-old son's succession. They may well have been relieved at the removal of 'evil' influences from government, and the deterrent effect which the convictions might have on future councillors and courtiers. Certainly the Prince's deathbed injunctions, as reported by the Anonimalle Chronicler and Walsingham too, were much concerned with the problem of good government.[37]

In extremis, on or before 7 June 1376, the Prince had himself rowed over to Westminster Palace, the historic heart of royalty and seat of government, where the Lords were still meeting in parliament. On that day he made his will, with Gaunt, 'our dear and beloved brother' named as first executor. Among the Prince's concerns were that the bulk of his chattels should go to pay his debts and provide for his poor servants.[38] To Joan he left items of great luxury which may have been especially dear to her. One was the magnificent silver vessel which had been a wedding present; the other a tapestry depicting eagles and griffins, with borders of swans with the heads of ladies.

The Prince died on 8 June – appropriately, on his favourite feast day, Holy Trinity. In his life of the Prince, Chandos Herald has a deathbed scene in which the Prince commended his wife and son to the king and Gaunt, and they swore to uphold his son's rights – as did other nobles who were present. That is credible, though, writing in 1385, the poet may have pointedly recalled the Prince's exhortations in the light of recent tensions between Richard and his magnates. The poet also recalled the grief-stricken reactions of those who witnessed the Prince's death:

But never, God help me, was such sore grief beheld as there was at his departing. The lovely and noble Princess felt such grief of heart that her heart was nigh breaking. Of lamentation and sighing, of crying aloud and sorrowing there was so great a noise that there was no man living in the world, if he had beheld the grief, but would have had pity at heart.[39]

Allowing for poetic licence, it is, indeed, likely that the Prince's kinsfolk, friends and retainers lamented wholeheartedly – not least because of fears of how his demise would affect their future and the realm's. It is credible, too, that the Princess appeared broken-hearted. Genuine recollections may lie behind the Herald's hyperbolic scene-painting. Though he was writing years later, he was probably doing so when the Princess was still alive, and for circles connected with her.[40]

The Prince had willed to be buried in Canterbury Cathedral, a place closely connected with the legitimisation of his marriage. Froissart says that the corpse was embalmed and enclosed in a lead coffin, but remained unburied until Michaelmas (30 September). A delay of several months in the burial of magnates was not unknown. The chronicler implies that the delay was in order that the Prince could be laid to rest with greater magnificence and fuller noble attendance. In fact the funeral was on 6 October. Perhaps there had been hopes that the king might recover sufficiently to make the journey to Canterbury for the Requiem Mass. There may have been problems about arranging the place of burial in the cathedral. The Prince had wished to lie humbly in the crypt, in the Chapel of St Mary Undercroft, near its miracle-working statue of the Blessed Virgin. Instead, he was laid to rest in the awesome setting of the choir, well placed to receive the prayers of pilgrims processing to and from the shrine of St Thomas (see Plate V). The exequies are, indeed, likely to have been attended by most of the magnates, as well as the Prince's widow and son: Gaunt was certainly among the mourners.[41] The day after the funeral, Edward III made his own will, at his house at Havering in Essex, one of his rural retreats where he was staying in a parlous state of health. There were only three people to whom he made financial bequests: his daughter Isabel and one of her daughters, and Princess Joan, who was to receive 1,000 marks. In his anguish at his son's death, one of his prime concerns was to aid the daughter-in-law who had more than once given him cause for anger.[42]

Order was made for payment of the fee of the earldom of Kent to Joan shortly before the Prince's funeral, and a week after it she was assigned dower from the Principality of Wales, the duchy of Cornwall and the earldom of Chester. The document assigning dower was dated at Havering. It stated that John of Gaunt had taken her oath not to marry without the king's licence: in this case, especially needful, in view of the princely estate she would receive – and her past marital history. The calculation was made that the properties assigned to her from the Prince's estate should yield just over £2,351 p.a., an income fit for an earl. Together with her income from the parts of the earldom of Kent she received, this placed her in wealth among the leading magnates.[43] That prospect may have eased her financial situation – when the earl of Arundel died the same year, she was among his debtors, for as much as 1,000 marks.[44]

The Principality of Wales was administered in two parts, North and South. In the North, Joan's principal assignment was Merionethshire, with Harlech Castle, one of the imposing fortresses built by Edward I. In the South, among a variety of rich properties were the castle and town of Cardigan. So Joan was put in charge of two important coastal fortifications, in a period when it was a possibility that Wales might be threatened with invasion. A few properties were granted to her in the County Palatine of Chester and Flintshire, including the fee farm of Chester and, also in the Palatinate, the lordship of Macclesfield and the manors of Frodsham and Middlewich. She received many properties in Devon and Cornwall. One of them may have had romantic significance for her: Tintagel Castle in Cornwall. For, according to what was received history, King Arthur was conceived and born there, and the tragic lovers Tristan and Iseult had died there. The castle was supposed to have been founded by Corineus, the first earl of Cornwall, during the time of the origins of Britain. The castle may have had great historical and symbolic significance, but it was remote and ruinous.

Of more practical use was the grant of Wallingford Castle in Berkshire, with its honour (see Plate VIII). The castle was the grandest residence Joan received. She received, too, properties not far distant from Wallingford – the manors of Nettlebed and

Watlington (with its park), and a rent from Princes Risborough. In London, there was the duchy of Cornwall's Inn of Wardrobe in Old Jewry. This was off Poultry, the eastern extension of Cheapside. Perhaps her own Wardrobe was already stored at the inn. Joan's retention of Wallingford Castle, from which access to Windsor Castle and Westminster Palace was easy, and of the Prince's Wardrobe, signalled her intention to be familiar with her son's court, rather than living in rural obscurity far from the city.

We have a tantalisingly brief glimpse of Joan some time in 1376, at St Albans Abbey, being received into the confraternity of the monastery together with twenty-eight companions. These comprised her widowed daughter Maud Courtenay, twelve knights and clerics, four *domicellae*, four female servants and seven male ones. Their reception ensured that they would all be included in the prayers of the community in perpetuity. In the enrolment of this in the abbey's 'Book of Benefactors', compiled by Thomas Walsingham, no precise date is given for her visit (see the appendix to this chapter for the list of companions). One of its principal purposes may have been to solicit prayers at the great shrine of St Alban, Protomartyr of Britain, for the Prince's recovery.

On the other hand, if the visit occurred after the Prince's death, it is likely to have been made in part to solicit prayers in aid of the repose of his soul. The presence of the cleric William Pakington may be an indication of this, for he was the Prince's receiver-general, and was a witness to the king's grant of dower to Joan on 13 October.[45] He must have been a key figure in negotiations over her dower.

The gathering at the abbey was certainly an important one for the Holand family. Perhaps Joan's Holand children were supporting her on their way to or from the Prince's funeral. Some of those in attendance were probably their retainers and servants. Clifford, Sharnesfeld, Bonde and Trivet had been among the Prince's retainers.[46] In and after Joan's widowhood, Clifford, Worthe and Clanvowe were among the knights on whom she particularly came to rely.[47] Agnes de Corby and Joanna Peverel were among her ladies-in-waiting; the latter had served her in Aquitaine.[48] Pontfret, Norton and William Corby were among servants of Joan of lesser status, presumably with offices in her household. Pontfret had given good service to her husband

Sir Thomas Holand, and had been retained by the Prince, too, as a yeoman.[49] Norton was to become a great favourite of hers, if he was not already so.[50]

Joan clearly had a particular devotion to St Alban. Like him, her father had been beheaded (in her eyes, doubtless for righteousness' sake). She was a good friend of the house, and probably a personal one of Abbot Thomas de la Mare (c. 1309–96), who had founded the confraternity of St Alban. The Prince had been close to this outstanding abbot, a stern defender of his house's rights, keen on encouraging scholarship and on reforming the English Benedictine communities. He was austere in adherence to the Regular life.[51] In the house's 'Book of Benefactors', Thomas Walsingham wrote that 'The Lady Joan the princess honoured the martyr frequently with great offerings, among which was a necklace of gold, and for charity she gave the convent 100s.'[52] (See Plate I.) She could have been kept well informed about the abbey's affairs by the prior of Wallingford, since the priory was a cell of the abbey. In 1384, Thomas de la Mare was pardoned at her supplication for escapes from his gaol – the abbey possessed a 'liberty' over part of Hertfordshire in which the abbot was responsible for administering justice.[53] That year he was in dispute over some local property rights with Sir William Windsor (the estranged husband of the disgraced Alice Perrers). Among witnesses in the suit who testified for the abbot were three of Joan's leading servants – Sir Lewis Clifford, Sir John Worthe and Sir Thomas Morewell.[54]

It is curious that Richard of Bordeaux was not with his mother on her visit to St Albans – he was to be admitted to the confraternity the following year, together with a distinct set of attendants. Yet, in her early widowhood, he was a member of her household. In 1378 she was compensated by the Crown for the great charges of accommodating him after the Prince's death.[55] Mother and son were both residing at Kennington on 25 January 1377, when a lavish entertainment was laid on by the citizens of London for Richard, who had been created Prince of Wales the previous month. A procession, 130 strong, rode through and then out of the city, passing along Cheapside and across London Bridge, and alighting in the precinct of Kennington Manor. The company were arrayed and masked as players ('mummers'), with visors over their faces, and costumed like people of various high ranks. An anti-papal edge was provided by those dressed as the pope's legates, for they sported devil-masks. This provocative behaviour could have been prompted by the fact that all popes for the last seventy-two years had been French and more pertinently that Pope Gregory XI's relatives had fought against the English. The riders were illuminated by torches, and they were accompanied by a great noise of minstrelsy.

That must have made a fine and strange impression if they came glimmering through the park at Kennington. The mummers entered the Great Hall of the palace. The Prince, coming from the Chamber, made his entry together with his mother, his three princely uncles (Gaunt, Langley and young Thomas of Woodstock), the earls of Warwick and Suffolk, and other lords. The mummers set up a gaming table, and gave Richard three throws with a loaded dice with which he won (unsurprisingly) golden presents. Joan, Gaunt and the other lords were presented with gold rings. Richard called for drinks all round, and then minstrels were bidden to play. The Prince and his lords formed a dance line facing one formed by the mummers. They danced away for a long time before more drinks were called for, and the visitors took their leave.[56]

Among the motives behind the mumming in honour of the new Prince was the aim to promote unity among the magnates and leading estates of the realm, dangerously fractured in the previous year – or at least to project a reassuring image of the restoration of harmony among them. In the six months or so since the end of the Good Parliament, tensions had resurfaced, for some of those most conspicuously condemned in parliament had received royal pardons, including Alice Perrers. She returned to court and resumed her influential position in the frail king's bedchamber. On the other hand, the well-respected bishop of Winchester, William Wykeham (an executor of the Prince), who had encouraged the Commons in their complaints about the court and about royal policy, was convicted by a Great Council, presided over by Gaunt, of having committed malversations when he had held leading Crown offices. The former Commons speaker Sir Peter de la Mare, who had acted vigorously as their spokesman, was arbitrarily imprisoned.[57]

In the new parliament which commenced a few days after the mumming, Gaunt was the dominant influence. He failed to assuage the discontented: his intransigence on his father's behalf once more caused controversy. The citizens and populace of London (among whom there had been vociferous supporters of the Commons in 1376) became convinced that he intended to launch an attack on the city's privileges. To add fuel to the fire, he and his ally Henry Lord Percy behaved imprudently on a separate issue. John Wycliffe, the Oxford theologian, widely admired as a would-be reformer of the Church and castigator in his sermons of its defects, was summoned to appear before an ecclesiastical tribunal headed by Bishop William Courtenay of London, convened in St Paul's Cathedral on 19 February 1377. Wycliffe was to be examined on his apparently unorthodox propositions, but he was menacingly accompanied by Gaunt and Percy, who proceeded to disrupt proceedings. When rumours about what happened spread, a riot ensued in the city.[58] Joan is likely to have approved of Gaunt's desire to protect Wycliffe. She had probably shared her late Prince's impatience with aspects of the Church's claims and privileges. Like some of the knights associated with her, she was to show herself an admirer of Wycliffe, though it is doubtful whether she fully embraced his burgeoning heresies and the radicalism of his views on the true nature of the Church and the Sacraments. At least one can say she was sympathetic to his calls for reform and spiritual regeneration.

The ferment in the city did not easily subside: next day it boiled over again. Lord Percy had made an arrest which was regarded as an infringement of civic liberty. Gaunt and he were dining on oysters in the city when they had to rise hastily from the table on news of a new riot. They were rowed across the river, landing near Kennington, seeking refuge in the manor. Walsingham described their appearance before Joan and Richard. In his depiction of the scene, his quill doubtless flowed with the malicious glee he felt at the discomfiture of his current *bête noire*, John of Gaunt. 'When they [Gaunt and Percy] stood before them [the Prince and his mother], not without great fear, as was evident from the sweat pouring down their quivering limbs, they bewailed all that had happened.' This was very different from the leaping lords of the mumming. The Princess spoke consolingly to them, and promised to settle the whole matter to their advantage.[59]

However, the situation was made worse by the intemperate actions of some Londoners, who broadcast assertions that Gaunt was a traitor and in fact an impostor, substituted for a dead royal infant. Joan, wishing to restore peace between the duke and the citizens, sent a delegation of knights to the civic rulers of London. As we have seen, she seems to have had good relations with the Londoners in recent years, and had received them graciously at the mumming. Her representatives now were former leading knights of the Black Prince – Aubrey de Vere, Simon Burley, Lewis Clifford. They had served the Prince on his last campaigns in Aquitaine, and are likely to have become well acquainted with the Princess there. Vere was a younger son of the late earl of Oxford. He was apparently moderate and mild by nature. He was her constable at Wallingford Castle. The more dynamic Burley was among those in charge of Prince Richard's education, and perhaps something of a father-figure to him. Clifford, one of Joan's favourites, was to become notorious for his unorthodox religious devotion.[60]

The message the knights conveyed was that the Princess requested the citizens to be reconciled with Gaunt, on the grounds that she, who loved them, was pleading for this, and that the disturbances needed to be ended before they escalated, with the distinct likelihood of civil strife. The citizens replied that, out of regard for her, they would do whatever she commanded – but they made verbal stipulations for her knights to pass on to Gaunt about the more lenient treatment they wanted for Bishop Wykeham and Sir Peter de la Mare. The citizens must surely have realised that Gaunt was not going to accept conditions from them concerning such high affairs of the realm. Moreover, he was holding out for the city's abject submission. Joan's attempt at arbitration failed.[61]

Walsingham's account of the episode is remarkable. He assumes that it was natural, and wholly acceptable to the parties, for a woman to act through her servants as mediator in a major national political crisis. Indeed, the times were out of joint, with the king physically and mentally enfeebled, and with royal authority clumsily wielded by Gaunt, who was now threatened with disobedience and contempt. Desperate remedies were needed. Joan had recently become a leading magnate. 'Cometh the hour, cometh the woman.' The ways in which Walsingham depicted her, and how she was regarded, suggest that she was the woman for a crisis – clear-sighted and idealistic in her aims, politic and emollient, respected and trusted by all men. She did not have the knee-jerk reaction of backing Gaunt, with whom she and her husband had been close. If the Black Prince had indeed been critical of the conduct of government in his last days, her attitudes were of a piece with his.

A shaft of light on Joan's new – and, for a woman, exceptional – roles in government in this period is thrown by a report written for her in French by a high-ranking official who, with three colleagues, went late in March on a tour of inspection of the southern parts of the Principality of Wales. The official had set out from London, in receipt of verbal instructions as well as letters from her and her son the Prince. He reported that he and his colleagues had successfully negotiated on behalf of the Prince with local officials, gentlefolk and townsmen for the grant of subsidies. They had also inspected his and his mother's castles there, and were sending for their approval and that of her council the text of an indenture which they had drawn up with the Chamberlain of South Wales, providing for repairs. They suggested that she order her council to purvey arbalasts and quarrels in London in all haste, since there were none available to defend the castles in those parts.

The information which they had received indicated that men-at-arms were urgently needed to be sent from England as well. They had been handed a letter written at Bordeaux by Sir Thomas Felton – royal lieutenant in Aquitaine – to local officials, dated 8 February. He said that the 'Bastard of Spain' (Enrique II of Castile) had concentrated an invasion fleet which he intended to land at the port of M. (Milford Haven in Pembrokeshire?), to support the claim of 'Oweyn of Wales' to be by rightful descent the Prince of Wales. Owain Lawgoch ('of the Red Hand'), a formidable soldier, had long ago forsaken the English cause when he was serving it in France, and sought the aid of the French and Castilian Crowns for his princely aspirations.[62] Fears of foreign invasion were doubtless stoked up in England as well as Wales by the failure of negotiations for peace or the further prolongation of the general truces with the French Crown and its allies, which were due to expire on 1 April. Joan's correspondent said that recent reports from Gascony which had been received in Wales reinforced the gravity of the threat. He urged her, and her son and council, to impress on the

King's Council the need to provide specific numbers of men-at-arms to garrison two castles at royal costs, and stressed the need for close co-operation between officials to concert measures.

The King's Council did, indeed, take measures to meet the possible threat. Privy Seal letters were dispatched to magnates owning castles and manors in the Marches of Wales, telling them to stock their properties with sufficient victuals for a siege. An order was made to arrest the prior of the alien priory at Pembroke – presumably he was a Frenchman, and therefore it was suspected that he might aid an invasion. An experienced soldier, the Welshman Sir Degory Sais, was dispatched to Wales with a retinue of thirty men-at-arms and thirty archers.[63] However, the feared invasion fortunately failed to materialise.

The report suggests that, at this juncture, the Princess and her council were taking a leading part in supervising the affairs of the Principality, and were doing so with some efficiency and success. Moreover, it also suggests that her commissioners considered that she had a grasp of the practical steps needed for defence, and that she and her council were well qualified to impress the needs on the king's councillors. Indeed, she was one of the few highborn English ladies who had experience of being involved in a large-scale invasion. She had observed and been caught up in the French reconquest of much of Aquitaine, especially when she had been at Angoulême seven years before. Moreover, marriage to two of the greatest soldiers of the age, and years spent in the company of the stars of the English military elite, may have given her more knowledge of warfare than just table talk. Spurs to her efforts in response to the report are likely to have been alarm and anger, for the despised 'Bastard of Spain', toppled from his usurped throne by her husband at the battle of Nájera in 1367, but since reinstated, was now attempting to deprive their son of his Principality in favour of (in English eyes) a traitor and impostor.

Besides instigating defence measures against a Spanish threat to Wales, royal councillors set out trying to seize the initiative in the warfare once again looming with the French Crown. They vigorously planned a summer expedition, and concentrated shipping in the port of London. The projected army was to be notable for the intended number of eminent retinue leaders – including Prince Richard (knighted by the king at Windsor in April on the vigil of the Garter

Feast), Gaunt, his younger brother Thomas of Woodstock, Joan's former husband the earl of Salisbury, her son-in-law the duke of Brittany and the earl of Warwick. One intention was to establish the Prince's military reputation as nominally the commander, surrounded by his united nobility, both veterans and fellow novices. Knights closely connected with Joan, her late husband and her family were among those who contracted to go – Philip and Peter Courtenay (former brothers-in-law of her daughter Maud), Lewis Clifford, John Clanvowe, Richard Stury and Aubrey de Vere.[64] Joan cannot but have been apprehensive about her son's involvement, much as it promised to enhance his honour. No one was safe on a battlefield or in a seafight. Gaunt had been in danger when, aged ten, he had been with his father in a particularly hard naval battle, and the Black Prince had been at risk too, when sixteen, at the battle of Crécy.

Surely Joan felt relief for her son's safety when, on 21 June 1377, Edward III died in his manor of Sheen (Richmond, Surrey), necessitating the cancellation of the expedition. Sorrow at the death of a king who, in his reign of fifty years, had provided a remarkable degree of stability, and opportunities to win honour and profit, was widely mingled with apprehension at the succession of a ten-year-old boy, especially when there was to be war with the French and Castilian Crowns. In the circumstances, as the king's mother, a particular burden of responsibility was to fall on Joan.

APPENDIX

List of companions of the Princess of Wales received with her into
the confraternity of St Alban in 1376 (*Liber Benefactorum*, BL, Cotton
Nero D. VII, fol. 129r)

Matilda Courtenay
Sir Thomas Holand
Sir John Holand
Sir William Neville
Sir Lewis Clifford
Sir John Worthe
Sir Nicholas Sharnefeld
Sir Nicholas Bonde
Sir John Trivet
Sir Theodoricus vandale
Sir John Clanvowe
Sir William Pakintone
Sir William Desforde
Mondene de la fy't
Agnes de Corby
Johanne Peverel
Cristina Wr'yt   domicellae
Reymunda
Dionisia Sutton
Margaret Bigge
Johanna ffollet
Richard Mews
Richard Pontfret
Warin Waldegrave
Henry Norton
John hankyn
William Corby
Edward nowell

·: 8 :·

The King's Mother

MOST ENGLISH PEOPLE LIVING IN 1377 had known no other king than Edward III. It is not surprising that the shock of his death had a salutary effect on domestic politics. The day after it occurred, an apprehensive delegation of London citizens went to Sheen, to pay their respects at the bier. They found Richard, his mother and his uncles grouped around it. The scene was carefully staged. Gaunt took the lead in making a formal reconciliation with the Londoners. It was agreed that there would be royal arbitration of the outstanding issues dividing them, and that concessions would be made on both sides.[1] The following month, on 16 July, Joan was present at her son's coronation in Westminster Abbey and at the customary banquet held the same day in the adjacent palace, in the awesome setting of Westminster Hall. The exhausted boy was carried out from the banquet on the shoulders of Sir Simon Burley. Burley had been one of his father's former knights, and was to be one of Richard's closest confidants. Joan seems to have approved of what many came to regard as his malign political influence, for she was to appoint him as one of her executors.[2]

It is not clear for how long, after the start of Richard's reign, his mother continued to live in his house at Kennington, or when she made Wallingford Castle (see Plate VIII) in Oxfordshire her principal residence, as it was to be for the rest of her life. In August 1380 she received royal licence to make purveyance within about nine miles (three leagues) of Wallingford for herself, her household and horses whenever she came to the castle: the licence was to run for one year. In form the castle was a Norman motte and bailey on a large scale. Principal place of the honour of Wallingford, it had been founded by no less a person than William the Conqueror. It was adjacent to the north gate of the borough, with one frontage overlooking the

Thames; a postern gate gave access from the castle to a quay. The Tudor antiquary John Leland was impressed by the castle's three great ditches, its keep and the domestic buildings in the bailey, including the royal range of apartments which Joan would have occupied, adjoining the collegiate chapel of St Nicholas.

Edward III had assigned the castle to the Black Prince, who spent a lot of money on improving it. The collegiate chapel was repaired in 1361–62, and provided with new statutes in the latter year. Between 1363 and 1370 the Prince spent £500 on repairs to the great tower, great chamber and other buildings, and in 1375 £200 on the great hall, great chamber and chapel. The Prince's fondness for the chapel, and reverence for St Nicholas, a very popular and protective saint, are reflected in his sumptious bequests for the chapel's furnishings.

Wallingford Castle was therefore a fittingly impressive and domestically modernised residence for a king's mother, with easy access to Windsor and Westminster.[3] Many of Joan's surviving letters patent issued on her sole authority as Princess of Wales were dated at Wallingford or places not far distant, in Buckinghamshire, Middlesex and Hertfordshire. There are also some notices of her visiting Windsor, Sheen, Westminster and London. If, as is likely, she had a custom of visiting the tombs of her two lawful husbands on the anniversaries of their deaths, a visit to Canterbury would suggest that she was there offering prayers for the repose of the Prince's soul (see Plate V).

The composition of circles specially connected with her in her second widowhood reflected both changes and continuities, as one would anticipate in the case of a middle-aged princess. For instance, Sir Donald Hazelrigg, who had served her first husband, died in her service in 1384.[4] Indeed the Princess kept some of those in her personal service for many years. After the Princess's death, Denise de Sutton said that she had served her for fifteen years.[5] Some of Joan's leading officials were in post throughout her second widowhood – Sir John Worthe, steward of her estates, and William Fulburne, receiver-general, are two such.[6] She valued and maintained a stable administration, and was loyal to familiar faces about her.

Former knights of the Prince and his father, elderly or middle-aged, kept various sorts of connections with her, some receiving her help in gaining minor royal favours. Some of them had residences within easy reach of Wallingford, domiciled in the Thames Valley or in other nearby counties, or at court. However, we have not found hard evidence that her own 'court' at Wallingford was a notable political or cultural focus especially for Berkshire or a wider region. This great household does not appear to conform all that closely to the well-known stereotype of a magnate's regional power bases. However, local notables from Berkshire and Oxfordshire were expected to be staying with her in the summer of 1385, but that was in exceptional circumstances. Joan was apparently not interested in developing a political role as the leading noble influence thereabouts, and as the principal regional intermediary between court and country. Her principal focus was on her son, the king, and on the well-being of his kingship. That was what she concentrated her declining energies on – as befitted her princely status as well as her maternal ambitions.

Joan must have been heartily relieved that, after Edward III's death, Gaunt was prepared to act more moderately in politics, and did not inflame hostile and suspicious opinion by pressing for some form of regency for himself during the royal minority. The duke – and the political community – were, as we have seen, galvanised into a semblance of unity by the renewal of war with the French and Castilian Crowns, which formally recommenced in the same month as the coronation. Gaunt was determined to take a lead against these formidable opponents, and also in deterring Robert II of Scotland from allying offensively with them and, besides, in pursuing his own claim to be king of Castile. These were Herculean tasks. Gaunt's international experience of war and diplomacy, his unique wealth and huge magnate retinue for service in war and peace made him the best qualified noble to defend the interests of the realm in the eyes of his brothers and, with some ambivalence, his fellow magnates.

The formal exercise of royal power was confided, with parliamentary authority, for the duration of the minority to a council which met regularly, and on which a series of lords served together with the usual leading royal officials. Gaunt and his brothers Edmund of Langley and Thomas of Woodstock did not receive any formal appointments to the King's Council. This was probably because their close kinship with Richard was considered to entitle them to an automatic right to give counsel, though it is unlikely to have been a right they were expected to exercise as continuously as the appointed councillors.[7] The minority came to be formally ended, and this precise form of continuous council discontinued, in 1380, when Richard was declared of age – at fourteen. During and after the minority it is likely that Joan could in some instances bring influence to bear on the conduct of affairs. She lacked the status that a dowager queen might have had in the minority of a son, but this lack of such formal authority may have worked to her advantage. For in the minority of Edward III, Queen Isabella's exploitation of her queenly office provided a dire precedent. In view of that, maybe it buoyed up Joan's influence that she did not have the sacred authority of a queen. Moreover, she had recently shown herself able and prepared to play an emollient, mediatory role in a crisis in the early months of her widowhood.

Closeness to Gaunt may have strengthened her voice. There are a few indications of their continued mutual goodwill. In 1379, at her petition, the abbot and convent of Leicester received a royal licence to alienate in mortmain the advowson of the church of Hathern (Leicestershire) to the sacrist and canons of the church of St Mary de Castro at Leicester. St Mary's was actually the main chapel of Leicester Castle, one of Gaunt's principal residences. So Joan's petition was a favour to Gaunt, agreed between them perhaps when she was staying at the castle. At New Year 1380 Gaunt gave her two presents – a covered cup of gold, and a cross with figures of Mary and Joseph, decorated with precious stones and pearls.[8]

Another reason for Joan's influence on affairs, especially after the minority was formally ended, was the reverence which Richard felt for her, which was to be strikingly demonstrated in 1385 by his mild reception of her efforts to mediate between him and Gaunt, and by his determination to see that she was properly protected whilst he was abroad. She wished to affirm and nourish her relationship with her son. This is reflected in the terms of a royal licence of 1378 for the alienation in mortmain of land in Beverley (Yorkshire) for a proposed hospice for poor men, which Richard de Ravenser, archdeacon of Lincoln and a leading royal official, intended to found. First named among those for whom the denizens were to pray daily were the king and his mother.[9] In the chantry which the canons of Leicester Abbey undertook to found in Hathern, the pair were singled out among the living for whom the chaplain was to pray.[10]

The connections between Joan and her son, and between her and the king's councillors, were probably oiled especially by some knights of the king's chamber, mostly former retainers of the Prince, some of whom can be grouped as having various ties with each other, and occasional connections with Joan. Maybe particular individuals were seconded from the royal household to attend on her. Most closely connected with her, as we have seen, was Sir Lewis Clifford. He came of minor gentry origins in Devon, and had worked his way up in the Prince's service. His marriage to Eleanor de la Warre (between 1372 and 1374), since she was of royal descent, had brought him into kinship with Joan – as well as making his landed fortunes.[11]

Clifford was Joan's spokesman in 1377 in her most bold and controversial public intervention in national – and, indeed, international – affairs. Gaunt's and Percy's prevention the previous year of the examination of John Wycliffe in St Paul's Cathedral had frustrated leading clerics who found his propositions suspect. The threat of prosecution failed to silence the irrepressible theologian. The bishops had sent a list of his alleged errors to Pope Gregory XI. In accordance with the bull which the pope issued in response to Archbishop Sudbury of Canterbury and Bishop Courtenay of London, Wycliffe was summoned to appear before an ecclesiastical tribunal to answer the charges. Towards the end of March, he came before the bishops in the chapel of the archbishop's residence at Lambeth. There, according to Walsingham, his trial was abruptly terminated by the arrival of a messenger from the court of Princess Joan, Lewis Clifford, 'who pompously forbade them from taking it upon themselves to pass sentence'. The chronicler denounced the bishops for being struck dumb with fear – and not even by a message from a nobleman or potentate. However, with unwonted circumspection, he refrained from a direct denunciation of the Princess – who, as he was to record, was a devoted benefactress of his house.[12]

Clifford was high in Joan's favour. A few weeks before then, on 3 March, at her manor house at Bushey, she made him the biggest life grant of her widowhood – the keepership for her life of Cardigan Castle, part of her dower, together with the very large sum of £100 p.a. from the profits of its lordship. This was an earnest of her trust in Clifford, since the castle was the administrative hub of South Wales, and a key point in coastal defences.

The disrespectful haughtiness before the bishops attributed to Clifford, if accurate, may have sprung not just from reverence for the Princess, but also from a sense of puritanical virtue probably inspired by the teachings of John Wycliffe. In the will which he was to make in 1404, Clifford displayed the sort of self-abnegation which, as K. B. McFarlane showed, was typical of those gentlefolk influenced by Wycliffe, and the intense engagement with the New Testament which he enjoined. Clifford castigated his own sinfulness, and decreed that he should have meagrely furnished exequies and a humble burial place. He was in the groups of knights who, with some variants, were to be accused by the chroniclers Walsingham and Henry Knighton, the chronicler of Leicester Abbey, of being Lollards, the appellation which came to be given to those suspected of stubbornly clinging to those propositions of Wycliffe which were definitively condemned as heresies between 1378 and 1382.[13]

In the light of these condemnations, patronage of Wycliffe by the Crown and by prominent nobles declined. The 'Lollard knights', according to these two monastic chroniclers, remained obdurate. They were mostly knights of the king's chamber, who, as McFarlane demonstrated, had many close connections with each other and, in some cases, enduring friendships. Several of them, besides Clifford, had some connections with Joan too. Like Clifford, John Clanvowe and William Neville were with her at St Albans Abbey in 1376. Neville was a younger son of a leading family in the Borders with Scotland; he and Clanvowe were so closely linked in their careers that they were probably formally contracted as 'brothers in arms', pledged to share the profits of any ransoms they might gain. All three were among Joan's executors, as was another 'Lollard knight' attached to the royal chamber, Richard Stury, who had apparently, as we have seen, had a memorably painful audience with the Black Prince in 1376.[14]

What may we conclude about Joan's religious beliefs and attitudes from her defence of Wycliffe in 1378, and her associations with suspect knights? We must bear in mind that the Lollardy attributed to some of her knights appears to have been mostly a matter of personal conviction rather than a movement that gripped her household. What is apparent is that Wycliffe's sermons appealed to the evangelical piety of the period, reflected, for instance, in her closely associated kinsman Roger de la Warre's provisions in 1368 for a humble funeral. The Orders of friars exemplified and preached the virtues of poverty, and some friars allied with Wycliffe in criticising the wealth of the 'possessioner' clergy – but only supported him before he formulated and expounded his unorthodox views on the nature of the Eucharist.[15]

We have no firm evidence that Joan was anything but firmly orthodox in her beliefs. It is likely that she sympathised with Wycliffe's reformatory early phases of his campaign, and perhaps with some of the particular emphasis which he placed on scriptural authority. As we have seen, Joan, like some of her kinsfolk, had a reverence for Franciscan piety, whose exaltation of holy poverty and proselytising diligence contrasted with the higher secular clergy's typically lordly lifestyles and delegation of their cures. Clifford's alleged brusqueness with the bishops, if it had her approval, chimed too with her husband the Prince's anticlerical outbursts in his latter days. Moreover, in her protection of Wycliffe in 1378, Joan was acting in precisely the same way as Gaunt had recently done – and as he was to continue to do, despite his perceived repudiation of what became clearly defined as heretical doctrine. Indeed, she may have been acting as the duke's surrogate in her dispatch of Clifford from her household. Gaunt was probably that month away from London, on his own estates, much preoccupied with planning the defence of the realm and its interests abroad against the threats posed by the French Crown and its allies. If Joan was then staying at Kennington, it would have been more convenient for her rather than her brother-in-law to gag the bishops.[16]

In August 1378 relations between the English Church and Crown became more critical as a result of a high-profile sacrilege. It may be that this was incidentally the result of a possible scheme in which Joan was involved, with the aims of defending the realm, helping to resolve Gaunt's Spanish impasse and marrying off her widowed daughter Maud Courtenay. What happened was that the royal council ordered two squires, Robert Hauley and John Shakell, military hard men, to hand over a young Spaniard in their custody, the count of Denia.

Instead, they concealed him, with his co-operation, in London. They were consequently arrested and imprisoned in the Tower of London, whence they escaped on 10 August, and sought sanctuary in the precincts of Westminster Abbey. The next day they were pursued into the abbey church during Mass by royal officials. Weapons were drawn: Hauley and Richard, an unarmed sacristan, were slain, and Shakell was captured and hauled out of sanctuary. William Courtenay, bishop of London (whom Gaunt had frustrated over the first trial of Wycliffe), excommunicated those responsible for the outrage, to the fury of the royal council. Gaunt himself could hardly be held responsible as he was then out of the realm, besieging St Malo in Brittany, but he was to express his anger with the bishop.[17]

The hostage, Alfonso, count of Denia in Valencia, in the kingdom of Aragon, was particularly important. He was of the royal blood of the ruling house of Aragon, and was in England as a pledge for the ransom of his father Alfonso (also styled count of Denia in English sources). The latter had been captured fighting against the Prince in the rout of Enrique II of Castile's army at Nájera in 1367. He had been, and remained, a leading supporter of Enrique, who had created him marquis of Villena in Castile.[18]

Why did the royal council suddenly take such an interest in young Denia? There were, indeed, disputes as to who had the right to shares in the ransom, which the council was being pressed to resolve. Perhaps the councillors considered that the Crown had conceded too much of the ransom to the squires, and wished the Crown to resume possession of the young man and the lion's share of the ransom. That was to be the eventual outcome. An exchange of the ransom for an English prisoner in Castile may have been under consideration.[19] But there may have been more pressing motives for the council's action, connected with war and diplomacy – and with Joan's aspirations for her daughter. Indeed, contemporaries were puzzled as to the council's motives, according to Walsingham, who was well placed to hear rumours from court:

> Some think the councillors' action was intended to gain the favour of the duke of Lancaster, who had a just claim to the kingdom of Spain (Castile), to enable him to gain possession of

this kingdom more easily now that he held so important a count [Denia]. Others declared that it was done on behalf of Lady Matilda (Joan's daughter Maud), the king's sister, the widow of Lord P. Courtenay, so that if she was betrothed to the count and was urged to marry so important a man, peace and harmony would grow between the two kingdoms (England and Castile) through the marriage.[20]

Maybe there was some truth in one or both of these surmises. Indeed, Gaunt's claim to the Castilian throne was a massive stumbling-block to peace with Castile, but one cannot rule out the possibility that he was willing to compromise his claim, as, indeed, he did in 1387–88, making his peace with Enrique's son and successor Juan I. Moreover, the strategic situation in the renewed warfare in 1377 demonstrated the imperative need to detach Castile from the French alliance, one way or another. As soon as warfare recommenced, Enrique invaded Gascony. Furthermore, a Castilian galley fleet, transferred to the port of Harfleur in Normandy, posed a formidable threat, the first in decades, to the coasts of England. In the summer the fleet, with French soldiers on board, ravaged down the Channel coasts. For their summer campaign of 1378, the Spaniards targeted Cornwall, provoking complaint by its communities in the October parliament.[21]

For Joan, the Castilian offensives since the renewal of the war must surely have been galling. 'The Bastard of Spain', as the Prince had officially termed Enrique, had invaded his former Principality of Aquitaine. In March 1377 Joan had shown herself keen to prepare against a rumoured Castilian plan to invade Wales. Her appointment of Clifford to the keepership of Cardigan Castle in March 1378 was probably in part prompted by fear of a recurrence of such a threat. But she was not well positioned to prepare defences in vulnerable English regions where she held properties. In 1377 the sack of Plymouth, which she knew well, and of ports of the duchy of Cornwall, where she had dower lands, are likely to have been bitter blows for her. Obsolete Tintagel was the only castle she held in the West Country. She may have also feared that her earldom of Kent, where she had no castles to provide for defence, would be attacked – as it was to be. In such dire circumstances, she may well have been prepared to pressurise her daughter into a diplomatic marriage – in contrast to her own love matches.

There is one piece of documentary evidence which suggests that the council was in negotiation with Alfonso of Villena. In August 1377 a safe-conduct had been issued to him (styled count of Denia) to come to England for up to a year to negotiate concerning his ransom. He was allowed an entourage of three knights, six esquires (including his favourite, the poet Pere March) and valets, with a total of thirty horses.[22] It may be that straightforward negotiations to alter the terms of the ransom were envisaged, or conditions for the substitution of Villena for his hostage son.

But solely negotiations over the ransom terms would not have required Villena's presence. The irascible marquis does not strike one as the sort likely, in the midst of war, to be at last prepared to submit himself to imprisonment, even for the sake of his son. More, perhaps, was at stake in the proposed visit. But we cannot be sure that he ever came, or that his vitriolic denunciations of the English over the ransom were the sour fruit of such a visit.[23]

PRUDENCE, REWARDS AND GRACE

As the king's mother, Joan was careful not to dissipate the resources of her royal dower lands to the possible future detriment of her son, the king. The substantial grants of these resources which she made to her servants to hold for her lifetime were few. In 1380 one of her favourite squires, Henry Norton, received Old Shoreham on the Sussex coast (perhaps with stern injunctions to defend it against raids). In April 1385, several months before her death, she granted her esquire William Clifford the manor of Trewarnaill in Cornwall.[24] Examples of minor grants were those in 1380 to her butler William Giles of the office of a water bailiff in Devon, and to William and Joan Pope of land in that shire.[25] In the 1380s, wishing to make more secure the position of some of her grantees in view of her advancing age, she secured from the Crown the right for them to hold these grants for their lives. Her favourite Sir Lewis Clifford, the most substantial grantee, was one of them.[26]

Joan appears not to have tried to enrich herself at her son's expense by seeking the keeping of other Crown lands, and of lands which came temporarily into the king's hands, notably through the wardships of minors, with which often went the valuable right to arrange their marriages. She does not seem to have been inclined to run a residential nursery and school in her household for young kinsfolk in ward, as her aunt Blanche Wake had done. In 1380 Joan was granted fines imposed for some sorts of feudal offences against the Crown within her princely dower lands.[27] Richard made a substantial grant to her in 1384 of Llanbadarn (Aberystwyth) Castle: she promptly granted its keepership for her life to Richard Stury, knight of the royal chamber with whom she had close associations.[28] So, in effect, this was an indirect royal grant to Stury, which made him beholden and answerable to Joan for his charge. This suggests that Richard trusted his mother's judgement in some military matters. The intention may also have been to make this seasoned royal chamber knight her retainer as well as the king's, with other special responsibilities to her – perhaps in communicating between mother and son.

There were, indeed, some royal grants made to her servants which were not said to be at her request, such as the generous ones made in 1379 and 1381 to her esquire Garcius Arnaud. Many of the favours which she received for herself were routine ones, in connection with her property-owning. For instance, in 1377 the council authorised John Payn, carpenter, of Watford (Hertfordshire) to impress carpenters, stonemasons and other workmen for the repair of her manor at Bushey.[29] She complained to the council in 1379 that a group had trespassed in her estate at Cottingham, carrying away 'earth, fish, trees, hares, rabbits, pheasants, partridges and deer'. Allegedly, they had also taken her corn and assaulted her servants. The council appointed a commission of oyer and terminer, on which Joan was weightily represented by Sir John Worthe, steward of her estates, and her long-standing retainer, Sir Donald Hazelrigg.[30]

So Joan set her son the king a good example (which he was to ignore) by refraining from enriching her friends and servants excessively at royal expense. Unusually, in 1379 she attempted to provide Joan de la Warre with a husband by getting a grant to her of a royal ward. If he died under age, and she had not married him, the young lady was to have the right to determine to marry any of his putative heirs, if under age. The assumption was that she would want to marry one of these successive boys although the arrangement seems to have left her, theoretically, with the choice not to do so, but to marry the heir to someone else. Joan de la Warre was a kinswoman of the Princess, possibly her goddaughter.[31] In this case, Joan seems to have favoured some freedom of choice for a prospective bride.

In the same year, royal provision was made for the retirement of one of the Princess's *domicellae*, Agnes de Corby. She was sent to Crowland Abbey (Lincolnshire) to receive a corrody there.[32] This was a lifetime's allowance of board and lodging attached to a religious house. Another of her damosels, Katherine de Cologne, apparently received a corrody in the Hospital of St Katherine by the Tower in London, which is mentioned in 1380.[33] Some others of Joan's domestic servants received royal tit-bits at her request. In 1377, her servant Henry Ferour was granted the office of porter at the royal castle of Portchester, on the Hampshire coast, and the keeping of the warren there – potentially onerous responsibilities in view of Franco-Castilian invasion threats. The following year, Giles, keeper of the Wardrobe in her household, received a plot of land in Wycombe (Buckinghamshire) which had escheated to the Crown.[34] At no cost to the Crown, Joan procured some exemptions from summonses to serve on commissions and assizes. One of the recipients (1377) was William Hazelrigg of Hazelrigg in Northumberland, whose brother Sir Donald had been retained by the late Sir Thomas Holand. At least in his sixties, William was a veteran soldier who had fought in Edward III's great victory over the Scots at Halidon Hill, near Berwick, in 1333. His participation in major campaigns in Brittany and France in the 1340s may well have brought him into contact and comradeship with Sir Thomas.[35] Another recipient of a like favour through Joan was Robert de Louthe, esquire (1379), who may have been a relative of the rector of the same name of Cottingham who adorned the church so strikingly to honour Edward III and his family.[36]

Why was Joan so moderate in her financial demands on the Crown, especially in view of her past extravagances? We can assume that the 'continual' council of the minority was well disposed to her, and that her son the king continued to be so, too, after he was declared of age. In the early years of his majority, he was to bestow some patronage in ways which were thought profligate and excessively partial. Joan is likely to have been anxious not to burden her son's embattled government, or to be vilified for exploiting her position as Queen Isabella or Alice Perrers had been. It is possible that, now in middle age, she was moved to adopt a more austere way of life by Franciscan or Wycliffite precepts, or by the examples set by her late husband's friend, Abbot de la Mare of St Albans.

It was considered especially appropriate for women, in pious imitation of the role of the Blessed Virgin Mary, to seek grace for suitors from their lord. Joan was active in petitioning Richard for pardons for offenders. This was, indeed, an important function of queenship, which Joan in some measure took on in the absence of a queen. After Richard's marriage to Anne of Bohemia in 1382, Joan's role in seeking pardons declined.[37] Joan had not, as a queen would be expected to do, petitioned generally for suppliants from the whole realm: hers were mainly people associated with her in one way or another or from places and regions where she had propertied interests. The total number of pardons she procured, enrolled on the Patent Rolls, was not large – a total of twenty-one between 1377 and 1385. Thirteen of them were for manslaughter. Besides, some of those in her service, in seeking pardons for manslaughters in which others were responsible or involved, considered that their petitions would carry weight if they mentioned their connection with her. There were two of her clerics, Thomas Walton and William Desseford, who petitioned separately in this way in 1379; two of her demosels, Agnes de Corby and Margaret de Lodewyk, who did likewise in 1380, and another of her clerks, William Fulburne (her receiver-general), who did so in 1381.[38]

Joan procured pardons for a variety of other offences, such as negligence over escapes from gaols, alleged robberies (including the case of a recent prisoner in Wallingford Castle in 1378), failures to procure royal licences for the alienation ('in mortmain') of property to religious houses, and an assault on a castle in Kent.[39] In 1383 she got a pardon for one of a group who had released Thomas Cheseman from the stocks at Birdham (Sussex), where he had been put for stealing thirty-nine sheep from the dean of Chichester.[40] In Wallingford, Joan's right of purveyance may not have been popular, but she did its burgesses a good turn when, at her petition, in 1384 they were pardoned payment of an annual farm owed by the town, in arrears for seven years. John Leland was to note that the town had been 'a considerable one with a good wall'; he reckoned it had had as many as fourteen churches, but in his day there were only three. Decline had probably set in as a result of plague pandemics in Edward III's time, Leland thought.[41]

The favours Joan granted and sought in her widowhood give some hints as to the circles she then moved in. The evidence which they provide as to the gentlefolk she cultivated and patronised is, indeed slight and fragmentary. For what they are worth, the favours suggest that she was not interested, as we have surmised, in building up an English regional power base, as, for instance, her younger kinswoman Joan de Bohun, countess of Hereford, did in Essex. The Princess was, indeed, as vulnerable as any other landowner to assaults on her property and challenges to her property rights. But, being the king's mother, she needed less local support to promote her interests. She could anticipate that her favourers would be prominent on commissions of enquiry involving her interests. Her political orientation was fixed on the court – as witnessed by her cultivation of its chamber knights.

Favours to kinsfolk and others with whom she had, in some cases, long connections were clearly of particular concern to her. In 1378 we find her allaying the concern of her aged aunt Blanche Wake about provision after her death for her chamberlain, John Dessex. Blanche had granted him for her lifetime fifteen acres of land in Colne Wake, in return for a wash of oysters, to be delivered to her annually on the first Sunday of Lent, and had also granted him the keepership of the gate of Bourne Castle, with wages of 2d a day. Joan now confirmed these grants for her own life by letters patent.[42] As we have seen, in 1379 she was concerned with the future welfare of a de la Warre kinswoman. In the same year, Joan interceded jointly with Elizabeth Audley, wife of Nicholas and daughter-in-law of James Lord Audley, of Heleigh and Red Castle (Shropshire), for a pardon for the death of a Welshman. Elizabeth was Joan's kinswoman, a descendant of Henry earl of Lancaster, Blanche Wake's father.[43] In the month before Joan's death in 1385, she and her kinsman and close friend Robert Braybrooke, bishop of London, secured from the Crown acquittances for a former leading servant of the Prince, on the grounds of his old age and good service. This was Sir Nigel Loring, of Hargrove (Bedfordshire). He must have been familiar to her in Aquitaine as one of the Prince's most trusted knights, who served as his chamberlain. He had been knighted at the naval battle of Sluis in 1340, and fought in the Prince's division at Crécy. He was a founder member of the Order of the Garter (1348) and a member of the Prince's Council, c. 1356.⁴⁴ Loring made his will on 14 March 1385, with Bishop Braybrooke as its supervisor. He feared that he would be prosecuted for his failure to maintain properly the castle and park of Trematon (Cornwall) which the Prince had originally granted him. Joan secured for him an acquittance for her lifetime as regards the castle, and the bishop as regards the park. Loring died in 1386.⁴⁵

Joan secured a few pardons and favours for religious houses and their heads. In some cases, these may simply have been exercises in lordship, in her capacity as lay patron, a position inherited from a house's founder. For instance, in 1381, soon after she had inherited the patronage of Ware Priory from Blanche Wake, at her instance the prior, who was a Frenchman, and therefore in danger of being deprived of his office as an enemy alien, was confirmed in it by the Crown.⁴⁶ At the same time she had inherited the patronage of Bourne Abbey, which soon received a royal licence to appropriate the advowson of a parish church which she had granted to the house.⁴⁷ This grant appears to reflect a personal reverence and concern for a community of canons. That may have been the case too with her benevolence to canons of another Order who followed the Rule of St Augustine, the Bonshommes. This grant demonstrates, too (like her concern for the frail and anxious Loring), her reverence for the Prince's memory. He had revived the house at Ashridge (Hertfordshire) of this obscure Order. He seems to have visited the house in 1374, and he bequeathed it one of the most precious relics he possessed: a fragment of the True Cross in a jewel-encrusted setting. He stipulated that it was to remain on the High Altar of the canons' church in perpetuity. In 1378 Joan procured a royal licence for the rector and community to receive land in mortmain, and, the following year, a pardon for the rector's servant, for manslaughter.⁴⁸

A WEDDING AND TWO FUNERALS

W E HAVE FEW NOTICES of Joan's whereabouts in 1378 and thereafter. She was at her manor house at Bushey on 13 March 1378, probably with Sir Lewis Clifford among her company, and on 1 September she was at Rockingham Castle (Northamptonshire), where she made her promissory grants to Blanche Wake's chamberlain. Like Marlborough Castle, it was a royal residence which had been held by the late Queen Philippa. It sits above a ford across the River Welland. Two drum towers guarding the gate had been added in Edward I's time, and remain distinctive features of the castle. Parts of the thirteenth-century hall and chamber survive. Joan probably stayed there on the way to or from visiting Blanche in Lincolnshire.[49]

On 23 April 1379 Joan was present at Windsor Castle at a large gathering of the king's family to celebrate the Feast of St George in the saint's chapel there. She was granted robes of the Order of the Garter for the occasion, as were her daughters Joan duchess of Brittany and Maud Courtenay, also Gaunt's Spanish wife Constance and his two elder daughters (by Blanche of Lancaster), Edmund of Langley's wife Isabel (Constance's younger sister), Philippa countess of Oxford, and her mother Isabel, countess of Bedford, a daughter of Edward III.[50] The public association of these ladies with the Garter ceremonies may have reflected hopes that they would act as symbols and forces for unity among the king's close kin.

Unity of opinion among the ladies was to be sorely tested. The year was especially fraught for Joan because mismatched passion blossomed in her family – perhaps recalling embarrassingly her own indiscretions as a young woman. Her widowed daughter, Maud Courtenay, displayed waywardness and determination in love. The object of her affections was the young and impulsive Waleran de Luxembourg, count of St Pol. A leading landowner in northern France, he had been captured in 1374 on a raid into the March of Calais. Edward III had bought him from his captor, but attempts to arrange with the French Crown for his exchange for an important Gascon prisoner had failed.[51] Froissart, who tells the story in romance mode, says that St Pol was held on easy terms in Windsor Castle. He was allowed out to hawk. Maud, whom the chronicler describes as the most beautiful woman in England, and her mother, stayed at the castle. There the couple met and fell in love, being frequently in one another's company, at dances, carolings and other court revels. The chronicler Walsingham, who reflected English disillusion with St Pol, said that Joan, and Maud's friends, tried to dissuade her from marrying him. Incensed by her intransigence, they refused to help her plans.[52] However, the King's Council saw some merit in the alliance with a landowner whose support might strengthen the defence of Calais. A treaty was made with him which fixed his ransom at a lower rate than hitherto. He agreed to switch to the English allegiance, and to mount a campaign at home in support of Richard II. This turned out to be a fiasco. Charles V of France forfeited him and occupied his castles. St Pol returned to England.[53]

Nevertheless, in accordance with the agreement, St Pol and Maud were married at Windsor Castle on 2 April 1380, entertained by 'a host of pipers and actors'. On her wedding day, Gaunt gave the bride a silver cup and ewer on a stand.[54] Presumably Joan had not withheld her blessing. In view of her own past marital waywardness, her alleged opposition appears hypocritical. However, she may have thought the marriage unhelpful to Richard, the fostering of his interest being paramount in her eyes. In fact, as far as the war was concerned, the marriage was a resounding failure. Soon after the accession of Charles VI to the French throne that year, St Pol made his peace with him, and returned with his bride to his ancestral homes. However, in the long run he was to have mutually satisfactory relations with Richard, and was, apparently, after Richard's death, devoted to his memory, and indignant at his fate.[55] Perhaps the young Richard had been less censorious than his mother about his sister's love match.

Soon after the wedding, Joan (perhaps piqued) was absent from court, for on 20 April she was party to an indenture dated at Missenden (Buckinghamshire).[56] This was near Princes Risborough, from which Joan received a rent as part of her princely dower, and also near the house of Bonshommes at Ashridge. Perhaps she was staying at Missenden Abbey, belonging to the Arroasian Order of Augustinian canons – an Order probably familiar to her at Bourne Abbey, another of their houses. She was now in mourning for an old acquaintance from her Aquitaine days, Guichard d'Angle, who, as we have seen, had been greatly admired by the Prince, and had acted as one of Richard's masters. He died between 5 March and 4 April. Joan attended the exequies at the Blackfriars in London, as did Richard and her two other sons, Sir Thomas and Sir John Holand.[57]

Joan was soon to have a much closer bereavement. Blanche Wake died early in July.[58] As we have seen, she was interred in the Franciscan friary at Stamford, as Joan was to be; her will directed that her tomb should be in the choir. She left 20s to every recluse in the town, thus displaying warmth towards a strong contemplative trend in contemporary devotion. Her confessor, Dr William Folville, was a brother in the Franciscan friary. In 1539 a marble tomb in the former friary, with an effigy of copper gilt on it, was identified as that of Blanche duchess of Lancaster – it was in fact Blanche Wake's place of burial. Tomb and effigy disappeared, but in 1963 their monumental inscription was discovered in a chimney breast in a house in the High Street at Stamford. The brief request for prayers for the lady's soul described her as the wife of Lord Wake – and as the daughter of the earl of Lancaster: hence the sixteenth-century misidentification.[59] Joan is likely to have attended the burial service. On 24 July, she was granted custody of the dower lands which her aunt had held, ensuring her secure tenure until her right to them as countess of Kent was duly processed.[60]

LITERARY AND INTELLECTUAL CONNECTIONS

IT IS DISAPPOINTING THAT no surviving books have been identified as having been possessed by Joan. We know of only one work which she commissioned. There is also the possibility that Chaucer's poem 'The Complaint of Venus' was composed for her. It is a translation of a ballad by the Savoyard poet Oton de Granson, who was on the English courtly scene. Son of the lord of Sainte-Croix (now in Switzerland), in 1372 he had been captured by the Castilians when fighting under the earl of Pembroke in the naval battle off La Rochelle. In 1374 he was retained by John of Gaunt. There is a possible social connection between Granson and Joan. His fellow countryman Jean de la Grivière was retained by Gaunt on the same day as he was. He and Granson may well have been brothers-in-arms who had set out together to seek their fortunes in the English cause. In 1376 they were both in the entourage of the Dame de Neuchâtel, travelling to Neuchâtel with her. In 1379 Joan secured a pardon for Grivière's son Ralph. With one blow he had slain John de Markeby, the king's water bailiff at Calais. Both Grivière and Granson were in the garrison at Calais that year.[61]

In Granson's poem, a male narrator eulogises the female focus of his love. Chaucer reverses this, having a female narrator as the panegyrist. His 'Envoy' is dedicated to a 'Princess'. There were three ladies in England to whom the title 'Princess' would have been appropriate in the late 1370s and early 1380s: Edward III's daughter, the countess of Bedford, Edmund of Langley's wife Isabel, who was an *Infanta* of Castile, and Joan. The countess of Bedford's husband, the Frenchman Enguerrand de Coucy, had deserted her and reverted to his native allegiance in 1377. She died in 1382. The poem has been dated as 'probably from the 1380s', but, if made for Joan, would have been written before the Prince's death in 1376, since the lover characterises her beloved as if he were living.[62]

Tantalisingly, some of the knights of the king's chamber who had associations with Joan had literary connections too. Sir Lewis Clifford, it is generally thought, was a friend of Chaucer. Sir Philip la Vache of Chalfont St Giles (Buckinghamshire), another trusty friend of the poet, was a knight of the royal chamber who married Clifford's daughter Elizabeth: Joan gave her a covered cup on her wedding day.[63] Sir Philip was one of Joan's executors. Chaucer was to address to him his 'Balade de Bon Conseyl', in which he urged him to shake off his habitual depression about the false values of the world, and its pitfalls, and stick to godly precepts. Sir John Clanvowe – in Joan's entourage in 1376 and later slated as a Lollard knight – was an author in two contrasting genres. He wrote a debate on courtly love, 'The Book of Cupid', in the 1380s, and, later, *The Two Ways*, an orthodox homiletic treatise in which K. B. McFarlane detected Lollard undertones.[64]

We have a surer indication of Joan's intellectual interests in the *Kalendarium* of John Somer, a Franciscan from the friary at Bridgwater (Somerset), who was attached to the Order's Oxford house. He was one of the leading astrologers of his day. This calendar, like others, listed the days of the month, with saints' days and with astrological data and separate tables. The dedication says that Somer composed it in 1380 at the request of Thomas Kingsbury, Provincial Master of the Franciscan Order in England, for Princess Joan. It was written in honour of God, the Virgin and Franciscan saints, including St Louis of Toulouse (1274–97). His cult appears to have been little celebrated in England. It was very much a Franciscan devotion, and likely to have been a personal one of Somer's. The cult would surely have appealed to Joan, too, if she became aware of it. She shared with the saint a common descent from Louis VIII of France (d. 1226).[65]

St Louis of Toulouse was the son and heir of Charles II, king of Sicily, but he renounced his prospective inheritance (in imitation of St Francis) in order to become a friar. The miracles recorded in the years after his death – to which the witnesses were nearly all from Provence – were concerned with recoveries of health. In 1317 he was canonised, and in 1343 Pope Clement VI granted the Franciscan Order the same indulgences for his feast as for those of St Francis and St Antony of Padua. The cult was strongly promoted by the Angevin kings of Naples, and was taken up by ruling houses with which the Black Prince was to form or strengthen links. When the life of Philip VI of France's son, the future John II, was despaired of, Philip prayed to St Louis of Toulouse, and, after John's recovery, went on pilgrimage to the saint's shrine at Marseilles, in company with the kings of Navarre and Majorca. Pere III of Aragon was a devotee, too, defying Pope Urban VI in 1366 by carrying off some relics of the saint.[66] So Joan had been on the periphery of continental princely circles in which St Louis was reverenced. It seems likely that she would have sought her saintly kinsman's aid during the Prince's illness. No presentation copy made to her of the *Kalendarium* is known to survive, though a copy composed in the period 1397–1400 was associated with her grandson Thomas Holand. It is curious that the surviving copies all start with the year 1387, two years after Joan's death, which has led to the supposition that no copy may have ever been given to her. But it has also been surmised that Somer provided her with astrological predictions.[67]

As Derek Pearsall has pointed out, Chaucer had a keen astrological interest, reflecting scientific trends at Oxford, which is manifested especially in his *Treatise of the Astrolabe*. Joan appears to have been interested in these matters, as was John of Gaunt. The Carmelite friar

Nicholas of Lynn was to compose a *Kalendarium* at his request in 1386.[68] Chaucer dedicated his *Treatise of the Astrolabe* to 'Lyte [little] Lowys my sone'. Could it be that Joan, Chaucer and Lewis Clifford shared a devotion to St Louis of Toulouse as well as absorption in planetary studies? We should not let Clifford's Lollardy stand in the way of such a speculation about devotion to the cult, for early Lollards did not necessarily shed all orthodox beliefs and practices in the ways which the more sharply defined sect later did. But we can at least say of Joan that her behaviour and connections, where religion, social behaviour and intellectual interests were concerned, suggest that she was at the cutting edge of some innovative trends, and by her example, patronage or protection provided encouragement and stimulus to them.

So, though our information about Joan's possession of books is meagre, it can be inferred from her behaviour that her literary interests were not necessarily all conventional in their pious or romantic content, but struck out in challenging directions on sometimes fundamental issues. She appears to have had decided and well-grounded opinions, sometimes at odds with traditional orthodoxy, on some of the great religious and cultural issues of the day. Her patronage of Wycliffe is likely to have been based on unorthodox interpretations of scriptural authority. Her attitudes to gender relations appear to reflect a diversification in current views, such as were reflected in Chaucerian dilemmas. And her keen interest in planetary divination shows her eager to embrace science.

·: 9 :·

Terrors and Tribulations

A CONSOLATION FOR JOAN, in the midst of her mourning for Blanche, was that she received the Wake properties which Blanche had held as dower, including those in Lincolnshire, where the centre of Joan's family piety as the widow of Thomas Holand was at Stamford. The favours which were bestowed by the Crown in June 1381 on Bourne Abbey and Ware Priory at Joan's petition suggest that she may have travelled as far north as Lincolnshire in order to be greeted as 'the lady', to inspect the estates, and receive petitions from the monks, canons and tenants newly come into her lordship. If she thought that all augured well for the immediate future, she could not have been more mistaken.[1] For 1381 was to be an *annus horribilis* for Joan. It was the year of the Peasants' Revolt (see Plate VII). The rebel bands from Kent and Essex, who briefly occupied London, were stung to fury by attempts to collect the harsh poll tax granted in parliament. Some of their leaders promoted reforms which, at their most drastic, would have undermined the dominance of the nobility and, at their most moderate, would have adversely affected the estate profits and related labour costs of landowners. There were also some regional and many localised risings directed against the unpopular regimes of particular landowners and urban elites, especially in parts of southern England. On those hot, turbulent June days in rebel-controlled London, Joan must have feared for her life, and the lives of her son the king, of her other two sons and her daughter Joan, and other vulnerable kinsfolk, friends and servants. She must have wondered whether John of Gaunt, a particular target for the commons' wrath, and his family would escape death, as, indeed, they did after various vicissitudes. The duke was widely blamed for the poll tax, and the failures in war. He was fortunate to have been distant from London, negotiating with the Scots, when the revolts broke out.[2]

There was, indeed, a reason why Joan is likely to have been especially fearful of a popular rising. She had gone to live in Aquitaine six years after the Jacquerie, when French peasants had risen in arms and tortured and massacred nobles of both sexes with extreme cruelty. True, this had taken place far away from where she had stayed, in parts of northern France centring on the Île-de-France. However, the Jacquerie was long remembered with horror in French noble circles, and it is likely that Joan heard of its excesses when she was Princess of Aquitaine. Two nobles with whom she was most probably well acquainted, Gaston Fébus, count of Foix, and Jean de Grailly, captal de Buch, had rescued noble ladies besieged in Meaux in 1358, and put the 'Jacks' who threatened them to flight.[3]

Joan may have been apprehensive that the Kentish rebels' animus might be specially directed against her. The comings and goings of great nobles as they frequently moved residence and visited one another with conspicuous trains – impressive carriages, great wagons, banners displayed – must have been of special interest to peasants and townsmen. They provided temporary employment to carters, blacksmiths, victuallers, innkeepers and prostitutes. They brought colour and excitement into the commons' lives. Joan's closeness to John of Gaunt was surely widely observed. Besides, the previous summer, the Franco-Castilian fleet had sailed up the Thames estuary, sacking places on its banks. The Kentish rebels of 1381 were fearful that there would be a repetition of this, and ordered men living near their coasts to stay behind, not joining the army of protest which went up to London. Perhaps Joan thought that the rebels might apportion her some blame, as countess of Kent, for not ensuring that the county's defences were sufficiently prepared to resist invasion. But since she held few properties in Kent, it was difficult for her to act forcefully, as she had had to defend South Wales from invasion a few years before.[4]

Indeed, the Princess was one of the first great nobles to be accosted by rebels – some of the main band of Kentishmen. Froissart says that, the same day that they were on the way to London, she was returning thither from a pilgrimage to St Thomas's shrine at Canterbury. 'She ran great risks from them, for these scoundrels attacked her carriage, and caused much confusion, which greatly frightened the good lady, lest they should do some violence to her or her ladies.' Froissart said that she travelled from Canterbury to London in just one day, without making a stop – an uncomfortable and nerve-racking ordeal for a middle-aged lady. So different from her usual stately progress, it must have been especially humiliating to be run out of her own earldom by the lowlier of its inhabitants. But Froissart was surely exaggerating when he asserted that it took only one day to cover a journey of fifty-six miles up Watling Street.[5]

If Joan had left Canterbury after the rebels entered the city, she had another reason for terror at the thought of encountering them on her flight. Despite its stout city walls, the rebels took control there on 10 June, where, according to an indictment made before her son Thomas Holand, titular earl of Kent, the following month, they pillaged, extorted, assaulted and killed, then set out for London.[6] Joan had probably gone to Canterbury, not only to offer at St Thomas's shrine, but to attend the annual anniversary Mass for the Black Prince on 8 June. Reverence for Joan and goodwill towards her among the citizens of Canterbury may have helped her to survive unscathed. The previous year, at her petition, the king had granted a privilege to the mayor and citizens of his special grace, for the honour of St Thomas of Canterbury, and because his father was buried in the cathedral.[7]

Joan, having escaped from the rebels, took refuge in the Tower of London, arriving there just ahead of the Kentish bands, who had encamped on Blackheath on 12 June. She was reunited in the Tower with the king, then aged fourteen, and with many of his close kinsfolk and leading councillors. According to the chronicler Henry Knighton, Joan's daughter, Joan duchess of Brittany, was in there as well as many other ladies.[8] Circumstances rapidly became dire, for on 13 June the rebels from Kent and Essex were admitted within the gates of London. They surrounded the Tower. An additional terror for the ladies was that the galaxy of eminent knights – unlike the defenders of Meaux – concluded that the Tower was indefensible. The king felt compelled to agree to go to Mile End, outside the city walls beyond Aldgate, the following day to meet the rebel leader Wat Tyler. There he perforce agreed to the demands Tyler made. The commons were permitted to seize all 'traitors', who were to be punished at law. Serfdom was to be abolished, land let out at a uniformly low rent and no man was to be compelled to serve another.[9]

There are various versions of the confusing events of that day. According to the *Anonimalle Chronicle*, the king had arrived at Mile End by seven o'clock in the morning, accompanied by his mother in a carriage. Presumably, she was desperate to plead for her son if there was trouble; he was surely aware that it would be unsafe for her to be left in the Tower. They were accompanied by the flower of chivalry, ready to defend the king and his mother to the death. According to the Anonimalle Chronicler, present were his fire-eating uncle, Thomas of Woodstock earl of Buckingham, her son the earl of Kent, the earl of Warwick, a seasoned soldier well known to her, the king's untried youthful companion Robert de Vere, earl of Oxford, William Walworth, the pugnacious mayor of London, and many knights and squires. Sir Aubrey de Vere, Oxford's uncle, well known to Joan as the Black Prince's former secretary, carried the king's sword.[10]

After the meeting, the chronicler says, Wat Tyler and the commons went to the Tower to seize Simon Sudbury, archbishop of Canterbury, and others whom they held responsible for oppressive government, whilst the king remained at Mile End. They executed the 'traitors'. An official record of the city of London corroborates the presence of Joan in a carriage with the king at Mile End, and also says that the commons went thence and broke into the Tower, whilst the king retired to the King's Wardrobe. This storehouse was situated near the west end of the city, just south of St Paul's Cathedral. Froissart says that Richard was accompanied to Mile End by his two half-brothers, Sir John Holand and Kent, as well as the earls of Salisbury (Joan's former husband) and Warwick, and two foreign lords, Robert of Namur and John, lord of Gommegnies. They were from the county of Hainault; they may have been among their compatriot Froissart's informants about the revolt. Robert of Namur, who had married a sister of the late Queen Philippa, was among his former literary patrons. These two may have provided Froissart with some of his vivid eyewitness vignettes of events, including those about the Princess, for whom he had a particular reverence.[11]

Froissart says that Richard dismissed his brothers and Gommegnies at Mile End, 'as they dared not appear before the commons'. An accusation of knightly cowardice was a rare charge, and is suggestive of the quaking hearts among Richard's companions. Perhaps the commons of Kent particularly blamed the Holands rather than their mother for their failure to defend the shire, from which the family title derived, against foreign raids. Gommegnies had been captain at Ardres, a castle in the March of Calais; in the parliament of 1377 he had been condemned for treason for surrendering it, but received a pardon. The rebels' animus against him suggests the importance of failures in the war to them, and the influence of soldiers among them in the formation of their opinions.[12] Approval by the rankers of Thomas of Woodstock's aggressive leadership on the recent expedition to France may account for why he was not tarred with the same brush as a failure in war, despite his close association with Gaunt and his abhorrence of the rebels, demonstrated by his subsequent harsh suppression of the commons' cause. Why was Joan able to escape rougher treatment from the rebels? Above all, the fact that she was the Black Prince's widow probably gave her a benevolent aura in the eyes of the outraged veterans, peasants and artisans.

The late Barrie Dobson pointed out the contradiction between the assertions about Joan's movements on that frantic day in June 1381 in the *Anonimalle Chronicle* and the London record, on the one hand, and Froissart's and Thomas Walsingham of St Albans Abbey's account, on the other. Whereas the first two mention her presence at Mile End, the others locate her in the Tower when the rebels entered it. Walsingham says that some of them broke into the royal apartments 'with their filthy sticks' and, after they 'arrogantly lay and sat on the king's bed while joking', several had even dared to ask her to kiss them. Froissart says that the commons 'entered into the Princess's chamber and smashed her bed, as a result of which she was very afraid and fainted; and then she was taken up by her servants and carried to the waterfront and put in a barge and covered up and conveyed to a place called the Queen's Wardrobe; and there she was all that day and night like a woman half dead, until she was comforted by her son'. Richard stayed there that night, according to the chronicler.[13]

Next day there occurred Richard's final confrontation with the commons in Smithfield, outside Aldersgate. Wat Tyler, after presenting even more radical demands to the king, and acting in a boorish fashion in his presence, became involved in a fracas with members of the king's retinue, and was mortally wounded. This confused and disheartened the rebels. The timely appearance of more military support for the king led to their submission to the royal mercy.

As Professor Dobson indicated, the account of Joan's movements in the *Anonimalle Chronicle* and in the official record is to be preferred. However, both Froissart and Walsingham, though generally more polemical and less accurate in their accounts of the Revolt than the Anonimalle Chronicler, had good sources of information about events in London. Perhaps we have here a case of mistaken identity. It may have been the Duchess Joan and not her mother who was left in the Tower. Outrageous treatment there of the king's mother made a much better story than outrage to his half-sister. There was a possible reason for animus against her. Thomas of Woodstock's expedition to France had ended up in Brittany. It had had to be abandoned because the duchess's husband once more reverted to the French allegiance. It would have made sense to leave her in the Tower rather than expose her at Mile End, in case some of the commons had heard about the outcome of the campaign from soldiers who had returned from Brittany the previous month, after wintering miserably there.[14]

An alternative explanation for the Princess's alleged presence in the Tower is that she had been escorted back there from Mile End before the king's negotiations with the rebels were concluded. Perhaps the king, seeing her disquiet at the menacing aspect of the commons (of which she had had a foretaste in Kent), ordered that she should be taken back. Despite the reluctance she would have felt at leaving her son in such dreadful circumstances, she would have had strong incentives to return, besides her terror. That presumably was where her daughter, most of her servants and her household gear were located. A possible objection to this suggestion is that both Froissart and a highly reliable chronicler, the Monk of Westminster, say that the Tower was broken into by rebels before the end of the Mile End conference.[15]

Within a few days of the suppression of the Revolt in London, the council ordered the construction of a new barge for Joan – perhaps her existing one had been damaged or stolen in the mayhem.[16] Doubtless, Richard was eager to please his mother after her tribulations. Like many other landowners, she had suffered material damage, too. Some of the properties which she held in dower in Essex had been entered and presumably damaged by rebels – North Weald, where she had had the manor house improved, among them. On her complaint to the king about this, Thomas of Woodstock was appointed in September 1381 to enquire into the matter.[17] By contrast, about eighteen months after these dire experiences, Joan procured a pardon for one of the rebel leaders – though not one involved in the disturbances in London or Kent. Thomas Sampson, who hailed from her manor of Kersey in Suffolk, had led the rebels who rioted and destroyed in Ipswich. He was imprisoned there under penalty of death for treasons and felonies, but he managed to evade execution by turning 'approver' – that is, accusing others of crimes. At Joan's petition he was pardoned in January 1383.[18] This is a striking instance of princely mercifulness on her part, and suggests that she appreciated that she could have fared much worse at rebel hands.

Joan had endured terrible shocks in the Great Revolt, but afterwards she had reason to thank God for the near miraculous escapes she and her family had had. Her son the king had demonstrated his ability to rule by his cool and sensible conduct during the crisis in London. Soon afterwards, he was to be exalted by making an illustrious marriage. His bride, Anne of Bohemia, was the sister of Wenzel, who, as king of the Romans, was nominal ruler of the Holy Roman Empire. Joan was well informed about the marriage proposal and negotiations, as her son Thomas Holand and her kinsman and confidant Robert Braybrooke were involved in them. So were knights of the king's chamber well known to her – Simon Burley and Richard Adderbury. The marriage appeared to be a big diplomatic coup, since Anne's family, the House of Luxembourg, had inclined to support the French Crown. Richard's bride landed at Dover shortly before Christmas 1381. Joan is likely to have been present at the wedding in Westminster Abbey on 20 January 1382, at which Braybrooke, newly promoted to the see of London, officiated.[19] She is likely to have been, too, at the queen's coronation there two days later. It turned out to be a happy marriage, though not one blessed with offspring. The mild and unobtrusive Anne would have shown due deference to her mother-in-law.

In the light of recent events, Joan planned to be less frequently at court, and to lead a more retired life at Wallingford Castle. In October 1381, she was envisaging future sojourns there. She then received royal licence for her officials to purvey goods for herself, members of her household and their horses within a radius around Wallingford whenever she came to stay at the castle. The privilege was granted for three years, in contrast to a previous grant of it, which had been restricted to one year.[20] Perhaps now less robust in health, Joan was concerned to make provision for her affairs after her death. In 1382 her great friend and servant Sir Lewis Clifford received royal confirmation of her grant to him in 1378 of the keeping of Cardigan Castle, now to be held by him for life.[21] In 1383 the Crown granted that her dower in the late Prince's properties should be held by her executors for two years after her death in order to settle her affairs. But these terms were considered excessively generous, and speedily amended: the period was cut down to a year, and guaranteed remuneration to her former servants in the period was excluded.[22]

Joan continued to procure royal pardons and privileges for petitioners, but not so frequently as hitherto. She received some privileges herself to boost her patronage for life in her Welsh dower lands. They were custodies of the temporalities of bishoprics and appointments to church livings belonging to them there, during episcopal vacancies, and the right to appoint justices under her own seal.[23]

We also find Joan associated with the affairs of her children. She had already in 1380 presented a petition, jointly with her son Sir Thomas Holand, for a pardon for the keeper of the gaol in Wallingford Castle, for the escape of five men. Apparently, the keeper was at Southampton, waiting to go abroad in Sir Thomas's military retinue, abandoning his responsibilities to his mistress for the challenge of soldiering.[24] Sir Thomas, in the immediate aftermath of the Peasants' Revolt, headed the justices who presided at Canterbury over presentments of rebels. In February 1382 Joan was pardoned for having alienated to him and his wife Alice a rent of £30 from the manor of Wickhambreux in Kent without royal licence. She had wanted to give this dutiful son a material stake in the earldom of Kent. Many years later, Alice alleged that Joan had granted Woking to her husband and herself. The couple already held some Wake properties in Yorkshire as part of their marriage settlement, but Joan was determined to bolster their landed estate, showing generosity to her eldest son, as her Holand mother-in-law had done to her younger sons many years before. Joan's behaviour contrasted with that of some widows who tenaciously clung to the whole of their dower or jointure, leaving their son or other heir penurious.[25]

Joan was involved too with the affairs of her daughter Joan duchess of Brittany, with whom she is likely to have socialised when she was living in England with the duke. One of their houses, where they stayed in the 1370s, was at Cheshunt (Hertfordshire).[26] It may have been for the convenience of visiting them there that Joan had repairs to her manor house nearby in North Weald in hand in 1378. Now the duchess, fresh from the ordeal she had endured with her mother in the Great Revolt, was in an unhappy and embarrassing situation. She was living in England, separated from her husband, who was staying in his duchy, now a vassal of Charles VI of France. Her difficult position seems to have aroused the sympathy of John of Gaunt, who was fond of her. Probably for a New Year's present in 1381 he gave her a covered gold cup which he had had made, and the following December he had a tun of Gascon wine sent to his 'very dear cousin'. She was the recipient, like his son Henry of Bolingbroke, his three daughters and three ladies to whom he was close, of a covered gold cup each at New Year 1382.[27]

Richard was concerned too for his half-sister's situation. His council was doubtless reflecting his wishes in making provision for her welfare. In December 1381 she was granted three Sussex manors, in aid of her maintenance, whilst she stayed in England.[28] Then, in May 1382, a delegation from the duke of Brittany arrived at court, one of whose requests was that the duchess should be returned to him. Richard referred them to his council, who directed the principal envoy, Jean de Bazvalen, to visit her at Byfleet, and put her husband's request directly to her. She told him that she was willing to return, if it was pleasing to her uterine brother the king and to her mother, in whose governance she was, she said, at present. If they agreed, she was pleased to do so of her own free will, and wholeheartedly. Next day Bazvalen and his fellow envoys were given an audience by Princess Joan at Wallingford Castle. In reply to his question, Joan said that she approved her daughter's return, and wished that what was done and ordained by her son the king as regards the matter should be put into effect. The duchess was duly reunited with her husband. She continued to have cordial relations with Richard.[29]

This episode sheds some light on Princess Joan's family relationships. We can infer that the king had no objection to his sister's return to Brittany, as well he might have done, in view of her husband's treachery. But the duchess wished to defer to her mother, to whom she had been much beholden in recent years – though the Princess had no formal right to keep her daughter from the husband to whom she had been married for many years. The duchess wished to be seen as the dutiful daughter, in contrast to the Princess's conduct as a teenager in defying her mother over her marriage – and in contrast as well to her own sister Maud's marriage a few years before to Waleran de St Pol, against the Princess's wishes.

So both of Joan's daughters ended up living abroad – not an unusual fate for English ladies of royal blood. What was a sign of changed times, of the decline of English fortunes in France, was that both their husbands – like the spouse of Edward III's daughter Isabel de Coucy – had recently abandoned the Plantagenet allegiance for that of the king of France. Isabel, one of Joan's principal remaining links with the heyday of Edward's court, died in London on 5 October 1382. She was buried in Greyfriars, the Franciscan house there. One would expect Joan to have been at the exequies.[30]

The course of public affairs over the next few years, domestic as well as international, doubtless continued to give Joan cause for concern. No more 'continual' councils had been appointed to govern after 1380 (when Richard was aged thirteen): nominally, he ruled as an adult, but, it was assumed, heavily guided by his chief kinsmen and leading officers. However, after the Great Revolt he increasingly asserted his will in the bestowal of royal patronage, sometimes imprudently, and especially to the benefit of favourites such as his boon companion Robert de Vere, earl of Oxford.[31]

What may Joan have felt about her son's early rule? It is likely that she was relieved that he had gained personal authority with ease, in contrast to the young Edward III, who had not been able to save her father from execution. Probably, she placed too much faith in the prudence and self-restraint of those about him who had served his father. The latter, indeed, was in some ways not a good example for his son to emulate – extravagant, impulsive and sometimes heedless of good counsel. Surely, however, Joan was concerned at growing tensions between Richard and the magnates, though comparisons with what she may have heard about Edward II's confrontational rule may have been clouded by the hagiography which now veiled the manifold blemishes in the martyred king's rule.

Tensions between Richard and his lords might have been relieved had he imitated his father by giving a decisive lead in opposing the military might of the French Crown, even if his role in the field had been merely formal. As we have seen, his participation in war had been planned as long ago as 1377. It may be that Richard grew up pessimistic about the chances of success in warfare in France. Some of his earliest memories may have been from the bleak times of reverses in Aquitaine. Former knights of his father who served the Prince there, and who had been caught up in the debacles, may have relayed to Richard sour memories of campaigning in France, and reckoned that a peace with the French Crown involving considerable concessions was the most realistic option. Richard's trusted vice-chamberlain, Sir Simon Burley, and his retainers Sir William Neville and Sir John Clanvowe (both of whom served Joan) had all, as we have seen, been captured in Aquitaine. The poem extolling the Black Prince, composed in 1385 or earlier by Chandos Herald, celebrated his victory in Spain in 1367, but dismally glossed over his later reverses in France.[32]

Richard cannot have been impressed by the results of the costly expeditions which Gaunt and Woodstock led to France early in his reign. As an adult, he was to be a lukewarm patron of Gascon knights and squires. In 1391 he was planning to have the remains of his brother Edward exhumed from Bordeaux Cathedral, and reburied in Westminster Abbey. In the mid 1390s he was to attempt to give up the duchy of Aquitaine: in 1399, when confronted by English revolt, he summarily dismissed the suggestion that he should take refuge there.[33]

We may speculate that Richard's indifference to claiming the territorial rights in France which Edward III had claimed and exercised was influenced by his mother's recollections of the miseries and reverses she had experienced there, during the decline of the Principality of Aquitaine. She certainly failed to inspire him with an ambition to revive his father's Principality. Her lack of sentimental attachments to the region is suggested by the apparent absence in her later years of anyone from there among her ladies-in-waiting and other leading servants.

One of the king's knights whose star rapidly rose at court in the 1380s, and who had served in Aquitaine in 1370–71, was Sir Michael de la Pole, whose father, Sir William, of Hull, had been one of the richest merchants and financiers in the realm under Edward III. Sir Michael was involved in the negotiation of Richard's marriage. In March 1383 he was appointed Chancellor of the Realm. In this role, he continued to ingratiate himself with the king, to whose often maladroit exercises of patronage he seems to have made no objection. Moreover, he showed no enthusiasm for launching attacks in France, and failed to inspire the king with any, either. He made a baleful and substantial contribution to creating conditions for the crises of 1386–88. These crises were, firstly, the threats of French invasion in 1385–86, and, secondly, the gathering movement to curtail the king's use of prerogative. They led to the impeachment of De la Pole (now earl of Suffolk) by the Commons in the parliament of 1386, an armed rising led by Thomas of Woodstock in 1387, the reduction of the king's status to that of a minor, and the execution of some of his closest friends, including Burley, condemned for treason in the 'Merciless Parliament' of 1388. Suffolk escaped abroad. Some knights formerly closely connected with Joan were among those forced to abjure the court – John Worthe, Richard Adderbury and Aubrey de Vere. In these tumultuous years, Richard may have regretted the absence of Gaunt, abroad pursuing his Iberian ambitions, and have recalled how relatively amenable he had been, as we shall see, in moderating his opposition to the king – at Joan's behest.[34]

Fortunately for her, she did not live to witness the French threat at its height, and the domestic upheavals which undermined her son's control of government which turned him into a man with an ultimately self-destructive mission to put royal authority on an unassailable basis. In 1383 she had had a connection with Michael de la Pole, helping him in her capacity as a local landowner with the endowment of a charitable foundation in Hull. In a charter dated at Wallingford on 20 November, she waived her rights as his feudal superior over lands in Cottingham and Willerby, which he wanted to grant to a Maison

Dieu, an almshouse for poor men, near the house of Carthusian monks which he had founded. She referred to him in the charter as 'dear to us'. Perhaps this was more than a flourish for a man who showed himself dedicated to her son's service. If so, her approval was to prove sadly misplaced.[35]

In her last years, family troubles too crowded in upon Joan. The autumn of 1384 was a time of conflicting emotions for her. The health of her daughter the duchess of Brittany failed. At Nantes, in bodily sickness, on 25 September 1384, the duchess made a will. She commended her soul 'to God our blessed Saviour, the glorious Virgin Mary His Mother, St Michael (patron saint of Brittany) and all the company of Paradise', and her body to be buried in the Cistercian house of Nôtre Dame de Prières in the bishopric of Vannes. She made her brother the earl of Kent heir to everything she had inherited in England from her parents. Otherwise, her husband the duke was the main beneficiary, as well as being executor. She died a few weeks after making the will. On 27 November, a solemn Mass was held for her in St Paul's Cathedral.[36] The following day a sliver of sunshine appeared when a daughter was born to Joan's son Thomas; she was christened Eleanor.[37]

It seems highly likely that a major source of worry for Joan at this time was the deterioration of relations between Richard and his uncle John of Gaunt. In essence, it stemmed from Richard's resentment at Gaunt's uniquely great landed power and influence, and his tendency to behave as an omniscient elder statesman. The depth of the king's hostility had been publicly revealed in an incident during the parliament held at Salisbury in April 1384. Richard had apparently reacted to an unsubstantiated accusation of treason against his uncle, made by a Carmelite friar, by ordering the duke's summary execution. A witness to this episode was a knight well known to Joan, John Clanvowe. Afterwards, Joan's son Sir John Holand vowed that he would make the friar confess who had put him up to tell the story. Holand and prominent knights of the king's chamber proceeded to inflict mortal tortures on the friar – an episode revealing the seamy side of supposedly devout and chivalrous court society.[38]

Intemperate behaviour continued to prevail at court. In January 1385, some of the king's friends allegedly plotted Gaunt's assassination.

The duke certainly became dangerously alienated and disaffected. The following month, he concluded an audience with the king at Sheen Manor on the Thames by asserting that he would not give future attendance because of the presence at court of those who wished to kill him. He was then rowed across the river, to rejoin and head off with the military retinue accompanying him.[39]

According to the well-informed Westminster Abbey Chronicler, when Joan was informed about these events, she 'was very much shocked and distressed, and hurried without loss of time to the king, whom she urged always to avoid quarrelling with his nobles and especially with his uncles'. She induced him to go to Westminster, where he arrived on 6 March. She hastened to visit Gaunt, probably then at his castle at Hertford, and persuaded him to accompany her to London to meet the king again. It may be in the course of these journeys that she visited her manor of Bushey, within easy reach of St Albans Abbey, where Thomas Walsingham may have gleaned her version of events for his chronicle: she was at her manor on 8 April. Another sympathetic chronicler, the Monk of Westminster, says that 'through her good offices harmony was soon restored between them'. Joan's intervention may indeed have done more than paper over the cracks: there was to be only one more serious, but brief, flare-up (that summer) between the king and his uncle. Her intervention became widely known, and she was long remembered, as we shall see, as a restraining influence on her headstrong son in this period. Thomas Walsingham reported the episode admiringly, stressing her determination and readiness to put herself out in order to resolve the matter to her satisfaction. Joan 'refused to put up with the troubles of the kingdom, and, though not strong, and used to luxury, and hardly able to move because she was so fat, nevertheless neglected her own tranquil way of life, took upon herself the troublesome journey first to the duke and then to the king, sparing no expense whatsoever'.[40]

A semblance of political unity was restored, too, because of the growing threat of invasions by both the French and the Scots. It was planned that Richard should at last be exalted as a military leader by taking an exceptionally large expedition, in which the magnates co-operated, to invade Scotland, where a French expeditionary force was based. There were fears that, while he was out of the realm, the main French army might invade southern England from its Flemish bases. To meet this threat, a proclamation was made that all knights, esquires and gentlefolk were to be armed and arrayed, ready to serve for the defence of the realm. But on 12 June, the king and council made important exceptions. Joan's favourite, Sir Lewis Clifford, was ordered 'upon his allegiance as he loves the king and his honour under pain of forfeiture to assist continually about the person of the king's mother for her comfort and security wherever she shall abide within the realm, rendering other services befitting the estate of so great a lady'. Similar orders were sent to other knights and esquires.[41] They were:

> Richard Stury
> John Worthe
> Thomas Latimer
> Thomas Morewell
> Philip la Vache
> William FitzRauf knights
> Gilbert Wace
> Laurence Sebroke
> William Harpele
> Henry Norton
> Garcius Arnaud
> Richard Mews

Joan was, presumably, in a state of high anxiety, concerned that, in the event of invasion, she would be vulnerable, since the king, her two other sons and the magnates were likely to be out of the realm, far away. She had recently had a nerve-racking time trying to prevent the outbreak of civil war. In the aftermath of the Peasants' Revolt, as localised rural discontents rumbled on, she may have had fears that there would be new risings of the commons. Maybe the appointment of Sir Hugh Segrave as constable of Wallingford Castle in 1382 had been intended to reassure her on that score. He had been one of the most highly rewarded officers of the Black Prince: he became steward of his lands, and was appointed one of his executors. From 1378 to 1382, Segrave was steward of the royal household, and in 1385 he was treasurer of the Exchequer. Perhaps this eminent royal councillor had a hand that year in arranging for Joan's safeguard.[42]

Joan's connections with some of her protectors appear tenuous. Sir Gilbert Wace held the manor of Ewelme, near Wallingford. He was about Joan's age, active in the public administration of Oxfordshire and as a knight for the shire in parliament. His campaigning experience appears to have been well in the past; he had been on Edward III's expedition to France in 1359, and on Gaunt's limited incursion there in 1369. Wace is likely to have been well placed to bring a local contingent to her defence if she stayed in the castle at Wallingford. By contrast, Laurence Sebroke's origins and career are obscure. He was returned as a knight of the shire for Gloucestershire in 1382, probably as a result of his marriage to a local heiress. Maybe he was recommended to safeguard Joan by Sir William Neville, a knight of the royal chamber close to Joan, under whose command he had served as captain of a retinue on a naval expedition in 1374.[43]

Was Joan reassured by the protection of her paladins? The group was mainly composed of knights and esquires in her service, familiar faces about her. Most of the knights appear to have been middle-aged; they did not merit the description of an outstanding group of soldiers. On the whole, they were probably rusty in the use of arms, and unused to working together in warfare. However, Clifford had experienced campaigning as recently as 1378: he was in Sir William Beauchamp's retinue on Gaunt's expedition to Brittany. La Vache was also on it, in Sir William Neville's retinue. There the army engaged in a gruelling and unsuccessful siege of St Malo. That would have given the two knights useful lessons in how to repel besiegers if they had to plan for the defence of Wallingford Castle. However that may have been a daunting prospect: repairs undertaken there in the years 1385–89 suggest that its ancient defences were dilapidated.[44]

Should we conclude that Richard failed to protect his mother adequately? His defence of her – as of the realm – hinged on the strategy of dealing with the threat from Scotland to the Marches before the French main invasion of southern England occurred. Had this gamble failed, hopefully shire levies could contain the French until Richard arrived back with his formidable 'army royal'. The strategy worked, as the French invasion did not materialise.

An event which happened in the king's army as it progressed northwards through Yorkshire in July had brought the now disquieted

Joan to what one commentator thought was a state of terminal grief. It concerned her unruly son Sir John Holand, who may have already been causing her anguish if by then he had seduced Gaunt's teenage daughter Elizabeth, who was betrothed to the heir to the earldom of Pembroke, a mere lad. According to the monk-chronicler of Westminster, Holand 'fell violently in love with her at first sight and pursued his wooing night and day, until she succumbed to him'.[45] However, on campaign Holand did far worse than this. He slew Ralph, son and heir of the earl of Stafford, in a quarrel over billets, and then fled from the army. On hearing the news, the king 'abandoned himself for some time to tears and mourning, since he had loved the lad all the more tenderly for having been a contemporary and comrade in the heyday of his own youth'. He promised Hugh, earl of Stafford that he would not stand in the way of his brother being subjected to the full rigour of the common law.[46]

When Joan heard the news she dispatched messages to the king with piteous pleas for mercy for Holand. At this point, Richard quite rightly thought that he could not soften. The messengers returned to Wallingford empty-handed. Walsingham wrote that 'it may be because she was weighed down by too much grief that she collapsed on her bed and after four or five days she died'. This was on 8 August. The Princess had made a will, dated the day before her death. This tardiness suggests that she had enjoyed moderately good health, despite the obesity to which Walsingham alludes. Perhaps this blow, on top of her recent anxieties and unaccustomed exercise, induced a heart attack or a stroke.[47]

The will is quite short. She started by stressing her religious orthodoxy, making the will in the name of the indivisible Trinity (to which the Black Prince had had a particular devotion). She asserted that she was of sound mind and faithful in the Catholic faith, leaving her soul to God Almighty her Saviour, the Virgin Mary and all the saints. Her emphasis on her orthodoxy may have stemmed from a need to repudiate Wycliffe's teachings, to which she had once been drawn.[48] Joan was to be buried in her chapel in Stamford friary, next to (*iuxta*) the tomb of her late lord and husband, the earl of Kent. There were only three beneficiaries – her three sons, whose future well-being and relationships, in view of present circumstances, were doubtless much on her mind – to the exclusion of their sister Maud countess of St Pol. Each son was to receive a luxurious bed and its furnishings. Richard was to get the best one – 'my new bed of red velvet, embroidered with ostrich feathers of silver, and heads of leopards of gold, with boughs and leaves issuing from their mouths'. So she had recently had a set of hangings made in which the Black Prince's badge of ostrich feathers was prominently worked. They were a highly suitable heirloom for Richard, bringing to mind his father as well as his mother. Perhaps the leopards with stems coming from their mouths expressed a hope that Richard would be blessed with children. Her son Thomas earl of Kent she termed 'well beloved', and John Holand 'most dear'. She left the rest of her goods and rents for her executors to pay off her debts, to reward her servants, according to the merits of their service, and to garner prayers for her soul: all conventional provisions.

Joan's executors were:

> Robert Braybrooke, bishop of London
> William Wykeham, bishop of Winchester
> John Lord Cobham
> William Beauchamp
> William Neville
> Simon Burley
> Lewis Clifford
> Richard Adderbury
> John Clanvowe
> Richard Stury
> John Worthe, 'steward of my lands'
> Philip la Vache   knights
> William Fulburne
> John de Yernemouth
> William de Harpele
> Henry Norton

The bishops were described as 'my most dear friends'. Braybrooke, as we have seen, was a long trusted kinsman. The aged Wykeham had been eminent in Edward III's government. As a result of the support which he had given to the Commons' campaign against the 'sleaze' of royal ministers in the Good Parliament of 1376, as we have seen, he had been imprisoned and prosecuted at Gaunt's instigation. The lords and knights appointed by Joan were described as being beloved by her. Lord Cobham was mature and well respected; his wife, like Joan, was a descendant of Edward I. Joan may have cultivated Cobham because he was an extensive landowner in Kent; she may have admired his construction of a fine castle at Cooling – in defence of the country, as the inscription on its outer gatehouse records. He had received a royal licence to crenellate in 1379; the castle was complete in 1385.[49] Lollard knights, Wycliffe's disciples, were conspicuous among the knights of the royal chamber who were her executors – Neville, Clifford, Clanvowe, Stury. Adderbury was another knight of the royal chamber. He had previously been retained by the Black Prince, and had served him in Aquitaine: he had been one of Prince Richard's masters, concerned with his education. He was a landowner in Oxfordshire and Berkshire, who strengthened the defences of his castle at Donnington, near Newbury, by the addition of an imposing gatehouse – presumably, like Cobham, in case of a French invasion.[50]

Two witnesses to Joan's will reflect her local connections. One of them was the prior of Wallingford. The Benedictine priory of the Holy Trinity was near the castle.[51] It may have been from the prior or another of the monks there that their *confrère* Thomas Walsingham at St Albans Abbey heard an account of the Princess's last days and the treatment of her remains. The body was wrapped in waxed linen and encased in lead, to remain at Wallingford until the king returned from Scotland, when it could be honourably interred in her chosen burial place.[52] Maybe the body was given a temporary appropriate resting-place in Wallingford Priory – or in the collegiate chapel of St Nicholas in the outer ward of the castle, a chapel on which the Black Prince had lavished attention. The other local witness to the will, John James, held properties in Wallingford and its honour, and in Oxfordshire as well as Berkshire. He sat for the borough and for both shires in parliament. He had been receiver-general for Enguerrand de Coucy, husband of Edward III's daughter Isabella. In 1382 Joan had procured an exemption for him from sitting on commissions. James is likely to have been her principal man of business within the honour of Wallingford.[53]

A later chronicler has a vignette of Richard receiving news of his mother's death in Scotland, and returning home clad in mourning clothes with his army.[54] By a writ dated Durham, 21 August, Richard ordered the county escheators to take the lands she had held into their hands, to hold inquisitions post mortem.[55] Gaunt had returned from the expedition to his castle at Leicester when he received a Privy Seal letter requesting him to come to London for Joan's exequies – presumably held in St Paul's.[56] Her remains were interred at Stamford Franciscan friary in a fitting ceremony, though it is not clear when this occurred: what we know of Richard's itinerary gives no firm clues as to when he was in the vicinity. One chronicler wrote that her tomb was in a most sumptuous chapel adjacent to the newly built choir of the friary – presumably the chapel which she mentions in a proprietorial way in her will.[57] On 29 June 1386, royal orders were made for glaziers to be taken to repair the windows and other parts of the chapel founded at Stamford for the soul of Joan. This was to be done immediately, before her anniversary occurred.[58]

In September 1385 the Crown had ordered escheators to give Thomas Holand possession of the lands of the earldom of Kent. In the same month confiscation of his brother John's possessions was decreed.[59] When Sir John was ordered to appear in the Court of King's Bench, which convened in Westminster Hall, on a charge of homicide, he failed to turn up.[60] To avoid the reach of the common law, the monk-chronicler of Westminster had heard, he had taken refuge in Lancashire. There he would not have been under the jurisdiction of the king's justices, but of those appointed in the County Palatine by John of Gaunt as duke of Lancaster. The duke had good reason either then or several months later to protect him, and work for his pardon, for before Gaunt left for Spain in July 1386 it was clear that his daughter Elizabeth was pregnant. Her marriage to John was hastily arranged. Gaunt was well placed to help with his reconciliation with the earl of Stafford and the latter's brother-in-law, the earl of Warwick, and their kin.[61]

On 2 February 1386 the court was at Windsor: on that day, in a solemnly choreographed public ceremony, the king pardoned his half-brother. The Westminster Chronicler was moved by the occasion:

Sir John Holand, attired in mourning and supported on the arms of the archbishop of Canterbury [William Courtenay] and the bishop of London [Robert Braybrooke] entered the king's presence. Three times, before reaching him, he flung himself to the ground on his knees and stretched his hands upwards and with tears and wails humbly begged the king for mercy, entreating him to overlook his rash and thoughtless offence against the king himself and his prohibition, by committing so grave a crime. Some of the bystanders were in tears as they watched. At the third obeisance the two bishops knelt by his side before the king.[62]

At the supplication of the lords present, especially the earls of Stafford and Warwick, the king forgave his brother. A pardon was issued six days later, and in the following months orders were made for John to receive his chattels and lands back. Gaunt made him constable of the army he took to Spain.[63] Clearly, he was considered to have inherited some of his father's military talent – as well as the reckless pursuit of love. The ceremony of his forgiveness had certain poignancies. It was held on the Purification of the Blessed Virgin Mary: mercy was shown, appropriately, on her feast, which had not been shown at Princess Joan's behest. One would have thought that at the ceremony her demise would have been in the thoughts of her sons, and of her old friend, Bishop Braybrooke. Joan would have been delighted that Richard and Gaunt were now on good terms. We do not know what role Gaunt played behind the scenes in aid of John, but it may have been one which the king– normally friendly with his brother – appreciated.

As we have seen, in 1383 Joan's executors had received the privilege of holding Joan's dower lands for a year after her death, but with the proviso that they were not to remunerate any of her former servants. Presumably in expectation of continued service from the same recipients to himself, Richard confirmed a few of the grants which his mother had made from her dower lands. For instance, the grant which she had recently made to the esquire William Clifford was confirmed in November 1385. Moreover, the executors were concerned that they should make fitting rewards to her former servants, each according to merits, as she had charged them to do. In return, the executors agreed to pay 100 marks from Joan's chattels to the king. Among the beneficiaries to this agreement were two of her former female servants. In 1386, Denise Sutton claimed that she had served Joan for fifteen years without reward. Her claim was accepted, for she was granted a life annuity of up to £10 from Joan's former dower in Cornwall, with the assent of the royal council. William FitzWalter's widow Alice received a life annuity of £10. These generous settlements on Joan's former ladies were tangible tokens of Richard's reverent and affectionate memories of his remarkable mother.[64]

Joan's eldest son, Thomas Holand, died well respected in 1397, before the possibility that he could be tarred with some of the excesses of Richard's period of tyranny in the last years of the reign. On the other hand, John Holand fully revealed his lawless and extortionate character in exploiting the tyranny for his own aggrandisement. He was lynched by peasants in 1400, after the failure of a plot to restore Richard to the throne. Joan's daughter Maud of St Pol had a daughter, appropriately christened Jeanne. Like her mother, and her mother's mother, she was accounted outstandingly beautiful: they were a family tree of fair maids.

·: IO :·

Venus Ascending?

WHAT MEMORIES WERE PRESERVED about Joan? Just a few vivid cameos and impressions remain recorded. If Richard II had not been deposed, and had left an heir of his body, her memory would have doubtless been honoured as a matriarch of royal lines. However, the Yorkist dynasty (keen to honour Richard's memory) commemorated Yorkist ties with Joan. Among the banners which accompanied Edward IV's coffin in 1483 was one depicting a white hind, called 'of the Fair Maid of Kent'. Her granddaughter Joan Holand, daughter of Thomas, earl of Kent, and second wife of Edward's forbear, Edmund of Langley, the first duke of York, also had the hind as her badge.[1]

It was crucial for Joan's lack of lasting fame that her tomb was destroyed at the Reformation – in contrast, for instance, to the first two dukes of York buried in the church of the dissolved college of Fotheringhay (Northamptonshire), which remained the parish church. Their monuments survived partly because they were ancestors of Henry VIII. Had Joan's doubtless conspicuous monument and chantry remained at Stamford, they are likely to have renewed interest in her from Tudor times onwards in an era of proliferating antiquarian studies. Had she been buried next to the Black Prince in Canterbury Cathedral interest in her would never have faded. Indeed if the prince had not predeceased his father by barely a year she would have been queen, but these conjectures, though tempting, add nothing to Joan's story and should be resisted.

We lack evidence that Joan's Holand descendants associated themselves conspicuously with her memory, except for her eldest son Thomas, earl of Kent and his family. Like his daughter, he had a hind badge, depicted on the seal which he used in 1387 and 1396.[2] None of the Holands was buried in her chapel in the Franciscan friary at

Stamford. Her son Thomas willed to be buried in Bourne Abbey, as did his grandson Edmund, earl of Kent. Perhaps continuing tittle-tattle about the marriage of Joan and Thomas induced a wish among their descendants to be distanced from them in death. For, as we have seen, the scandal the couple had caused was long remembered, as were the negative circumstances of her marriage to the Prince. The adult Richard II was well aware of how the proof of his legitimacy and that of his siblings rested on a series of papal judgements and dispensations. Before he went on campaign to Ireland in 1394, he entrusted Thomas Arundel, archbishop of York, with the task of putting a chest containing crucial documents into the safe-keeping of the abbot and convent of Westminster. Apart from his will, the contents comprised the bulls and instruments confirming the validity of Joan's marriages to Holand and the Prince. Among the six high-ranking royal officials who witnessed the hand-over of the chest in the chapter house of Westminster Abbey was Joan's old servant Sir Philip la Vache. Perhaps he had personal knowledge derived from Joan about what documents should be there.[3]

The persistence of denigratory anecdotes stemming from Joan's marital dramas is evident from the way in which they had surfaced and were broadcast during the rebellion of 1399, and were used to support Richard's deposition in favour of his cousin Henry of Bolingbroke. Richard had exiled him, but he invaded England after the death of his father, John of Gaunt, ostensibly to claim his Lancastrian inheritance. Adam Usk, a Welsh cleric well positioned in London to observe the process of Richard's deposition, recorded in his chronicle gossip current after Henry had captured Richard in Wales: 'concerning whose (the king's) birth much evil report was noised abroad, as one not sprung from a father of royal race, but from a mother given to slippery ways of life, to say nothing of much that I have heard'.[4]

The spread of such speculations receives some corroboration from Froissart's account of Bolingbroke's alleged conversation with the captive Richard in the Tower of London, already alluded to:

> Now the rumour is, throughout England and beyond, that you are not the son of the Prince of Wales, but of some clerk or canon. I have heard from certain knights who were in the

household of my uncle the Prince that when the Prince felt that his marriage was a failure because your mother was a first cousin of King Edward and he was beginning to conceive a great dislike for her because she bore him no children ... she, who had won him in marriage by guile and cunning, was afraid that my uncle the Prince would find some pretext for divorcing her. So she arranged to become pregnant and gave birth to you, and to another before you.[5]

Froissart was not in England in 1399, and his account of events there is in important respects vague, uncorroborated and questionable. However, a French writer who probably was there wrote that Londoners rejoiced at Bolingbroke's capture of 'this wicked bastard who has governed us so ill'.

It seems likely that Richard's enthusiastic use of the white hart as his principal badge, a variant on the one adopted by his mother, was intended to exalt her memory, and to proclaim his faith, in the teeth of calumnies, in her spotless conduct. It is, indeed, odd that he did not make at least equal use of his father's badge of ostrich feathers, which would have emphasised his intentions to emulate his martial deeds.

The diverse highlights in Joan's life clearly generated contrasting memories of her. Adam Usk had an earlier passage in his chronicle showing her as a praiseworthy figure, trying – in 1387, actually two years after her death – to wean Richard away from flatterers, and to deflect him from plotting against the councillors who (in Usk's garbled account) had risen in protest against his rule. She is shown here as a prophet whose advice the king only feigns to take. The episode is possibly transposed from an account of her mediation between Richard and Gaunt in 1385, of which it may have some unique echoes:

with heavy grief in her heart, and not sparing to toil even by night, [she] hastened from Wallingford to London, to allay the discord. And on her knees she prayed the king her son as he looked for her blessing, in no wise to bend to the wishes of flatterers, and especially of those who were now urging him on, or otherwise she would bring down her curse upon him. But the king with reverence raised her up and promised that he would willingly be guided by the twelve [guardians imposed upon him]. To whom his mother replied: 'At your coronation, my son, I rejoiced that it had fallen to my lot to be the mother of an anointed king; but now I grieve, for I foresee the fall which threatens you, the work of accursed flatterers.' Then the king passed with his mother to Westminster Hall, and there, seated on his throne, by her mediation, made his peace with the twelve guardians; yet he did it falsely and with deceit.[6]

In contrast to this edifying image of Joan, some other fifteenth-century writers referred to her cryptically, without praise, in a way which suggests that they expected their readers to know about her scandals. This was so, as we have seen, in the case of John Hardyng.[7] Similarly neutral in tone, but telling in matter, was his contemporary John Capgrave, Augustinian prior at King's Lynn. In his *Chronicle of England*, he noted that in 1361, 'Prince Edward wedded Joan, the countess of Kent, which was before departed from the earl of Salisbury, and wedded after to Sir Thomas Holand, knight.'[8] One wonders whether Capgrave was treading carefully here in order not to offend the Holand descendants.

What of the real Joan? We can detect glimmerings of her sometimes unconventional piety, her polished courtliness, her exceptional personal magnetism – and steely determination. A devotee of the cult of courtly love, she was impulsive and wayward in her youth, and still capable of shocking behaviour in her thirties. However, marriage to one frequently absent husband and to another who became an invalid is likely to have honed her managerial talents, and taught her the worldly wisdom for which she was valued later, when for several years she became a major political influence.

The social subjection of women, as daughters, wives and widows, was prevalent in princely and noble society, but a series of developments in religious aims and attitudes gave greater respect and scope for ladies and their potentialities, and provided them with some significant new legal rights and protections. These developments complicated gender relations. Joan's clandestine marriages exemplify a consequent trend to indulge in romantic unions – of which the Church, whose legislation facilitated them, thoroughly disapproved. Moreover, despite Joan's scandalous past, she exemplified a tendency to allow widows ruling roles as magnates.

What changes in sensibilities had taken place? The theologians of the twelfth and thirteenth centuries had insisted that marriage, besides being the only valid context for procreation, was also an indissoluble sacred bond symbolising Christ's marriage to the Church. This high ideal of marriage was reflected in ecclesiastical legislation, which in important respects came into conflict with feudal custom. It spelled out some new and equivalent rights for both sexes. The Church repudiated the widespread practice among the nobility of children being married at a young age, at their father's or guardian's dictation. Marriage or making a commitment to do so informally, the canonists laid down, was only valid if both parties freely gave mutual consent, and if the girl was aged at least twelve and the boy fourteen. In 1344, the pope annulled the marriage of Richard earl of Arundel (with whom Joan was to be well acquainted) and Isabel Despenser. He did so on the grounds of their petition that they had been espoused at the respective ages of seven and eight, not by mutual consent, but through fear of their relatives. On coming to the age of puberty, they said, they had renounced their vows, but were forced by blows to cohabit. A son was conceived. This whole scenario, however, is somewhat suspect, as they had two daughters together as well, and, at the time of their petition, Earl Richard was in the throes of a passionate affair with a mistress, Eleanor of Lancaster (sister of Joan's aunt by marriage, Blanche Wake), whom he married as soon as his annulment came through.[9]

In pursuit of the principle that marriage required essentially free and mutual consent, the canonists, as we have seen exemplified twice in Joan's case, reluctantly kept the door open for marriages which had no ecclesiastical involvement, and which might be out of the control or even knowledge of overlord or family. Indeed, the clerical template for an ideal marriage ceremony remained one preceded by the calling of banns, and comprising the public making of vows and blessing by a priest, witnessed by kin-groups at the church door, followed by a Mass. The Church imposed penances for the omission of banns or of the blessing, but continued to recognise as lawful the more casual form of marriage. In these cases, either the groom made the legally binding oath, with the words, 'I promise to take you to wife here and now,' or promised to do so in the future, together with the bride's reciprocal oath. In the first case, the oaths in themselves instantly constituted marriage. Such marriages or promises to marry could take place anywhere. Instances have been cited of nuptials performed in bed, under an ash tree, in a garden, by an oak tree, in a tavern, in a small store room, in a field, on the king's highway.

Canonists extended principles of mutual consent and obligation with some caution in laying down rules for husbands' social conduct within marriage. In accordance with St Paul's injunction, 'Husbands, love your wives,' canonists insisted that they should treat their spouses with what they termed 'marital affection'. Ecclesiastical courts were prepared to receive wives' complaints on that score and provide remedies. For instance, in 1408 Sir William Rither swore before many witnesses to obey a series of articles that the archbishop of York had laid down as to how he was to treat his wife Sibelle. First: 'that he shall not do or get done to her no bodily harm nor maim nor beat nor imprison but keep her in full freedom as a man of his degree has to do to his wife without doing or saying anything that may be reproof or villainy to her person. Also that he shall void Marion Grydon out of his company and out of his and Sibelle's company.'[10]

Moreover the Church was prepared to investigate complaints by brides of their husbands' impotence, and, if it was proved, decree separations. It might also decree separation if a complainant proved a spouse's adultery, cruelty or unorthodox religious beliefs.

However inadequate the Church's recognitions of mutual rights in marriage were, they set standards and are likely to have raised female expectation. Their likely fulfilment is reflected in terms of endearment in wills, and in burial arrangements. In 1298, Guy de Beauchamp, earl of Warwick ordered that his heart was to lie 'wherever my dear consort will be buried'. In 1369 his daughter, Dame Maud de Say, willed to be buried 'near Edmund my loving husband'.[11] It became fashionable in the fourteenth century to depict couples together in tomb sculpture, united in death, facing the Last Judgement, as notionally they had been united in life. Sometimes this image of closeness was reinforced by depicting couples clasping their right hands, in the gesture they had made when reciting the marriage oaths. This is exemplified by the alabaster effigies of a knight and his lady on a tomb in Chichester Cathedral, which have been identified as those of Richard earl of Arundel and Eleanor of Lancaster. The earl had had the tombs made several years after her death in 1372; the couple were originally buried in Lewes Priory (Sussex).

So tomb sculpture, besides projecting lineage and status with increasing elaboration, came to emphasize the marital virtues of interdependence, fidelity, affection – and, also, projected sexual attractiveness. The effigies of wives often display elaborate coiffures, jewelled necklaces, tightly fitting gowns which sometimes emphasized the figure, and sleeves adorned with sets of buttons such as Joan acquired after her marriage to the Prince. This raiment reflected big changes in court fashions in the 1330s and 1340s. Hitherto, ladies had worn robes calculated to conceal what had been regarded as a principal source of human weakness – the female body. Indeed, denunciations of women's fashions became a staple of sermons. In like vein, Margery Kempe wrote penitently about how, as a young wife, she had worn a hat with gold braiding in order to attract men's attention when she went to church.[12]

Yet, despite the well-rehearsed temptations of adorning and revealing female flesh, the trend to do so may have been encouraged by some theologians keen to further marital affection and procreation. No less an authority than St Thomas Aquinas urged wives to adorn their bodies in order to encourage their husbands to discharge the 'marital debt'. Clerics may have been concerned that the husbands would be beguiled by unlawful counter-attractions. There was the ubiquity of prostitution, engaged in not only by professionals such as the Flemish girls who in 1381 staffed a brothel in Southwark, but as an occasional service offered by many poor women. Besides, military culture encouraged close personal ties between pairs of knights and esquires, which in some cases may have led to homosexual bonding. John Hastings, earl of Pembroke, as we have seen, served as one of the Prince's commanders in the defence of Aquitaine. Sir William Beauchamp, who was to have connections with Joan in her widowhood, served there too. As these young knights lay in bed together in France (a common habit among men), Pembroke promised that, if he did not have a son, he would leave Beauchamp his possessions. In the will which Beauchamp made over thirty years after Pembroke's death, he willed to be buried right under the earl's tomb.[13]

Besides the refinement by theologians of the proprieties of

marriage, there were more general religious trends challenging some of those attitudes and habits in gender relations which denigrated the nature, and depressed the status and dignity of women. New perceptions of womankind exalted and encouraged female capabilities. Doctrinal shifts had the likely effect of increasing among husbands a sense that wives might offer them a spiritual lifeline, so further encouraging mutual affection. In the thirteenth century, the doctrine of Purgatory was elaborated, and the torments to be anticipated there were graphically realised in sermons, literature and art. The belief was reinforced that prayers for souls in Purgatory could alleviate and curtail their sufferings. This led to the proliferation of chantry foundations, which had perpetual endowments to provide for frequent commemorative Masses and prayers for particular souls, to continue till Domesday. In England, the movement for such foundations peaked in the first decades of the fourteenth century. Considering that, among the nobility and gentry, wives were often younger than their husbands, and that the life expectancy of men was shorter, there was a presumption that a grieving widow might be available, willing and especially reliable in assisting and forwarding the implementation of provisions which husbands had made for their souls. Thomas Holand, son of the free-spirited bride Joan, and Alice, daughter of the also maritally unconventional earl of Arundel, were married off young in more conventional circumstance, at their parents' behest. In the will which Thomas made in 1397, thirty-three years later, he appointed Alice and their son to make arrangements for his burial. He prayed his wife to fulfil his will, 'for all the love and trust that has been between us'.[14]

More appreciative views of womankind were underpinned by other religious changes which had gathered pace from the twelfth century onwards. These had produced new perceptions about the nature of women, which had profound effects on gender relations. A crucial change was the exaltation of the Blessed Virgin Mary as the Queen of Heaven, and the proliferation of cults devoted to her virtues, sufferings and beneficence. They provided images of female perfection which all women could strive to imitate – particularly queens, and others (such as Joan, the king's mother) to whom men delegated aspects of their authority. However, a key component of Marian virtue was one which cut both ways: her obedience to God. That could be used to inculcate obedience to men, to whom God had entrusted authority. But not necessarily so. The cult of the Virgin, as Margery Kempe's spiritual dialogues show, could reinforce a conviction that Christ's personal injunctions to an individual must be obeyed, in preference to those of men in authority, even when they were priests.

The Virgin Mary was unequivocally unique, and as such could only be palely imitated. Nevertheless, it came to be accepted that women, allegedly enfeebled in their nature by their mixture of humours, could make leaps in spirituality necessarily greater than those confronting men. Validation was provided for such female muscularity by the rising cults in the west of early virgin martyrs, like St Catherine of Alexandria, exemplars who had typically refuted pagan philosophers, or defied their fathers and the governing authorities, and gave witness by enduring the fearsome and mortal torments visited on them.

Moreover, the new perceptions of the nature of Christ, as propagated by the Cistercian Order in the twelfth century, had provided a celestial path open to both sexes. Emphasis on the humanity of Christ and on contemplations of His Passion produced spiritual highs in women equally as in men. These were seen as transforming the material passions in their hearts, most sublimely in enabling sacred beings to lodge in souls and to communicate directly with individuals. Female mystics had their visions expounded. Priests compiled manuals explaining the exercises needed to progress in spirituality, copies of which were used by layfolk of both sexes as well as by religious. The burgess's wife Margery Kempe provides a notable example. Whereas in the early Middle Ages layfolk who wished to lead specially devout lives were expected to become monks and nuns, turning their backs on the temptations of the secular world, the Church came to accept that men and women in their contrasting natures had the capability of living a devout life outside the cloister. Couples could, indeed, together take vows of chastity before a bishop. Mutual consent was necessary. Margery Kempe tells how she ardently desired to become a bride of Christ, but for long was unable to get her husband John's agreement, before he finally capitulated, and went with her before a bishop to make the commitment.[15]

More significant in social and political consequences than mutual chastity was the Church's willingness to receive vows of chastity from recently widowed ladies, which stopped the pressure from kinsmen and overlord on them to remarry at their behest. We have seen how Joan allegedly resisted the Prince's pressure to marry one of his knights by threatening to take the vow, and how her sister-in-law Elizabeth countess of Kent resisted similar pressure that she was likely to have received from the king by taking the vow. Such a course might put great landed power into a woman's sole and perpetual control. One example, doubtless familiar to Joan, was that of Joan, daughter of Richard earl of Arundel and Eleanor of Lancaster, whose husband, Humphrey de Bohun, earl of Hereford, died in 1373, when she was young. She took a vow of chastity and, until her death in 1419, ruled vast estates in England and Wales. She appears to have resided mainly in Essex. Though ineligible to hold royal commissions and offices, she exercised patronage over important members of the shire elite. In her later years Henry IV was to rely on her political influence there.[16]

This brief survey of developments in gender relations, which gathered pace in the century or so before Joan's birth, illustrates how in some respects perceptions of women's nature and capacities, and recognition of their dignity and rights, had changed for the better – though in important respects traditional denigratory views and restrictive laws remained in place. Views of gender characteristics and of right relations between the sexes were in Joan's time now notably diverse and in some respects conflicted. These themes and divergencies are above all reflected in Chaucer's varied depictions of women and of gender relations. Repeatedly, he depicts women's reactions to the dominance which men strive to exercise – the heroic sufferings endured by some, the deceit and defiance characterised by others. To some extent, Chaucer may have reflected dilemmas and debates in circles which Joan knew, since his friend Sir Lewis Clifford was one of her closest confidants. In *The Franklin's Tale*, set in a mythical past, Chaucer was to provide a seemingly unconventional blueprint for a happy and successful marriage between a knight and a lady, which ostensibly met the ecclesiastical and secular requirements for male dominance, but covertly subverted them:

The lordship husbands have upon their wives
And to enhance the bliss of both their lives
He freely gave his promise as a knight
That he would never darken her delight
By exercise of his authority,
But he would obey in all with simple trust
As any lover of a lady must;
Save that his sovereignty in name upon her
He should preserve, lest it should shame his honour.

The Franklin commented that their agreement worked well for them. He thought the company would readily agree that love could not be constrained by mastery: men and women desired their liberty within marriage. In fact his tale exemplified the ways in which a loving couple adhered to their ideals, preserving their honour and mutual trust in face of dire threats to their marriage. However, what may have stirred up debate among the poem's courtly audiences was the notion that the husband surrendered the exercise of his legal sovereignty entirely to his wife. This was in accordance with the conventions of courtly romance, in which the ideal male lover surrendered himself entirely, emotions as well as body, in rapture to his mistress. Indeed, the Church condemned such love as idolatry. Yet Chaucer clearly indicates that this was the sort of love shared by the knight and his wife, not just a more restrained and formal marital affection.

The greater self-worth which the Church's revisionary attitudes had induced in women by the early fourteenth century inspired them with greater expectations of marrying for love, or finding love in marriage, or asserting freedom in celibacy after marriage ended. Joan, in her clandestine marriages, defied social norms in the search for love. Her wayward sister-in-law Elizabeth of Kent perhaps sought to emulate the freedoms of choice which Joan so patently valued, at first seeking independence as a widow, and later forbidden love. Joan's daughter Maud defiantly married for love too. A few years later, the Black Prince and Joan, in Chandos Herald's poem, were made to exemplify a marriage suffused by courtly love – as Chaucer had done for the marriage of John of Gaunt to Joan's kinswoman Blanche of Lancaster (d. 1368), in *The Boke of the Duchesse*.

Can we conclude then, particularly in the light of Joan's well-known example, that Venus was in the ascendant in the making and conduct of aristocratic marriages? There continued to be notable examples of marriage for love, such as the unconventional, ill-matched marriages of Henry V's widow, Katherine of Valois, to Owen Tudor, and Edward IV's secret marriage in 1464 to Elizabeth Wydeville. The popularity of Chaucer's works provided powerful lessons of how loveless marriages deteriorated. Yet in the fifteenth century there were no further changes in doctrine or religious outlooks which favoured the roles of women. Arranged marriages continued to be the norm. In fact, they remained vital for the well-being of aristocratic fortunes. In an era of epidemics, they were a particularly vital means of sustaining and increasing landed wealth, as rent rolls and other estate profits often tended to decline.

However, from around the fifteenth century, for the first time, considerable private correspondence of knightly and squirearchical families survives. These letters throw light on marriage negotiation and the relations of married couples. Social and affective values were highly prized, as well as monetary and political ones. Courtship was regarded as a crucial means of determining compatibility and, hence, the likelihood of affection and love developing. Correspondence between married couples, though typically businesslike, reveals indications of these qualities – though not in the transfer of sovereignty which the Franklin's knight made over to his wife.

It is no surprise that Joan liked to live in high style and to dress luxuriously. Nevertheless, like many of her class she also reverenced holy poverty. This was seen in her patronage of the Franciscans – towards whose Order she may have become well disposed, too, because of their charity to her disgraced father, and because her aunt Blanche Wake was enthusiastic about one of their houses. In later years, she may have been drawn to support and protect John Wycliffe in part because of his vision of a reformed clerical estate, characterised by penury and austerity. In view of the inveterate support Wycliffe's teachings were to receive from some of her knights, it is likely that 'conventicles' were held in her household for the expounding of the New Testament and of Wycliffe's writings. As for her son, the king, he took a more ambivalent approach to the Lollards. He neither uttered any fierce condemnation of them nor did he openly support them. He was, it seemed, prepared to tolerate the Lollard ambience in his mother's household but it must be remembered that his legitimate claim to the throne depended utterly on those papal documents he later had locked away in Westminster Abbey chapter house. It was certainly not in his interests as king to provoke a falling out with the papacy.

We have almost no indications of Joan's intellectual and literary interests, apart from her patronage of the Franciscan astrologer John Somer. No books which she possessed have been identified; nor have any poems written in her honour or at her request. Yet she was the lady who, on a favourable interpretation, had most conspicuously among contemporaries married for love. Moreover, when she was ageing, Chandos Herald did not think it incongruous to portray her as her younger self in verse as the exemplar of *amour courtois*. The handmaiden of courtly love was poetry. Sir Lewis Clifford, follower of Wycliffe, and perhaps Joan's favourite knight in her later years, was given a copy of the ballades of the French poet Eustache Deschamps to be conveyed to Geoffrey Chaucer. Elsewhere, Deschamps referred to Clifford as 'amoureux' – that is, an expert in the fine points of courtly love.[17] It was to be to Clifford's son-in-law, Sir Philip la Vache, that Chaucer addressed a ballad. In it, he urged the knight to be true to himself, but to shake off the melancholy induced by the trials of life at court.[18] Another court knight accused of Lollardy, who had served Joan, was Sir John Clanvowe. He was the author of both a religious treatise castigating sin, and a poem debating love, sometimes known as 'The Cuckoo and the Nightingale'. Joan may not have been fond of poetry, but she lived in a milieu where versifying was high fashion.[19]

A rare literary insight into Joan's self-imaging is the emblematic badge of the white hart, seated, with a crown-styled chain round its neck, which was famously adopted by Richard. He may have derived it from his mother, who, as we have seen, by 1372 possessed a golden goblet, on whose cover was depicted a white deer, lying down, encircled by a crown. Richard inherited a set of bed covers from his father on which were juxtaposed embroideries of the arms of Kent and Wake with a white hart. On a bed of that provenance, the blazons were appropriate to Joan. But why might she have chosen the hart to represent her?[20] In medieval imagery, a deer was in various ways projected as a Christian symbol, but a seated and royally collared image of one referred to the legend of Caesar's deer. According to this, Caesar put a collar on a deer which survived to a miraculous age. Caesar's deer came to be interpreted as a symbol of chastity, and of rejection of carnal pleasures. Perhaps Joan adopted this when she became what she wished to project as the untouchable and pure wife of the Prince. He, indeed, had proclaimed himself a modern Caesar, for he had adopted as his badge ostrich feathers displayed by the king of the Romans, John of Bohemia, who had been killed by the English at the battle of Crécy. If Richard did indeed adopt his mother's badge, in doing so he was implicitly refuting the calumnies which continued to be associated with her name, and was graphically proclaiming his legitimacy, so preciously enshrined in the documents in his strong box.[21]

We do not know enough about Joan to understand what led her to make the two most momentous – and outrageous – decisions in her life: to engage in clandestine marriages to men who were, for opposite reasons of status, unsuitable. Indeed, one must not exaggerate her singularity in determining that she would flout convention and precept by marrying whom she wanted, however unwelcome and inappropriate her choice appeared to her feudal superior or kinsfolk. Her sister-in-law Elizabeth of Juliers was another case in point: so were to be her own daughter Maud and her brother-in-law Gaunt's daughter Elizabeth (seduced by Joan's son John). Faced with the determination – or, as contemporary discourse had it, weakness – of some women, kings and noble families had on occasion to tear up their dynastic plans, and sometimes accept affronts to their will and derogations to their status. The Holands even found it necessary to bow the knee to the earl of Surrey, who blithely maintained Isabella Holand, young and unmarried, as his mistress.

It is tempting – but perhaps dangerous – to see Joan's first clandestine marriage as in some ways reflecting more general dislocations attendant on Edward II's uncertain rule, and consequent on his deposition. As a young girl, Joan surely had bitter experience of the humiliations stemming from her father's treason and ignominious fate. That may have given her empathy with the young Thomas Holand, as the victim of his father's failures and equally pitiful death. Yet this young man surely impressed her, like others, by his determination, self-confidence, prowess and high personal repute. Her second clandestine marriage lacked the excuse of teenage angst and romanticism. It wrecked the dynastic plans which Edward III had for the Prince, and was, on her part, grossly disobedient and ungrateful, for Edward had given priority to restoring her family's fortunes. He had tolerated her complicity with Thomas Holand in undermining the important dynastic alliance he had made for her, shaming one of his favoured families, the Montagues. He had eventually raised Thomas to the earldom of Kent. Could it be that she calculated that Edward would forgive her again, because of his strong affection for the Prince, to which Froissart (who had known the parties well) was to allude?

Perhaps in some respects, in Joan's second clandestine marriage, she replicated her teenage transgression, because the death of Thomas Holand left her not just bereft, but possibly in a state of panic about her future, potentially unappealing, prospects. She was now countess of Kent in her own right, a considerable marital prize. She could anticipate that once more, as when she was a girl, she would be pressed to make a marriage which suited others. As a giddy girl she had heedlessly chosen a husband of lower status, but now she was a countess verging on middle age, a lady of high status, whose husband had been a distinguished warrior and governor. The higher nobility had a historic concern that kings would use feudal overlordship to marry their daughters and widows to men in royal service who were 'raised from the dust'. These fears had been enshrined in the provisions of Magna Carta. In periods when kings were waging intense warfare abroad, such as during most of the first two decades or so of Edward III's reign, opportunities abounded for gentlefolk of lesser degree to gain status and prestige. The values of chivalry, sedulously promoted by Edward and the Prince, tended to blur the rigidities of status. In these circumstances, the higher nobility were more acquiescent than usual in the royal promotion of gentlefolk of inferior origins. Undoubtedly there were some tensions: John Hastings, earl of Pembroke, was unwilling to defer to Sir John Chandos on campaign in Aquitaine in 1371. On an earlier occasion on campaign, the Prince had abusively rejected the earl of Oxford's objection when he had passed his cup first to Chandos.

Furthermore the peace of 1360 left some English bachelors on service abroad eager to raise and consolidate their status at home, investing in property and brides. It appears that the Prince was eager to secure personally the hand of his kinswoman Joan for one of his knights of inferior status. Her transformation of the princely surrogate from emissary to suitor – a plot worthy of a nineteenth-century operetta – opened unrivalled prospects for her and for her children. The role of Princess was to fit her perfectly. Being pitchforked into presiding over a patchwork of alien and sometimes hostile principalities in Aquitaine was quite a challenge. Nevertheless the dearth of recorded criticism suggests that she acquitted herself well: Froissart had no fault to find.

Subsequently, she proved a highly respected force for stability in a shrunken England, whose 'empire' abroad lay in tatters, whose sound and vigorous rule declined due to the debility of both King Edward and the Prince, and whose stability was to be further threatened by the minority of her son, Richard, and the renewal of war with France, Castile and, eventually, Scotland. The role of king's mother had last been ignominiously filled by Isabella of France. Joan played it to perfection. She was a worthy substitute for a queen in making numerous and moderate requests for Richard's mercy, and for favours for a variety of petitioners. Yet she did not attempt to exploit her situation by amassing riches for herself, or for the king's knights and others in her service. Her prestige and her moderation, which had qualified her to mediate in a crisis in Edward's last months, enabled her to intervene when her son's fledgling rule was wavering. His queen, Anne of Bohemia, a meek foreigner, was not well suited to do so – but Joan could, still commanding the respect and affection of her son.

We have glimpsed tantalising facets of Joan's character and behaviour – of her allure, her ruthlessness, her princeliness, a distinct religiosity and remarkably good political sense. We can perhaps also attribute kindliness to her, reflected in favours she gave or procured, especially for some of her household servants. But, above all, Joan is to be remembered as a striking example of a medieval woman who was determined to be mistress of her fate, and to make her mark in challenging and changing times.

Notes

1 *Loosened Bonds*

1 For concepts of womankind I have relied principally throughout the text on H. Leyser, *Medieval Women: A Social History of Women in England, 450–1500* (London, 1996) and K. M. Phillips, *Medieval Maidens: Young Women and Gender in England, 1270–1540* (Manchester, 2003).

2 *Tragic Beginnings*

1 Version of *The Brut* (BL, Harley MS 2279) printed in Baker, 221–5.

2 S. L. Waugh, 'Edmund, first earl of Kent (1301–1330)', *ODNB*, vol. xvii, 760–2.

3 *Chronica Monasterii de Melsa*, ed. E. A. Bond, 3 vols, RS 43 (London, 1866–68), vol. ii, 359; Baker, 224–5.

4 *Complete Peerage*, vol. vii, 143–7.

5 CCR 1300–26, 412; CPR 1321–24, 81.

6 N. Fryde, *The Tyranny and Fall of Edward II* (Cambridge, 1979), 130–1.

7 CPR 1321–24, 215, 248, 404; *Complete Peerage*, vol. vii, 145.

8 *The War of Saint-Sardos (1323–1325): Gascon Correspondence and Diplomatic Documents*, ed. P. Chaplais, Camden Third Series, 87, RHS (London, 1954); Fryde, *Tyranny and Fall*, 143–4; M. G. A. Vale, *The Angevin Legacy and the Hundred Years War, 1250–1340* (Oxford, 1990), 237–40.

9 *Complete Peerage*, vol. vii, 145; Vale, *Angevin Legacy*, 241.

10 *War of Saint-Sardos*, viii, 217–18, 236–7; *Complete Peerage*, vol. vii, 145.

11 CPL, vol. ii, 246; *Complete Peerage*, vol. xii, pt 2, 296–304; W. M. Ormrod, 'Wake, Thomas, second Lord Wake (1298–1349)', *ODNB*, vol. lvi, 719–21.

12 CIPM, vol. ix, no. 219; R. Nicholson, *Edward III and the Scots: The Formative Years of a Military Career* (Oxford, 1965), 65, 67, 68, 69, 77.

13 'Annales Paulini', in *Chronicles of the Reigns of Edward I and Edward II*, ed. W. Stubbs, 2 vols, RS 76 (London, 1882–83), vol. i, 314.

14 CPL, vol. ii, 308.

15 *CPL*, vol. ii, 349; *Complete Peerage*, vol. vii, 147; *CPR 1330–34*, 178; J. C.
   Parsons, 'Margaret [Margaret of France] (1279?–1318)', *ODNB*, vol. xxxvi,
   635–6.
16 Fryde, *Tyranny and Fall*, 198–9.
17 *Complete Peerage*, vol. i, 242; *ibid.*, vol. vii, 146; *ibid.*, vol. vii, 147–8.
18 Nicholson, *Edward III and the Scots*, 22–3.
19 *Ibid.*, 61–2; *Complete Peerage*, vol. xii, pt 2, 303.
20 *Adae Murimuth Continuatio Chronicarum*, ed. E. M. Thompson,
   RS 93 (London, 1889), 253–7. John, Lord Maltravers, keeper of Corfe
   Castle and close ally of Mortimer, was heavily implicated in the plot
   to convince Edmund that Edward II was alive. In 1330 his lands were
   confiscated and given to Edmund's widow and to William Montague.
   C. Shenton, 'Maltravers, John, first Lord Maltravers (c. 1290–1364)',
   ODNB, vol. xxxvi, 372–3.
21 Fryde, *Tyranny and Fall*, 143, 194; Baker, 43–4.
22 le Bel, vol. i, 101.
23 *Complete Peerage*, vol. v, 416–19; *ibid.*, vol. v, 393–5; A. B. Emden,
   A Biographical Register of the University of Oxford to 1500, 3 vols (Oxford,
   1957–59), vol. iii, 157.
24 *CIPM*, vol. ix, no. 673; *Complete Peerage*, vol. i, 242.
25 *CPR 1330–34*, 99; *RP*, vol. ii, 55.
26 *CPL*, vol. ii, 349; *Complete Peerage*, vol. vii, 147.
27 A grant was made by Edmund on 18 January 1331, *CPR 1330–34*, 41;
   CPR 1334–38, 180; *CPR 1338–40*, 133. (Formally Countess Margaret had
   been granted custody of John's marriage by Edward III.)
28 J. Vale, 'Philippa [Philippa of Hainault] (1310×15?–1369)', *ODNB*, vol. xliv,
   34–7. For evidence of Joan's position in the queen's household see TNA,
   E 36/205, fol. 11. I owe thanks to Mark Ormrod for this reference in his
   Edward III (London, 2011), 144 n. 127.

3 Bigamy

1 *CPL*, vol. iii, 252–3; *Complete Peerage*, vol. vi, 531–2; M. M. N.
   Stansfield, 'Holland, Thomas, earl of Kent (c. 1315–1360)', *ODNB*,
   vol. xxvii, 694–5.
2 K. P. Wentersdorf, 'The Clandestine Marriages of the Fair Maid of Kent',
   JMH, 5 (1979), 202–19.
3 *Complete Peerage*, vol. xii, pt 2, 935–6.

Notes to pp. 23–34

4 *Complete Peerage*, vol. vi, 528–31; J. R. Maddicott, 'Thomas of Lancaster and Sir Robert Holland: A Study in Noble Patronage', *EHR*, 86 (1971), 449–72; quotation from *The Brut* in R. M. Haines, *King Edward II* (Montreal, 2003), 138–9.

5 *Complete Peerage*, vol. vi, 530 n.; M. Elton, 'Uncovered: London's Grim Tribute to a Medieval Martyr', *BBC History Magazine* (April 2015), 11–12; *Knighton's Chronicle, 1337–1396*, ed. G. H. Martin (Oxford, 1995).

6 C. H. Hunter Blair, 'Armorials upon English Seals from the Twelfth to the Sixteenth Centuries', *Archaeologia*, 2nd series, 89 (1943), 9–12, 15.

7 *Complete Peerage*, vol. vii, 150–1.

8 *Ibid.*

9 Froissart, *Œuvres*, vol. iii, 197.

10 *CPL*, vol. iii, 252–3.

11 *Complete Peerage*, vol. xi, 385–9.

12 *Ibid.*; G. A. Holmes, *The Estates of the Higher Nobility in Fourteenth-Century England* (Cambridge, 1957), 26.

13 *Complete Peerage*, vol. xi, 387 n.

14 Froissart, *Œuvres*, vol. iv, 411; le Bel, vol. ii, 82–3; Wentersdorf, 'Clandestine Marriages', 210.

15 *CPL*, vol. iii, 252–3.

16 A. Ayton, *Knights and Warhorses: Military Service and the English Aristocracy under Edward III* (Woodbridge, 1994), 182–3; Froissart, *Œuvres*, vol. iv, 174–5.

17 *Complete Peerage*, vol. xii, pt 2, 935–6; *ibid.*, vol. vi, 531–2; *CPR 1334–38*, 163; *CPR 1338–40*, 439.

18 P. E. Russell, *The English Intervention in Spain and Portugal in the Time of Edward III and Richard II* (Oxford, 1955), 7–9.

19 *Complete Peerage*, vol. xi, 388; Baker, 79.

20 A. Ayton and P. Preston, *The Battle of Crécy, 1346* (Woodbridge, 2005), 248; *Crécy and Calais from the Original Records in the Public Record Office*, ed. G. Wrottesley (London, 1898), 81, 100, 150.

21 Froissart, trans. Brereton, 75; *Adae Murimuth Continuatio Chronicarum*, ed. Thompson, 202–4; A. Verduyn, 'Burghersh, Bartholomew, the Elder, second Lord Burghersh (d. 1355)', *ODNB*, vol. viii, 798–9.

22 le Bel, vol. ii, 82–3.

23 *CPR 1345–48*, 337; le Bel, vol. ii, 198 n., 199 n.

24 *Récits d'un bourgeois de Valenciennes*, ed. J. M. B. C. Kervyn de Lettenhove (Louvain, 1877), 219–20.

25 Froissart, *Œuvres*, vol. iv, 79.
26 *Eulogium*, vol. iii, 208.
27 Froissart, *Œuvres*, vol. iv, 431–2.
28 Froissart, *Œuvres*, vol. v, 31, 76.
29 le Bel, vol. ii, 161; *Crécy and Calais*, ed. Wrottesley, 176–7.
30 G. F. Beltz, *Memorials of the Order of the Garter* (London, 1841), 54.
31 *Complete Peerage*, vol. xii, pt i, 508–11; *Test. Ebor.*, pt i, 41–5; S. L. Waugh. 'Warenne, John de, seventh earl of Surrey (1286–1347)', *ODNB*, vol. lvii, 399–403.
32 *CPL*, vol. iii, 116.
33 Wentersdorf, 'Clandestine Marriages', 202–19.
34 *CPL*, vol. iii, 252–3; *CPR 1348–50*, 213; Wentersdorf, 'Clandestine Marriages', 219–20.
35 Wentersdorf, 'Clandestine Marriages', 220–2.
36 J. S. Bothwell, *Edward III and the English Peerage* (Woodbridge, 2004), 122–4; *Complete Peerage*, vol. xi, 88–90; *CPR 1348–50*, 309.
37 *Chronicle of John Hardyng* cited in Wentersdorf, 'Clandestine Marriages', 203–4.
38 *Knighton's Chronicle*, ed. Martin, 185.
39 *Complete Peerage*, vol. xi, 388–90; J. L. Leland, 'Montague, William, second earl of Salisbury (1328–1397)', *ODNB*, vol. xxxviii, 775–7.

4 Married Bliss

1 *Complete Peerage*, vol. vii, 148–50; M. M. N. Stansfield, 'Holland, John, first earl of Huntingdon and duke of Exeter (c. 1352–1400)', *ODNB*, vol. xxvii, 674–5; M. M. N. Stansfield, 'Holland, Thomas, fifth earl of Kent (1350–1397)', *ODNB*, vol. xxvii, 695–6.
2 *BPR*, vol. iv, 87.
3 *CPR 1350–54*, 312.
4 É. Perroy, *The Hundred Years War*, trans. W. B. Wells (London, 1951), 125.
5 *Complete Peerage*, vol. vii, 148; *CPR 1354–58*, 543, 562; Froissart, *Œuvres*, vol. iv, 377; *Syllabus (in English) of … Rymer's Foedera*, ed. T. D. Hardy, 3 vols (London, 1869–85), vol. i, 350.
6 *CPL*, vol. iii, 268.
7 *CIPM*, vol. x, no. 46; *CPR 1350–54*, 383; Verduyn, 'Burghersh, Bartholomew, the Elder', *ODNB*, vol. viii, 798–9.

8 J. Nichols, *A Collection of All the Wills known to be extant of the Kings and Queens of England* (London, 1780), 212.

9 *Complete Peerage*, vol. vii, 149; Nichols, *Collection of All the Wills*, 215–16.

10 Beltz, *Memorials of the Order of the Garter*, 90–1; *le Bel*, vol. i, 14 and n.

11 *BPR*, vol. iv, 76, 128; Froissart, *Œuvres*, vol. v, 424; F. Bériac-Lainé and C. Given-Wilson, *Les prisonniers de la bataille de Poitiers* (Paris, 2002), 37, 41.

12 le Bel, vol. ii, 304; Froissart, *Œuvres*, vol. vi, 152–4.

13 Froissart, *Œuvres*, vol. vi, 162–75, 189, 190.

14 *Complete Peerage*, vol. vii, 152.

15 London, Lambeth Palace Library, Register of Simon Islip, fol. 167a; Nichols, *Collection of All the Wills*, 215–16.

16 *CCR 1364–68*, 97, 469.

17 *Complete Peerage*, vol. vii, 149–50; *CCR 1364–68*, 97, 469.

18 *BPR*, vol. iv, 524.

19 K. Fowler, *Medieval Mercenaries*, vol. 1: *The Great Companies* (Oxford, 2001), 104–5, 175–6; Froissart, *Œuvres*, vol. vii, 46–65, 95.

20 Fowler, *Medieval Mercenaries*, vol. i, 173 and n., 179, 187, 192, 198, 199.

21 *CCR 1369–74*, 408. Eustache was referred to as alive on 1 Dec. 1372; *Complete Peerage*, vol. vii, 149–50; Froissart, *Œuvres*, vol. vii, 8, 102–4, 115–16.

22 *Test. Vet.*, vol. i, 179–80.

23 *BPR*, vol. iv, 220; *CPR 1350–54*, 175, 189, 213; *CCR 1349–54*, 530.

24 *CIPM*, vol. x, no. 46.

25 *CCR 1349–54*, 530.

26 *Ibid.*, 552–4.

27 *BPR*, vol. iv, 456; *John Leland's Itinerary: Travels in Tudor England*, ed. J. Chandler (Stroud, 1993), 534.

28 *CCR 1341–43*, 133.

29 *BPR*, vol. iv, 422, 444, 450, 483, 519, 555.

30 *BPR*, vol. iv, 430, 482; *JGR 1379–83*, vol. 1, 56.

31 *BPR*, vol. iv, 450, 472.

32 J. Aberth, 'Crime and Justice under Edward III: The Case of Thomas De Lisle', *EHR*, 107 (1992), 283–301.

33 J. D. Birkbeck, *A History of Bourne* (Bourne, 1970), 24–5; *Early Lincoln Wills*, ed. A. Gibbons (Lincoln, 1888), 56–7.

34 *BPR*, vol. iv, 454, 507; *Test. Vet.*, vol. i, 64–6.

35 TNA, E 403/461/15.

36 *JGR 1371–75*, vol. ii, nos. 940, 1241; see also TNA, DL 29/4069/262.

37 *CCR 1349–54*, 393.

38 *CCR 1354–60*, 514–15.

39 *BPR*, vol. iv, 424; M. H. Dodds (ed.), *A History of Northumberland*, vol. 14 (Newcastle-upon-Tyne, 1935), 520; *The Controversy between Sir Richard Scrope and Sir Robert Grosvenor in the Court of Chivalry, AD MCCCLXXXV–MCCCXC*, ed. N. H. Nicolas, 2 vols (London, 1832), vol. ii, 325–7; *Test. Ebor.*, pt i, 265–7.

40 *CPR 1354–58*, 27; J. S. Hartley and A. Rogers, *The Religious Foundations of Medieval Stamford* (Nottingham, 1974), 56–8. I owe thanks for this reference to Dr Nicholas Bennett.

41 *Report on the Manuscripts of the Late Reginald Rawdon Hastings*, 4 vols, Historical Manuscripts Commission (London, 1928–47), vol. i, 172; B. Jennings *Yorkshire Monasteries: Cloister, Land and People* (Otley, 1999), 37; G. Poulson, *The History and Antiquities of the Seigniory of Holderness*, 2 vols (Hull, 1840–41), vol. ii, 10, 12 and n., 21; *Test. Ebor.*, pt i, 100–1.

42 *CCR 1360–64*, 352; *CPR 1354–60*, 145; D. Webb, *Pilgrimage in Medieval England* (London, 2000), 250.

43 *CCR 1354–60*, 145, 208; *CPR 1350–54*, 148; A. Verduyn, 'Burghersh, Bartholomew, the younger, third Lord Burghersh (*d.* 1369), *ODNB*, vol. viii, 799–800.

44 *CPR 1350–54*, 231, 383.

45 *BPR*, vol. iv, 537; R. G. Davies, 'Braybrooke, Robert (1336/7–1404)', *ODNB*, vol. vii, 416–18.

46 *ODNB*, vol. viii, 799. Some of those whose coats of arms were displayed may have been his companions in war.

47 R. Barber, 'Chandos, Sir John (d. 1370)', *ODNB*, vol. xi, 9–11; *BPR*, vol. iv, 537.

48 Froissart, trans. Brereton, 115.

49 *CCR 1360–64*, 372; cf. *CCR 1369–74*, 132; *CCR 1354–60*, 569; *CPR 1354–58*, 15; A. Gross, 'Pembridge, Sir Richard (*c.* 1320–1375)', *ODNB*, vol. xliii, 511–12.

50 *BPR*, vol. iv, 460.

51 *CPR 1349–54*, 585, 588. The Arundel loan for 200 marks was repaid. The Neville loan for 400 marks was to be repaid in two instalments.

52 K. Fowler, *The King's Lieutenant: Henry of Grosmont, First Duke of Lancaster, 1310–1361* (London, 1969), 140.

53 J. Sumption, *The Hundred Years War*, 4 vols (London, 1990–2015), vol. ii, 272–3.
54 *Catalogue des Rolles Gascons, Normans et François*, ed. T. Carte (London, 1748), 56, 58.
55 J. H. Le Patourel, *The Medieval Administration of the Channel Islands, 1199–1399* (London, 1937), 128.
56 CCR 1354–60, 372–3.
57 CIPM, vol. x, no. 557.
58 CCR 1354–60, 635; Le Patourel, *Medieval Administration of the Channel Islands*, 128.
59 Beltz, *Memorials of the Order of the Garter*, 84–5.
60 *Complete Peerage*, vol. vi, 531–2; M. M. N. Stansfield, 'Holland, Thomas, earl of Kent (*c.* 1315–1360)', *ODNB*, vol. xxvii, 694–5.
61 Sumption, *Hundred Years War*, vol. ii, 421.
62 Fowler, *King's Lieutenant*, 168.
63 *Foedera*, vol. iii, 509–10; Fowler, *King's Lieutenant*, 293 n. 84; Fowler, *Medieval Mercenaries*, vol. i, 26, 39
64 *BPR*, vol. iv, 536; *Chronique des Quatre Premiers Valois (1327–1393)*, ed. S. Luce, SHF (Paris, 1862), 123.
65 *Complete Peerage*, vol. vi, 530.
66 Hartley and Rogers, *Religious Foundations of Medieval Stamford*, 63–5; Royal Commission on Historical Monuments, *An Inventory of the Historical Monuments in the Town of Stamford* (London, 1977), 33.

5 A Whirlwind Romance

1 *Pageant of the Birth, Life and Death of Richard Beauchamp, Earl of Warwick, K.G. 1389–1439*, ed. Viscount Dillon and W. H. St John Hope (London, 1914), 44.
2 CCR 1360–64, 175, 189; CCR 1360–64, 171, 181; CFR 1356–68, 134; CIPM, vol. x, no. 657.
3 *BPR*, vol. iv, 442, 452, 453, 461–2.
4 *Ibid.*, 442.
5 *Ibid.*, 456.
6 *Ibid.*, 442.
7 Fowler, *King's Lieutenant*, 217–18; Froissart, *Œuvres*, vi, 358; *Test. Vet.*, vol. i, 64–6.

8 CCR 1349–54, 53.

9 M. Burrows, *The Family of Brocas of Beaurepaire and Roche Court* (London, 1886), 90–4; *Chronique des Quatre Premiers Valois*, ed. Luce, 122–5; H. Summerson, 'Brocas, Sir Bernard (*c.* 1330–1395)', *ODNB*, vol. vii, 740–1.

10 CPR 1358–61, 234.

11 *Chronique des Quatre Premiers Valois*, ed. Luce, 123–5.

12 Froissart, *Œuvres*, vol. vi, 366–7.

13 Roger de Clarendon, accused of plotting against Henry IV, was executed in 1402. In his will the Black Prince left him a silk bed. The Prince may have had at least one other illegitimate son: see C. Given-Wilson and A. Curteis, *The Royal Bastards of Medieval England* (London, 1984).

14 BPR, vol. iii, 418, 419, 420; BPR, vol. iv, 371, 387, 388, 389, 390; *King's Works*, vol. ii, 906.

15 TNA, E 403/409, (15 Oct. 1361). See Ormrod, *Edward III*, 451, n. 23 for this reference.

16 CPP, 376; P. Zutshi, 'Petitions to the Pope in the Fourteenth Century', in *Medieval Petitions: Grace and Grievance*, ed. W. M. Ormrod, G. Dodd and A. Musson (York, 2009), 95; Wentersdorf, 'Clandestine Marriages', 217–25.

17 BPR, vol. iii, 421, 422, 423; BPR, vol. iv, 391, 392, 393, 394.

18 Webb, *Pilgrimage in Medieval England*, 28, 32, 51, 82, 124, 136.

19 Beltz, *Memorials of the Order of the Garter*, 18 n.; London, Lambeth Palace Library, Register of Simon Islip, fol. 180 b.

20 *Complete Peerage*, vol. iv, 144–9; *Complete Peerage*, vol. i, 340.

21 Beltz, *Memorials of the Order of the Garter*, 18; J. Vale, *Edward III and Chivalry: Chivalric Society and its Context, 1270–1350* (Woodbridge, 1982), 53, 133 n. 203.

22 Froissart, *Œuvres*, vi, 366–7; *Knighton's Chronicle*, ed. Martin, 184–5; 'A Wigmore Chronicle, 1355–1377', ed. J. Taylor, in J. Taylor, *English Historical Literature in the Fourteenth Century* (Oxford, 1987), 292.

23 BPR, vol. iii, 423; BPR, vol. iv, 395, 396, 397, 399, 400, 403.

24 G. J. Dawson, *The Black Prince's Palace at Kennington, Surrey*, British Archaeological Reports, vol. 26 (Oxford, 1976), 1–53; *King's Works*, vol. ii, 967–9.

25 R. Barber, 'Jean Froissart and Edward the Black Prince', in *Froissart: Historian*, ed. J. J. N. Palmer (Woodbridge, 1981), 29–30; BPR, vol. iii, 426–38; *Froissart*, trans. Brereton, 470; *King's Works*, vol. ii, 561–3.

26 *A Descriptive Catalogue of Ancient Deeds in the Public Record Office*, 6 vols (London, 1890–1915), vol. i, A1400.

27 *BPR*, vol. iv, 428, 434, 476–7, 478, 500.

28 *Ibid.*, 500.

29 A. S. Harvey, 'Cottingham Church and its Heraldry', *Yorkshire Archaeological Journal*, 40 (1960), 265–97. I owe thanks for this reference to Mark Christodolou.

30 T. D. Grimke-Drayton, 'The East Window of Gloucester Cathedral', *Transactions of the Bristol and Gloucestershire Archaeological Society*, 38 (1915), 78, 82, 90.

31 *BPR*, vol. iv, 475.

32 *BPR*, vol. iii, 441; *BPR*, vol. iv, 442.

33 *BPR*, vol. iv, 508; Webb, *Pilgrimage in Medieval England*, 38, 95.

34 *Foedera*, vol. iii, pt ii, 667–70; TNA, E 30/1105.

35 *BPR*, vol. iii, 452, 453, 454, 458; *BPR*, vol. iv, 465, 481, 482, 486, 490; A. D. Fizzard, *Plympton Priory: A House of Augustinian Canons in South-Western England in the Late Middle Ages* (Leiden, 2008).

36 *King's Works*, vol. ii, 804–5; C. A. Ralegh Radford, *Restormel Castle* (London, 1977).

37 *BPR*, vol. iii, 454, 455; Webb, *Pilgrimage in Medieval England*, 81.

38 *BPR*, vol. iv, 497.

6 Princess of Wales and of Aquitaine

1 For a list of *sénéchaussées* ceded, including those of Bordeaux and Les Landes (Gascony), and for variant lists, see R. Delachenal, *Histoire de Charles V*, 5 vols (Paris, 1909–31), vol. iv, 16 n. 2. The English claimed that some places were wrongfully retained in the French Crown's allegiance, e.g. La Roche-sur-Yon (see below).

2 *Ibid.*, vol. iv, 18; Fowler, *Medieval Mercenaries*, 39–43; D. Green, *The Black Prince* (Stroud, 2001), 84; P. Tucoo-Chala, *Gaston Fébus, prince des Pyrénées (1331–1391)* (Pau, 1993), 117.

3 Delachenal, *Histoire de Charles V*, vol. iv, 4; *Chronica Johannis de Reading et Anonymi Cantuariensis, 1346–1367*, ed. J. Tait (Manchester, 1914), 222.

4 For Bordeaux, Gascony and their English connections, see Vale, *Angevin Legacy*.

5 J. A. Brutails, *Guide illustré dans Bordeaux et les environs* (Bordeaux, n.d.), 36–7. For parishes and other religious institutions in the city, see B. Guillemain, 'L'essor religieux', in *Bordeaux sous les rois d'Angleterre*, ed. Y. Renouard (Bordeaux, 1965), 128, 131–2, 145, 145 n.

6 The stone is in the Musée d'Aquitaine in Bordeaux.

7 Bordeaux, Archives Départementales de la Gironde, series G. Chapitre métropolitain Saint-André, anniversaires, G 317; Russell, *The English Intervention*, 8–9.

8 Brutails, *Guide illustré dans Bordeaux*, 27–32; Guillemain, 'L'essor religieux', 127–42.

9 F. Bériac-Lainé, 'Les défunts de la cathédrale au XIVe siècle', in *La cathédrale Saint-André: reflet de neuf siècles d'histoire et de vie bordelaise*, ed. M. Agostino (Pessac, 2001), 93–106.

10 *Collection générale des documents français qui se trouvent en Angleterre*, ed. J. Delpit (Paris, 1847), 86–121.

11 *Life of the Black Prince by the Herald of Sir John Chandos*, ed. M. K. Pope and E. C. Lodge (Oxford, 1910), 148.

12 *Ibid.*

13 Delachenal, *Histoire de Charles V*, vol. iv, 21 and note; Froissart, *Œuvres*, vol. vi, 368. For further descriptions of the court in Aquitaine and the process of acculturation, see D. Green, *Edward the Black Prince: Power in Medieval Europe* (Harlow, 2007), particularly ch. 6.

14 P. Capra, 'L'apogée politique au temps du Prince Noir (1355–1372)', in *Bordeaux sous les rois d'Angleterre*, ed. Renouard, 385–7.

15 Froissart, *Œuvres*, vol. viii, 62.

16 Froissart, trans. Brereton, 469–70; Froissart, *Œuvres*, vol. vii, 106.

17 Froissart, trans. Brereton, 460.

18 *Collection générale*, ed. Delpit, 104–6. Other homages were taken in Angoulême in March and Apr. 1364, including that of the count of Armagnac, in 'la sale' on 2 Apr. – *ibid.*, 121.

19 Tucoo-Chala, *Gaston Fébus*, 120–1.

20 P. Dubourg-Noves (ed.), *Histoire d'Angoulême et ses alentours* (Toulouse, 1989), 73–85.

21 *Eulogium*, vol. iii, 236.

22 A. Gransden, 'A Fourteenth-Century Chronicle from the Grey Friars at Lynn', *EHR*, 72 (1957), 276; T. Walsingham, *Historia Anglicana*, ed. H. T. Riley, 2 vols, RS 28 (London, 1863–64), vol. i, 301.

23 *CPR 1364–67*, 180; *Anon. Chron. 1333–81*, 51; *Chronica Johannis de Reading et Anonymi Cantuariensis*, ed. Tait, 164, 222; 'Wigmore Chronicle', ed. Taylor, 293.

24 Froissart, *Œuvres*, vol. vi, 393.

25 *Ibid.*, 378.

26 Gransden, 'A Fourteenth-Century Chronicle', 276.

27 *CPR 1377–81*, 372, 606; Green, *The Black Prince*, 129–30.

28 *CPP*, 522; *Complete Peerage*, vol. iv, 144–7.

29 *BPR*, vol. iv, 35–6, 266, 588 (for Louches); *ibid.*, 142–3 (for Peverel); *CPP*, 521–2.

30 *BPR*, vol. ii, 202; *CPP*, 456; *CPR 1360–64*, 197; *CCR 1360–64*, 197; *CPR 1358–61*, 446.

31 *CPP*, 456.

32 *BPR*, vol. iv, 442–3 (for Foljambe); *CPP*, 521–2 (for Braybrooke and Foljambe).

33 *BPR*, vol. iv, 456; *BPR*, vol. iii, 480–1; *BPR*, vol. iv, 545; *CPP*, 453; *Complete Peerage*, vol. iv, 324–5; Nichols, *Collection of All the Wills*, 118–19.

34 Beltz, *Memorials of the Order of the Garter*, 217.

35 M. Jones, *Ducal Brittany, 1364–1399: Relations with England and France during the Reign of Duke John IV* (Oxford, 1970), 18–19, 45 and 45 n. 4; Tucoo-Chala, *Gaston Fébus*, 117–19.

36 Froissart, *Œuvres*, vol. vii, 75–8; Jones, *Ducal Brittany*, 46 and n. 2.

37 *CPP*, 525, 456; *CPL*, vol. iv, 54–8.

38 For the backgrounds of the Companies, see Fowler, *Medieval Mercenaries*.

39 For Spanish affairs, see Russell, *The English Intervention*, chs 2 and 3.

40 *Lettres secrètes et curiales du pape Urbain V (1362–1370) se rapportant à la France*, ed. P. Le Cacheux and G. Mollat, 2 vols (Paris, 1902–55), vol. 1, 126 n., 128 and n.

41 Russell, *The English Intervention*, 26–9.

42 *Lettres secrètes et curiales du pape Urbain V*, ed. Le Cacheux and Mollat, vol. 1, 143, 146–50.

43 *Ibid.*, 147.

44 *Ibid.*, 153–4.

45 *CPL*, vol. iv, 21; Emden, *Biographical Register*, vol. ii, 1195.

46 R. Barber, *Edward Prince of Wales and Aquitaine* (London, 1978), ch. 8; Froissart, *Œuvres*, vol. vii, 90, 117.

47 Barber, *Edward Prince of Wales*, 188–91; *Foedera*, vol. iii, 799–807; Russell, *The English Intervention*, 56–69.

48 *Froissart*, trans. Brereton, 469–70.
49 *William Thorne's Chronicle of Saint Augustine's Abbey, Canterbury*, ed. A. H. Davis (Oxford, 1934), 591.
50 D. Abulafia, *A Mediterranean Emporium: The Catalan Kingdom of Majorca* (Cambridge, 1994), 17; Froissart, *Œuvres*, vol. vii, 146–7.
51 Barber, *Edward Prince of Wales*, 193; N. Housley, *The Later Crusades, 1274–1580: From Lyons to Alcazar* (Oxford, 1992), 182. I owe thanks to Professor Michael Angold for the suggestion that the existence of another claimant called Richard is plausible.
52 Nichols, *Collection of All the Wills*, 72; P. Rickard, *Britain in Medieval French Literature, 1100–1500* (Cambridge, 1956), 146–51.
53 For the date of the Prince's departure from Bordeaux, see Barber, *Edward Prince of Wales*, 262 n. 3; Russell, *The English Intervention*, 81.
54 *Life of the Black Prince*, ed. Pope and Lodge, 152–3.
55 Barber, *Edward Prince of Wales*, 197; Beltz, *Memorials of the Order of the Garter*, 54; Froissart, *Œuvres*, vol. vii, 169–70, 172–3, 214.
56 *Life of the Black Prince*, ed. Pope and Lodge, 153; Froissart, *Œuvres*, vol. vii, 148–9; A. Goodman, *John of Gaunt: The Exercise of Princely Power in Fourteenth-Century Europe* (London, 1992), 46.
57 Froissart, *Œuvres*, vol. vii, 214.
58 A. E. Prince, 'A Letter of Edward the Black Prince describing the Battle of Nájera in 1367', *EHR*, 41 (1926), 415–18.
59 *Life of the Black Prince*, ed. Pope and Lodge, 167; cf. Froissart, *Œuvres*, vol. vii, 239.
60 Barber, *Edward Prince of Wales*, 215–16; Sumption, *Hundred Years War*, vol. iii, 19–20.
61 Barber, *Edward Prince of Wales*, 220–1; Ormrod, *Edward III*, 506–7; Sumption, *Hundred Years War*, vol. iii, 18–20.
62 Froissart, *Œuvres*, vol. vii, 356.
63 Sumption, *Hundred Years War*, vol. iii, 27–9.
64 *St Albans*, vol. i, 33.
65 *Ibid.*
66 *Life of the Black Prince*, ed. Pope and Lodge, 167; *Eulogium*, vol. iii, 334. I also appreciate being made aware of David Green's discussion on Walsingham and the Black Prince's symptoms in D. Green, 'Masculinity and Medicine: Thomas Walsingham and the Death of the Black Prince', *Journal of Medieval History*, 35 (2009), 34–51.

67 Froissart, *Œuvres*, vol. vii, 388–90; Sumption, *Hundred Years War*, vol. iii, 47.

68 *Complete Peerage*, vol. ii, 427; Froissart, *Œuvres*, vol. vii, 251–2, 385–6.

69 Froissart, *Œuvres*, vol. vii, 386–7, 427–8; for Warwick, see *Test. Vet.*, vol. i, 79–80.

70 Froissart, *Œuvres*, vol. vii, 443–9, 459.

71 *Life of the Black Prince*, ed. Pope and Lodge, 169.

72 Froissart, *Œuvres*, vol. viii, 8–9.

73 *Complete Peerage*, vol. iv, 147; Sumption, *Hundred Years War*, vol. iii, 81.

74 *Test. Vet.*, vol. i, 75, 109, 158–9, 164.

75 *Complete Peerage*, vol. vi, 650–3; J. Sumption, 'Angle, Guichard (IV) d', earl of Huntingdon (c. 1308x15–1380)', *ODNB*, vol. ii, 160–2.

76 Green, *The Black Prince*, 129–30.

77 Delachenal, *Histoire de Charles V*, vol. iv, 284; *Froissart*, trans. Brereton, 176; Sumption, *Hundred Years War*, vol. iii, 79–81.

78 Froissart, trans. Brereton, 179; Froissart, *Œuvres*, vol. viii, 38; Sumption, *Hundred Years War*, vol. iii, 82–3.

79 Froissart, trans. Brereton, 179.

80 *Life of the Black Prince*, ed. Pope and Lodge, 169; *Collection générale*, ed. Delpit, 130–1; TNA, E 101/178/19; TNA, C 47/28/9/15.

81 Froissart, *Œuvres*, vol. viii, 60–4.

82 *CPP*, 397, 493, 505, 508, 522, 525, 527, 537.

7 Deaths of Princes

1 Sumption, *Hundred Years War*, vol. iii, 95.

2 *Calendar of Letter Books of the City of London*, ed. R. R. Sharpe, 11 vols (London, 1899–1912), vol. vii, 275.

3 *Anon. Chron. 1333–81*, 69.

4 G. Holmes, *The Good Parliament* (Oxford, 1975), 13.

5 *CPR 1381–85*, 297. Her husband granted her the revenues of Richmond in 1383 and she seems to have held them till her death (see also Jones, *Ducal Brittany*, 189); TNA, C 53/153 (1), m. 5; TNA, C 53/154 (2), mm. 8, 9. I owe thanks for these and other references to the Charter Rolls to Professor Christopher Given-Wilson.

6 Holmes, *Good Parliament*, 17.

7 J. I. Catto, 'An Alleged Great Council of 1374', *EHR*, 82 (1967), 764–71; *Eulogium*, vol. iii, 337–9.

8 Barber, *Edward Prince of Wales*, 228; *King's Works*, vol. ii, 734–8.

9 *Calendar of Letter Books of the City of London*, ed. Sharpe, vol. vii, 291.

10 *CPL*, vol. iv, 182, 185.

11 Froissart, *Œuvres*, vol. viii, 118–23, 207; J. W. Sherborne, 'Indentured Retinues and English Expeditions to France, 1369–1380', *EHR*, 79 (1964), 725.

12 Froissart, *Œuvres*, vol. viii, 205–6, 208.

13 *Ibid.*, 208; Joan's eldest son Thomas was listed under the command of Humphrey de Bohun, earl of Hereford, TNA, E 101/31/15, m. 1.

14 Y. Renouard, 'Nouvelles crises et dévastations', in *Bordeaux sous les rois d'Angleterre*, ed. Renouard, 407.

15 Goodman, *John of Gaunt*, 232–5.

16 Holmes, *Good Parliament*, 37–46.

17 *CPL*, vol. iv, 146; Sumption, *Hundred Years War*, vol. iii, 81–3.

18 *JGR 1371–75*, vol. ii, nos. 915, 1342.

19 Holmes, *Good Parliament*, 31, 33–4; *JGR 1371–75*, vol. ii, nos. 1343, 1429, 1431.

20 *Early Lincoln Wills*, ed. Gibbons, 52–3.

21 *Complete Peerage*, vol. vi, 531–2; vol. viii, 219–21; *CFR 1369–77*, 211. 238.

22 *CCR 1364–68*, 472. Thomas Latimer was also a witness.

23 K. B. McFarlane, *Lancastrian Kings and Lollard Knights* (Oxford, 1972), 166–7.

24 Stansfield, 'Holland, Thomas, fifth earl of Kent', *ODNB*, vol. xxvii, 695–6.

25 *BPR*, vol. iv, 545; *CCR 1374–77*, 52; *CIPM* , vol. xiv, no. 325; *Complete Peerage*, vol. iv, 324–5; *CPR 1374–77*, 524.

26 Stansfield, 'Holland, Thomas, fifth earl of Kent', *ODNB*, vol. xxvii, 695–6.

27 Holmes, *Good Parliament*, 68–9; *Test. Vet.*, vol. i, 152–3.

28 Goodman, *John of Gaunt*, 58–9.

29 *Anon. Chron. 1333–81*, 79–94; Holmes, *Good Parliament*, ch. 5.

30 *St Albans*, vol. i, 122 n.

31 C. Given-Wilson, *The Royal Household and the King's Affinity: Service, Politics and Finance in England, 1360–1413* (London, 1986), 57, 148–9.

32 *CPR 1381–85*, 453.

33 *St Albans*, vol. i, 32–5.

34 *Froissart*, trans. Brereton, 404, 407.

35 *St Albans*, vol. i, 46–9.

36 *Anon. Chron. 1333–81*, 92.

37 *Ibid.*, 94–5; *St Albans*, vol. i, 32–5.

38 Nichols, *Collection of All the Wills*, 66–77.

39 *Life of the Black Prince*, ed. Pope and Lodge, 170.

40 P. E. Russell, 'The War in Spain and Portugal', in *Froissart: Historian*, ed. J. J. N. Palmer (Woodbridge, 1981), 89.

41 Froissart, *Œuvres*, vol. viii, 380–1.

42 Nichols, *Collection of All the Wills*, 61.

43 *CPR 1374–77*, 374–6; *CPR 1377–81*, 21.

44 BL, Harley MS, 4840, fol. 393. This was the estimated value of a jewel deposited by her with him.

45 *CPR 1374–77*, 374–6; Given-Wilson, *King's Affinity*, 103–4. Pakington served the Black Prince, Joan and Richard. He was among those listed as receiving liveries of mourning for Joan's exequies. *Chaucer Life Records*, ed. M. M. Crow and C. C. Olson (Oxford, 1966), 104.

46 *CPR 1377–81*, 159 (for Bonde); *ibid.*, 237 (for Trivet); *ibid.*, 113, 163 and Green, *The Black Prince*, 45 (for Sharnesfield).

47 McFarlane, *Lancastrian Kings and Lollard Knights*, 164–5 (for Clifford); *ibid.*, 165–6 (for Clanvowe); Worthe was appointed steward of her lands in 1378; in 1385 he was one of those appointed by the king to safeguard Joan.

48 *BPR*, vol. iv, 522 (for Peverel); *CPR 1377–81*, 460 (for de Corby).

49 *BPR*, vol. iv, 461–2 (for Pontfret); *CPR 1350–54* and *CPR 1354–60*, several entries in both for Corby.

50 *CPR 1381–85*, 463.

51 J. G. Clark, 'Mare, Thomas de la (c. 1309–1396)', *ODNB*, vol. xxxvi, 620–2.

52 BL, MS Cotton Nero D VII, fol. 129 (St Albans Abbey *Liber Benefactorum*).

53 *CPR 1381–85*, 441.

54 Given-Wilson, *King's Affinity*, 144–6; *The House of Commons, 1386–1421*, ed. J. S. Roskell, L. Clark and C. Rawcliffe, 4 vols (Stroud, 1993), vol. iv, 779–80.

55 *CPR 1377–81*, 180; BL, MS Cotton Nero D. VII, fol. 129v.

56 *Anon. Chron. 1333–81*, 102–3; Richard issued letters dated at Kennington on 25 and 27 Feb. 1377 (*CPR 1377–81*, 163, 169).

57 Holmes, *Good Parliament*, ch. 6.

58 *St Albans*, vol. i, 88–9.

59 *Ibid.*, vol. i, 88–9, 90–1.

60 Goodman, *John of Gaunt*, 102–3; *St Albans*, vol. i, 93–5.
61 *St Albans*, vol. i, 93–5.
62 *Anglo-Norman Letters and Petitions from All Souls MS. 182*, ed. M. D. Legge (Oxford, 1941), 162–6.
63 TNA, E 403/462, m. 3–4, 10.
64 *Ibid.*; TNA, E 403/465, m. 20.

8 The King's Mother

1 *Anon. Chron. 1333–81*, 106; *St Albans*, vol. i, 128–9.
2 *St Albans*, vol. i, 114–15; *ibid.*, 187 n., 114, line 21; J. L. Leland, 'Burley, Sir Simon (1336?–1388)', *ODNB*, vol. viii, 869–70.
3 *CPR 1377–81*, 539; *King's Works*, vol. ii, 298–301; *John Leland's Itinerary*, ed. Chandler, 30; C. Simpson, *Wallingford: The Archaeological Implications of Development. A Survey* (Oxford, 1974), 7, 8, 11.
4 *CIPM*, vol. vi, no. 120.
5 *CPR 1385–89*, 130.
6 *CCR 1377–81*, 128.
7 The king's uncles frequently attested royal charters during the minority: TNA, C 53/155(1) – C 53/157(2).
8 *CPR 1377–81*, 371; *JGR 1379–83*, vol. i, no. 327.
9 *CPR 1377–81*, 112.
10 *Ibid.*, 371.
11 McFarlane, *Lancastrian Kings and Lollard Knights*, 162, 173–4.
12 *St Albans*, vol. i, 196–7.
13 *CPR 1377–81*, 185; McFarlane, *Lancastrian Kings and Lollard Knights*, 148–9, 207–20; *Test. Vet.*, vol. i, 164–5.
14 McFarlane, *Lancastrian Kings and Lollard Knights*, 162, 164–5, 176, 197–206.
15 *Test. Vet.*, vol. i, 75.
16 For Gaunt and Wycliffe, see Goodman, *John of Gaunt*, 241–4.
17 *Anon. Chron. 1333–81*, 121–4; *CCR 1377–81*, 26. Hauley was buried in the abbey; Goodman, *John of Gaunt*, 226–7.
18 Russell, *The English Intervention*, 98 n. 2, 103 n. 1.
19 *CCR 1377–81*, 482–3; *CCR 1381–85*, 487.
20 *St Albans*, vol. i, 239.
21 Russell, *The English Intervention*, 238–40, 242.

22 *Foedera*, vol. iii, 68a and 71b; cf. *ibid*. 112, 122 for further proposals over ransom with Villena.

23 Archivo del Reino de Valencia, Mestre Racional, 9,600; cf. *ibid*., ii, 599. I owe thanks to Dr Jorge Saiz Serrano for transcripts of these documents; see *Foedera*, vol iii, 68a and 71b; cf. *ibid*., 112, 122 for further proposals over ransom with Villena.

24 *CPR 1377–81*, 463; *CPR 1381–85*, 48–9 issued under the king's privy seal on 7 Nov. 1385.

25 *CPR 1377–81*, 592 for William Giles and William and Joan Pope.

26 *CPR 1381–85*, 185; R. A. Griffiths, *The Principality of Wales in the Later Middle Ages: The Structure and Personnel of Government. I. South Wales, 1277–1536* (Cardiff, 1972), 212.

27 *CPR 1377–81*, 528.

28 *CPR 1381–85*, 453; Griffiths, *Principality of Wales*, 232.

29 *CPR 1377–81*, 372, 606.

30 *Ibid.*, 357.

31 *Ibid.*, 385.

32 *Ibid.*, 255.

33 *Ibid.*, 483.

34 *Ibid.*, 82, 240.

35 *Ibid.*, 59; *Controversy between Sir Richard Scrope and Sir Robert Grosvenor*, ed. Nicolas, vol. ii, 325–7.

36 *CPR 1377–81*, 297.

37 W. M. Ormrod, 'In Bed with Joan of Kent: The King's Mother and the Peasants' Revolt', in *Medieval Women: Texts and Contexts in Late Medieval Britain: Essays for Felicity Riddy*, ed. J. Wogan-Browne, R. Voaden, A. Diamond, A. Hutchinson, C. Meale and L. Johnson (Turnhout, 2000), 289, 291.

38 *CPR 1377–81*, 396, 397, 460, 483, 626.

39 *Ibid.*, 267, 277.

40 *CPR 1381–85*, 229.

41 *Ibid.*, 449; *John Leland's Itinerary*, ed. Chandler, 30, 35.

42 *CPR 1385–89*, 21. This confirmed the earlier grant made by Blanche at Rockingham dated 1 Sep., 2 Richard II.

43 *CPR 1377–81*, 376.

44 Barber, *Edward Prince of Wales*, 89–90, 171, 181; Green, *The Black Prince*, 28, 45, 67.

45 CPR *1385–89*, 35; *Early Lincoln Wills*, ed. Gibbons, 55; C. L. Kingsford, 'Loring, Sir Neil [Nigel] (c. 1315–1386)', rev. R. Barber, *ODNB*, vol. xxxiv, 456–7.

46 CPR *1381–85*, 13.

47 *Ibid.*, 4.

48 CPR *1377–81*, 277, 335; Green, *The Black Prince*, 122–4; Nichols, *A Collection of All the Wills*, 71–2.

49 *King's Works*, ii, 815–18.

50 Beltz, *Memorials of the Order of the Garter*, 246–7.

51 Sumption, *Hundred Years War*, vol. iii, 366–8.

52 Froissart, *Œuvres*, vol. ix, 131–3; *St Albans*, vol. i, 348–9.

53 Sumption, *Hundred Years War*, vol. iii, vol. i, no. 366–7; *St Albans*, vol, i, 350–1.

54 Froissart, *Œuvres*, vol. ix, 133; *JGR 1379–83*, 463; *St Albans*, vol. i, 348–9.

55 *St Albans*, vol. i, 398.

56 BL, Add. Charter 27703.

57 *Complete Peerage*, vol. vi, 653; Sumption, 'Angle, Guichard (IV) d'', *ODNB*, vol. ii, 160–2.

58 *CIPM*, vol. xv, nos. 438–45.

59 *Early Lincoln Wills*, ed. Gibbons, 83; Hartley and Rogers, *Religious Foundations of Medieval Stamford*, 65.

60 CFR *1377–83*, 243.

61 *Ibid.*, 324; *Oton de Granson et sa vie et ses poésies*, ed. A. Piaget (Lausanne, 1941), 11–18, 41.

62 D. Pearsall, *The Life of Geoffrey Chaucer* (Oxford, 1992), 71, 181; *Oton de Granson*, ed. Piaget, 244–5. Cf. 248–9, 471–2 (here a princess is addressed).

63 Pearsall, *Life*, 181–3; E. Rickert, C. C. Olson and M. M. Crow (eds), *Chaucer's World* (London, 1948), 404–5 (for Vache wedding gift).

64 McFarlane, *Lancastrian Kings and Lollard Knights*, see ch. 5; Pearsall, *Life*, 130, 166–7, 182–3.

65 *The Kalendarium of John Somer*, ed. L. R. Mooney (Athens, GA, 1998), 2–34, 54–5; L. R. Mooney, 'Somer, John (d. in or after 1409)', *ODNB*, vol. li, 559.

66 M. R. Toynbee, *St Louis of Toulouse and the Process of Canonisation in the Fourteenth Century* (Manchester, 1929), 30, 101, 191–4, 201–30.

67 *Kalendarium of John Somer*, ed. Mooney, 34, 34 n., 54–5.

68 *The Kalendarium of Nicholas of Lynn*, ed. S. Eisner and G. Mac Eoin (Athens, GA, 1980); Pearsall, *Life*, 217–18.

9 *Terrors and Tribulations*

1 CCR *1381–85*, 26, 446, 576, 634; CIPM, vol. xv, nos. 438–45.

2 For the course of the revolt see *The Peasants' Revolt of 1381*, ed. R. B. Dobson (London, 1970).

3 Froissart, *Œuvres*, vol. vi, 44–57.

4 *Anon. Chron. 1333–81*, 136.

5 Froissart, *Œuvres*, vol. ix, 391.

6 *Peasants' Revolt*, ed. Dobson, 145–7.

7 8 Feb. 1380 – confirmation of an earlier charter dated Westminster 6 Apr., 22 Edward III; Ormrod, 'In Bed with Joan of Kent', 285 n.

8 *Knighton's Chronicle*, ed. Martin, 210–12.

9 *Anon. Chron. 1333–81*, 137–9.

10 *Ibid.*, 144–5.

11 *Ibid.*, 145; *Peasants' Revolt*, ed. Dobson, 209–10; Froissart, *Œuvres*, vol. ix, 398–406.

12 Froissart, *Œuvres*, vol. ix, 404.

13 *Peasants' Revolt*, ed. Dobson, 209 n.; Froissart, trans. Brereton, 220; Thomas Walsingham in *Peasants' Revolt*, ed. Dobson, 171–2.

14 *Peasants' Revolt*, ed. Dobson, 209 n.; *ibid.*, 161, 172; Ormrod, 'In Bed with Joan of Kent', 279.

15 Froissart, *Œuvres*, vol. ix, 398–406; *West. Chron.*, 6–7.

16 CPR *1381–85*, 18.

17 CPR *1377–81*, 105.

18 CPR *1381–85*, 226.

19 R. G. Davies, 'Braybrooke, Robert (1336/7–1404)', ODNB, vol. vii, 416–18; *West. Chron.*, 22–5.

20 CPR *1381–85*, 50; CPR *1377–81*, 530.

21 CPR *1381–85*, 185; Griffiths, *Principality of Wales*, 212.

22 CPR *1381–85*, 214.

23 CPR *1381–85*, 233, 567.

24 CPR *1377–81*, 546.

25 CPR *1381–85*, 98.

26 Nantes, Archives Départementales de Loire-Atlantique, E 117/34; TNA, E 101/31/3; *Calendar of Inquisitions Miscellaneous*, 7 vols (London, 1916–68), vol. vii, 23.

27 JGR *1379–83*, vol. i, no. 178; JGR *1379–83*, vol. i, nos. 688, 715.

28 *CPR 1377–81*, 227, 291, 297, 511.

29 Beltz, *Memorials of the Order of the Garter*, 200–1; *Mémoires pour servir de preuves à l'histoire ecclésiastique et civile de Bretagne*, ed. H. Morice, 3 vols (Paris, 1742–46), vol. ii, 380.

30 *West. Chron.*, 28–9.

31 A. Tuck, 'Vere, Robert, ninth earl of Oxford, marquess of Dublin, and duke of Ireland (1362–1392)', *ODNB*, vol. lvi, 312–15.

32 Fowler, *Medieval Mercenaries*, vol. i, 294; Froissart, *Œuvres*, vol. vii, 332; Sumption, *Hundred Years War*, vol. iii, 28–9. The poem may have been written earlier than 1385. Modern scholarship supports the view that an earlier date is likely.

33 J. Creton, 'Livre de la prinse et mort du roy Richard (1401–02)'; 'Translation of a French Metrical History of the Deposition of King Richard the Second', ed. and trans. J. Webb, *Archaeologia*, 20 (1824), 25; Davies, 'Braybrooke, Robert (1336/7–1404)', *ODNB*, vol. vii, 416–17; Edward of Angoulême's remains were transferred to King's Langley: Ormrod, *Edward III*, 508 n. 55.

34 A. Tuck, 'Pole, Michael de la, first earl of Suffolk (*c.* 1330–1389)', *ODNB*, vol. xliv, 709–13.

35 BL, Egerton Charter 2130; E. M. Thompson, *The Carthusian Order in England* (London 1930), 200–1.

36 *Mémoires*, ed. Morice, vol. ii, columns 478–80 citing original, now Nantes, Archives Départementales de Loire-Atlantique, E 24, 3. I owe thanks for this reference to Professor Michael Jones.

37 Jones, *Ducal Brittany*, 99 n 2.

38 *West. Chron.*, 68–81.

39 *Ibid.*, 110–11, 112–15.

40 *Ibid.* 114–15; *St Albans*, vol. i, 751.

41 *CCR 1381–85*, 553.

42 *CPR 1377–81*, 34, 239; *House of Commons, 1386–1421*, ed. Roskell, Clark and Rawcliffe, iv, 723.

43 *CPR 1381–85*, 283–4 (Wace); *House of Commons, 1386–1421*, ed. Roskell, Clark and Rawcliffe, iv, 723–4; *ibid.*, 328–9.

44 Sumption, *Hundred Years War*, vol. iii, 323–7; TNA, E 101/36/39, mm. 1, 2.

45 *West. Chron.*, 192–3.

46 *Ibid.*, 122–3; Froissart, *Œuvres*, vol. x, 387.

47 *St Albans*, vol. i, 758–9.

48 Nichols, *Collection of All the Wills*, 78–81. For further reading on Joan's religious beliefs, see Green, *Edward the Black Prince*, ch. 6.
49 R. Allen, 'Cobham, John, third Baron Cobham of Cobham (*c*. 1320–1408)', *ODNB*, vol. xii, 293–5; *Complete Peerage*, vol. iii, 344–5.
50 *Controversy between Sir Richard Scrope and Sir Robert Grosvenor*, ed. Nicolas, vol. ii, 378–80; M. Wood, *Donnington Castle, Berkshire* (London, 1964).
51 Nichols, *Collection of All the Wills*, 78–81.
52 *St Albans*, vol. i, 758–9.
53 *CPR 1381–85*, 155; *House of Commons, 1386–1421*, ed. Roskell, Clark and Rawcliffe, iii, 486.
54 *The Kirkstall Chronicle, 1355–1400: From MS. Dodsworth 140 in the Bodleian Library*, ed. M. V. Clarke and N. Denholm-Young (Manchester, 1931), 27.
55 *CPR 1385–89*, 143.
56 *Chaucer Life Records*, ed. Crow and Olsen, 103–5, list expenses of mourning robes provided for Joan's exequies dated 10 Sept. 1385; among the recipients is Pakington; TNA, E 403/511, m. 11.
57 *Kirkstall Chronicle*, ed. Clarke and Denholm-Young, 27; N. Saul, *Richard II* (London, 1997), 470.
58 *CPR 1385–89*, 188.
59 *Ibid.*, 18.
60 *West. Chron.*, 144–5.
61 *Ibid.*, 192–3.
62 *Ibid.*, 158–9.
63 *Ibid.*, 192–3 and n. 5.
64 *CPR 1385–89*, 48–9 (Clifford); *ibid.*, 130 (Denise Sutton); 155–6 (Alice Fitzwalter); TNA, E 101/511/5.

10 Venus Ascending?

1 M. P. Siddons, *Heraldic Badges in England and Wales*, 4 vols (Woodbridge, 2009), vol. ii, 151–2.
2 *Ibid.*
3 A. K. McHardy, 'Richard II: A Personal Portrait', in *The Reign of Richard II*, ed. G. Dodd (Stroud, 2000), 11–32; London, Westminster Abbey, Muniments, 9584.

4 *Chronicon Adae de Usk. A.D. 1377–1421*, ed. E. M. Thompson (London, 1904), 180–1, 181 n. 1.

5 Froissart, trans. Brereton, 460.

6 *Chronicon Adae de Usk*, ed. Thompson, 143–4, 144 n. 1.

7 See *The Chronicle of John Hardyng*, ed. H. Ellis (London, 1812), p. 331.

8 John Capgrave, *The Chronicle of England*, ed. F. C. Hingeston, RS 1 (London, 1858), 221.

9 For Arundel, see *Complete Peerage*, vol. i, 243 and n. (d).

10 York, Borthwick Institute for Archives, Archbishops' Registers 17: Register of Henry Bowet (1407–23), fol. 291.

11 *Test. Vet.*, 83.

12 Margery Kempe, *The Book of Margery Kempe, 1436*, ed. W. Butler-Bowden (London, 1936), 27.

13 *Test Vet.*, 171.

14 Nichols, *Collection of All the Wills*, 118–19.

15 A. Goodman, *Margery Kempe and Her World* (London, 2002), 69.

16 J. C. Ward, 'Joan de Bohun, Countess of Hereford, Kent and Northampton, c. 1370–1419: Family, Land and Social Networks', *Essex Archaeology and History*, 32 (2001), 146–53.

17 Pearsall, *Life*, 130–1.

18 *Ibid.*, 166–7.

19 *Ibid.*, 130.

20 N. H. Nicolas, 'Observations on the Origin and History of the Badge and Mottoes of Edward, Prince of Wales', *Archaeologia*, 31 (1846), 364.

21 M. Bath, 'The Legend of Caesar's Deer', *Medievalia et Humanistica*, new series, 9 (1979), 53–66.

Bibliography

MANUSCRIPT SOURCES

Bordeaux, Archives Départementales de la Gironde

Archives de la Gironde: Table alphabétique générale des séries G & H. –
table 1 sér. G – chapitre métropolitain Saint-André-anniversaires, C 317
(1389–1504).

Kew, The National Archives

Chancery	Exchequer
C 47/28/9/15	E 30/1105
C 53/153(1)	E 36/205
C 53/154(2)	E 101/31/3
C 53/155(1)	E 101/31/15
C 53/157(2)	E 101/36/39
	E 101/178/19
Duchy of Lancaster	E 101/511/5
DL 29/4069.262	E 117/34
DL 403/461/15	E 403/409
	E 403/461/15
	E 403/462
	E 403/465
	E 403/511

London, British Library

Additional Charter 27703
Egerton Charter 2130
MS Cotton Nero D. VII: *Liber Benefactorum* of St Albans Abbey
MS Harley 4840

London, Lambeth Palace Library

Register of Simon Islip

London, Westminster Abbey Muniments

Ms. 9584

Bibliography

Nantes, Archives Départementales de Loire-Atlantique

E 24, 3
E 117/34

Valencia, Archivo del Reino de Valencia

Mestre Racional, 9,600

York, Borthwick Institute for Archives

Archbishops' Registers 17: Register of Henry Bowet (1407–23)

PRINTED SOURCES

Adae Murimuth Continuatio Chronicarum, ed. E. M. Thompson, RS 93
(London, 1889).

Adam of Usk, *Chronicon Adae de Usk, A.D. 1377–1421*, ed. E. M. Thompson
(London, 1904).

Anglo-Norman Letters and Petitions from All Souls MS. 182, ed. M. D. Legge
(Oxford, 1941).

'Annales Londoniensis', in *Chronicles of the Reigns of Edward I and Edward II*,
ed. W. Stubbs, 2 vols, RS 76 (London, 1882–83), vol. i.

'Annales Paulini', in *Chronicles of the Reigns of Edward I and Edward II*,
ed. W. Stubbs, 2 vols, RS 76 (London, 1882–83), vol. i.

The Anonimalle Chronicle, 1307–1334, ed. W. R. Childs and J. Taylor, Yorkshire
Archaeological Society, Record series, 147 (Leeds, 1991).

The Anonimalle Chronicle 1333–1381, ed. V. H. Galbraith (Manchester, 1927).

Archives Municipales de Bordeaux, Livre de Bouillons (Bordeaux, 1867).

Baker, Geoffrey le, *Chronicon Galfridi le Baker de Swynebroke*,
ed. E. M. Thompson (Oxford, 1889).

Bel, Jean le, *Chronique de Jean le Bel*, ed. J. Viard and E. Déprez, 2 vols, SHF
(Paris, 1904–5).

Brown, R. A., H. M. Colvin and A. J. Taylor, *The History of the King's Works:
The Middle Ages*, 2 vols (London, 1963).

The Brut or the Chronicles of England, ed. F. W. D. Brie, 2 vols, Early English
Text Society, Original Series, 131 & 136 (London, 1906–8).

Calendar of Close Rolls Edward II–Richard II, 24 vols (London, 1892–1927).

*Calendar of Entries to the Papal Registers Relating to Great Britain and Ireland:
Papal Letters*, ii–iv (London, 1895–1902).

*Calendar of Entries to the Papal Registers Relating to Great Britain and Ireland:
Petitions to the Pope, 1342–1419* (London, 1896).

Calendar of Fine Rolls, Edward II–Richard II, 10 vols (London, 1912–29).

Calendar of Inquisitions Miscellaneous, 7 vols (London, 1916–68).
Calendar of Inquisitions Post Mortem, Edward I–Richard II, 17 vols (London, 1904–88).
Calendar of Letter Books of the City of London, ed. R. R. Sharpe, 11 vols (London, 1899–1912).
Calendar of Papal Letters to Scotland of Clement VII of Avignon, 1378–1394, ed. C. Burns and A. I. Dunlop, Scottish Historical Society, 4th series, 12 (Edinburgh, 1976).
Calendar of Patent Rolls, Edward II–Richard II, 27 vols (London, 1894–1916).
Calendar of Select Pleas and Memoranda of the City of London, 1381–1412, ed. A. H. Thomas (Cambridge, 1932).
Capgrave, John, *The Chronicle of England*, ed. F. C. Hingeston, RS 1 (London, 1858).
Cartulaire de l'Église Collégiale Saint-Seurin de Bordeaux, ed. J. A. Brutails (Bordeaux, 1897).
Castro, J. R., *Archivo General de Navarre*, Catálogo de la Sección de Comptos Documentos (Pamplona, 1954–59).
Chaucer, G., *The Complete Works of Geoffrey Chaucer*, ed. W. W. Skeat (Oxford, 1952).
Chaucer Life Records, ed. M. M. Crow and C. C. Olsen (Oxford, 1966).
Chronica Johannis de Reading et Anonymi Cantuariensis, 1346–1367, ed. J. Tait (Manchester, 1914).
Chronica Monasterii de Melsa, ed. E. A. Bond, 3 vols, RS 43 (London, 1866–68).
'Chronicle of the Grey Friars of London', ed. R. Howlett, in *Monumenta Franciscana*, ed. J. S. Brewer and R. Howlett, 2 vols, RS 4 (London, 1858–82), ii.
Chronicon Abbatiae de Parco Lude. The Chronicle of Louth Park Abbey, ed. E. Venables, Publications of the Lincolnshire Record Society (Horncastle, 1891).
Chronique des règnes de Jean II et Charles V, ed. R. Delachenal, 4 vols, SHF (Paris, 1910–20).
Chronique Normande du XIVe siècle, ed. A. and É. Molinier, SHF (Paris, 1882).
Les Chronique de Normandie (1223–1453), ed. A. Hellot (Rouen, 1881).
Chronique des Quatre Premiers Valois (1327–1393), ed. S. Luce, SHF (Paris, 1862).
Collection générale des documents français qui se trouvent en Angleterre, ed. J. Delpit (Paris, 1847).

Bibliography

The Controversy between Sir Richard Scrope and Sir Robert Grosvenor in the Court of Chivalry, AD MCCCLXXXV–MCCCXC, ed. N. H. Nicolas, 2 vols (London, 1832).

Crécy and Calais from the Original Records in the Public Record Office, ed. G. Wrottesley (London, 1898).

Creton, Jean, 'Translation of a French Metrical History of the Deposition of King Richard the Second', ed. and trans. J. Webb, *Archaeologia*, 20 (1824), 1–442.

A Descriptive Catalogue of Ancient Deeds in the Public Record Office, 6 vols (London, 1890–1915).

Dynter, E. de, *Chronique des Ducs de Brabant*, ed. P. F. X. de Ram, 3 vols (Brussels, 1854–60).

Early Lincoln Wills, ed. A. Gibbons (Lincoln, 1888).

The Edington Cartulary, ed. J. H Stevenson, Wiltshire Record Society, 42 (Devizes, 1987).

Eulogium Historiarum, ed. F. S. Haydon, 3 vols, RS 9 (London, 1858–63).

Foedera, Conventiones, Literae et Cujuscunque Generis Acta Publica, ed. T. Rymer, 3 vols in 6 parts (London, 1816–30).

Froissart, J., *Œuvres complètes: Chroniques*, ed. J. M. B. C. Kervyn de Lettenhove, 25 vols (Brussels, 1867–77).

—— *Chronicles*, trans. G. Brereton (Harmondsworth, 1968).

'Gesta Edwardi de Carnarvan auctore canonico Bridlingtoniensi, cum continuatio', in *Chronicles of the Reigns of Edward I and Edward II*, ed. W. Stubbs, 2 vols, RS 76 (London, 1882–83), vol. ii.

Les Grandes Chroniques de France, ed. J. Viard, 10 vols, SHF (Paris, 1920–53).

Gray, T., *Scalacronica, 1272–1363*, ed. and trans. A. King, Surtees Society, 209 (2005).

Hardyng, J., *The Chronicle of John Hardyng*, ed. H. Ellis (London, 1812).

John Leland's Itinerary: Travels in Tudor England, ed. J. Chandler (Stroud, 1993).

John of Gaunt's Register, 1371–1375, ed. S. Armitage-Smith, 2 vols, Camden Third Series, 20–1, RHS (London, 1911).

John of Gaunt's Register, 1379–1383, ed. E. C. Lodge and R. Somerville, 2 vols, Camden Third series, 56–7, RHS (London, 1937).

The Kalendarium of John Somer, ed. L. R. Mooney (Athens, GA, 1998).

The Kalendarium of Nicholas of Lynn, ed. S. Eisner and G. Mac Eoin (Athens, GA, 1980).

Kempe, Margery, *The Book of Margery Kempe, 1436*, ed. W. Butler-Bowden (London, 1936).

The Kirkstall Chronicle, 1355–1400: From MS. Dodsworth 140 in the Bodleian Library, ed. M. V. Clarke and N. Denholm-Young (Manchester, 1931).

Knighton's Chronicle, 1337–1396, ed. G. H. Martin (Oxford, 1995).

Letters, Orders and Musters of Bertrand du Guesclin, 1357–1380, ed. M. Jones (Woodbridge, 2004).

Lettres secrètes et curiales du pape Urbain V (1362–1370) se rapportant à la France, ed. P. Le Cacheux and G. Mollat (Paris, 1902–55).

The Life and Campaigns of the Black Prince, ed. R. Barber (Woodbridge, 1979).

Life of the Black Prince by the Herald of Sir John Chandos, ed. M. K. Pope and E. C. Lodge (Oxford, 1910).

Mémoires pour servir de preuves à l'histoire ecclésiastique et civile de Bretagne, ed. H. Morice, 3 vols (Paris, 1742–46).

Nichols, J., *A Collection of All the Wills known to be extant of the Kings and Queens of England* (London, 1780).

Oton de Granson et sa vie et ses poésies, ed. A. Piaget (Lausanne, 1941).

Pageant of the Birth, Life and Death of Richard Beauchamp, Earl of Warwick, ed. Viscount Dillon and W. H. St John Hope (London, 1914).

The Peasants' Revolt of 1381, ed. R. B. Dobson (London, 1970).

'Petite Chronique de Guyenne jusqu'à l'an 1442', ed. G. Lefèvre-Pontalis, *Bibliothèque de l'École des Chartes*, 47 (Paris, 1886), 53–79.

Récits d'un bourgeois de Valenciennes, XIVe siècle, ed. J. M. B. C. Kervyn de Lettenhove (Louvain, 1877).

Recueil des actes de Jean IV, duc de Bretagne, ed. M. Jones, 2 vols (Paris, 1980–83).

Register of Edward the Black Prince, ed. M. C. B. Dawes, 4 vols (London, 1930–33).

Report on the Manuscripts of the late Reginald Rawdon Hastings, 4 vols, Historical Manuscripts Commission (London, 1928–47).

Rotuli Parliamentorum, 6 vols, Record Commission (London, 1767–77).

Sir Christopher Hatton's Book of Seals, ed. L. C. Loyd and D. M. Stenton (Oxford, 1950).

Syllabus (in English) of … Rymer's Foedera, ed. T. D. Hardy, 3 vols (London, 1869–85).

Testamenta Eboracensia, Surtees Society, 4, 30, 45, 53, 79, 106 (1836–1902).

Testamenta Vetusta, ed. N. H. Nicolas, 2 vols (London, 1826).

Thorne, William, *William Thorne's Chronicle of Saint Augustine's Abbey, Canterbury*, ed. A. H. Davis (Oxford, 1934).

Wallingford, R., *Richard of Wallingford: An Edition of His Writings*, ed. J. D. North, 3 vols (Oxford, 1976).

Bibliography

Walsingham, T., *Historia Anglicana*, ed. H. T. Riley, 2 vols, RS 28 (London, 1863–64).

—— *Chronicon Angliae*, ed. E. M. Thompson, RS 64 (London, 1874).

—— *Ypodigma Neustriae*, ed. H. T. Riley, RS 28 (London, 1876).

—— *The St Albans Chronicle: The Chronica Maiora of Thomas Walsingham*, ed. J. Taylor, W. R. Childs and L. Watkiss, 2 vols (Oxford, 2003–11).

The War of Saint-Sardos (1323–1325): Gascon Correspondence and Diplomatic Documents, ed. P. Chaplais, Camden Third Series, 87, RHS (London, 1954).

The Westminster Chronicle 1381–1394, ed. L. C. Hector and B. F. Harvey (Oxford, 1982).

'A Wigmore Chronicle, 1355–1377', ed. J. Taylor, in J. Taylor, *English Historical Literature in the Fourteenth Century* (Oxford, 1987).

SECONDARY WORKS

Aberth, J., 'Crime and Justice under Edward III: The Case of Thomas De Lisle', *EHR*, 107 (1992), 283–301.

Abulafia, D., *A Mediterranean Emporium: The Catalan Kingdom of Majorca* (Cambridge, 1994).

Allmand, C. T., *The Hundred Years War: England and France at War, c. 1300–c. 1450* (Cambridge, 1988).

—— (ed.), *Society at War: The Experience of England and France during the Hundred Years War* (Woodbridge, 1998).

Armitage-Smith, S., *John of Gaunt* (London, 1904).

Ayton, A., *Knights and Warhorses: Military Service and the English Aristocracy under Edward III* (Woodbridge, 1994).

Ayton, A., and P. Preston, *The Battle of Crécy, 1346* (Woodbridge, 2005).

Barber, R., *Edward Prince of Wales and Aquitaine* (London, 1978).

—— 'Jean Froissart and Edward the Black Prince', in *Froissart: Historian*, ed. J. J. N. Palmer (Woodbridge, 1981), 25–35.

Bath, M., 'The Iconography of the Collared Deer', in *Proceedings of the International Colloquium Beast Epic, Fable and Fabliau*, ed. K. Varty (Glasgow, 1976).

—— 'The Legend of Caesar's Deer', *Medievalia et Humanistica*, new series, 9 (1979), 53–66.

Beltz, G. F., *Memorials of the Order of the Garter* (London, 1841).

Bémont, C., *La Guyenne pendant la Domination Anglaise, 1152–1453* (London, 1920).

Bériac-Lainé, F., 'Les défunts de la cathédrale au XIVe siècle', in *La cathédrale Saint-André: reflet de neuf siècles d'histoire et de vie bordelaise,* ed. M. Agostino (Pessac, 2001), 93–106.

Bériac-Lainé, F., and C. Given-Wilson, *Les prisonniers de la bataille de Poitiers* (Paris, 2002).

Birkbeck, J. D., *A History of Bourne* (Bourne, 1970).

Bond, M. F., *The Inventories of St George's Chapel, Windsor Castle, 1384–1667* (Windsor, 1947).

Bothwell, J. S., *Edward III and the English Peerage: Royal Patronage, Social Mobility and Political Control in Fourteenth-Century England* (Woodbridge, 2004).

Brown, S., *York Minster: An Architectural History, c. 1220–1500: 'our magnificent fabrick'* (Swindon, 2003).

Brutails, J. A., *Guide illustré dans Bordeaux et les environs* (Bordeaux, n.d.).

Burrows, M., *The Family of Brocas of Beaurepaire and Roche Court* (London, 1886).

Capra, P., 'L'apogée politique au temps du Prince Noir (1355–1372)', in *Bordeaux sous les rois d'Angleterre,* ed. Y. Renouard (Bordeaux, 1965), 369–404.

Catto, J. I., 'An Alleged Great Council of 1374', *EHR,* 82 (1967), 764–71.

Chambers, G. E., *The Bonshommes of the Order of St. Augustine at Ashridge and Edington* (Cambridge, 1979).

Clarke, M. V., *Fourteenth Century Studies,* ed. L. S. Sutherland (Oxford, 1937).

Cokayne, G. E., *The Complete Peerage of England, Scotland, Ireland, Great Britain and the United Kingdom,* rev. V. Gibbs et al., 13 vols (London, 1910–59).

Collins, H. E. L., *The Order of the Garter, 1348–1461: Chivalry and Politics in Late Medieval England* (Oxford, 2000).

Davison, B. K., *Sherborne Old Castle, Dorset* (London, 2001).

Dawson, G. J., *The Black Prince's Palace at Kennington, Surrey,* British Archaeological Reports, 26 (Oxford, 1976).

Delachenal. R., *Histoire de Charles V,* 5 vols (Paris, 1909–31).

Déprez, E., *Préliminaires de la Guerre de Cent Ans: La Papauté, la France et l'Angleterre, 1328–1342* (Paris, 1902).

Dodds, M. H. (ed.), *A History of Northumberland,* vol. 14 (Newcastle-upon-Tyne, 1935).

Doherty, P. C., *Isabella and the Strange Death of Edward II* (London, 2003).

Dubourg-Noves, P. (ed.), *Histoire d'Angoulême et ses alentours* (Toulouse, 1989).

Dunn, A., *The Peasants' Revolt: England's Failed Revolution of 1381,* 2nd edn (Stroud, 2004).

Bibliography

Elton, M., 'Uncovered: London's Grim Tribute to a Medieval Martyr', *BBC History Magazine* (April 2015), 11–12.

Emden, A. B., *A Biographical Register of the University of Oxford to 1500*, 3 vols (Oxford, 1957–59).

Eubel, C., *Hierarchia Catholica Medii Aevi*, vol. 1 (Münster, 1898).

Fairbanks, E. R., 'The Last Earl of Warenne and Surrey', *Yorkshire Archaeological Journal*, 19 (1907), 193–266.

Favreau, R., *La commanderie du Breul-de-Pas et la guerre de Cent Ans dans la Saintonge méridionale* (Jonzac, 1986).

——'La cession de La Rochelle à l'Angleterre en 1360', in *Actes du 111e Congrès national des Sociétés savantes, Poitiers, 1986, Section d'histoire médiévale et de philologie. La France anglaise au moyen âge* (Paris, 1988), 217–31.

Fino, J.-F., *Forteresses de la France médiévale: Construction, attaque, défense* (Paris, 1967).

Fizzard, A. D., *Plympton Priory: A House of Augustinian Canons in South-Western England in the Late Middle Ages* (Leiden, 2008).

Fowler, K., *The King's Lieutenant: Henry of Grosmont, First Duke of Lancaster, 1310–1361* (London, 1969).

—— *Medieval Mercenaries*, vol. 1: *The Great Companies* (Oxford, 2001).

Fryde, N., *The Tyranny and Fall of Edward II, 1321–1326* (Cambridge, 1979).

Galway, M., 'Joan of Kent and the Order of the Garter', *University of Birmingham Historical Journal*, 1 (1947), 13–50.

——'Chaucer, Graunson and Isabel of France', *The Review of English Studies*, 24 (1948), 273–80.

Gardelles, J., *Les châteaux du moyen âge dans la France du sud-ouest (1216–1327)* (Paris, 1972).

Gardner, A., *Alabaster Tombs of the Pre-Reformation Period in England* (Cambridge, 1940).

Given-Wilson, C., *The Royal Household and the King's Affinity: Service, Politics and Finance in England, 1360–1413* (London, 1986).

Given-Wilson, C., and A. Curteis, *The Royal Bastards of Medieval England* (London, 1984).

Given-Wilson, C., and F. Bériac-Lainé, *Les prisonniers de la bataille de Poitiers* (Paris, 2002).

Goodman, A., *John of Gaunt: The Exercise of Princely Power in Fourteenth-Century Europe* (London, 1992).

—— *Margery Kempe and Her World* (London, 2002).

Goodman, A., and J. L. Gillespie (eds), *Richard II: The Art of Kingship* (Oxford, 1998).

Goodwin-Austen, R. A. C., 'Woking Manor', *Surrey Archaeological Collections*, 7 (1874), 44–9.

Gransden, A., 'A Fourteenth-Century Chronicle from the Grey Friars at Lynn', *EHR*, 72 (1957), 270–8.

Green, D., *The Black Prince* (Stroud, 2001).

—— *Edward the Black Prince: Power in Medieval Europe* (Harlow, 2007).

—— 'Masculinity and Medicine: Thomas Walsingham and the Death of the Black Prince', *Journal of Medieval History*, 35 (2009), 34–51.

Green, M. A. E., *Lives of the Princesses of England*, 6 vols (London, 1849–55).

Griffiths, R. A., *The Principality of Wales in the Later Middle Ages: The Structure and Personnel of Government. I. South Wales, 1277–1536* (Cardiff, 1972).

Grimke-Drayton, T. D., 'The East Window of Gloucester Cathedral', *Transactions of the Bristol and Gloucestershire Archaeological Society*, 38 (1915), 69–97.

Guillemain, B., 'L'essor religieux', in *Bordeaux sous les rois d'Angleterre*, ed. Y. Renouard (Bordeaux, 1965), 127–72.

Haggard, J., 'The Ruins of Old Woking Palace', *Surrey Archaeological Society*, 55 (1958), 124–6.

Haines, R. M., *King Edward II: His Life, His Reign, and its Aftermath, 1284–1330* (Montreal, 2003).

Hartley, J. S., and Rogers, A. *The Religious Foundations of Medieval Stamford* (Nottingham, 1974).

Harvey, A. S., 'Cottingham Church and its Heraldry', *Yorkshire Archaeological Journal*, 40 (1960), 265–97.

Harvey, J., *The Black Prince and his Age* (London, 1976).

Hewitt, H. J., *The Black Prince's Expedition of 1355–1357* (Manchester, 1958).

Higounet, C. (ed.), *Histoire de l'Aquitaine* (Toulouse, 1971).

Hilton, R. H., and T. H. Aston (eds), *The English Rising of 1381* (Cambridge, 1984).

Holmes, G., *The Order of the Garter: Its Knights and Stall Plates, 1348 to 1984* (Windsor, 1984).

Holmes, G. A., *The Estates of the Higher Nobility in Fourteenth-Century England* (Cambridge, 1957).

—— *The Good Parliament* (Oxford, 1975).

Housley, N., *The Later Crusades 1274–1580: From Lyons to Alcazar* (Oxford, 1992).

Hunter Blair, C. H., 'Armorials upon English Seals from the Twelfth to the Sixteenth Centuries', *Archaeologia*, 2nd series, 89 (1943), 1–26.

Bibliography

James, M. R., *A Descriptive Catalogue of the Manuscripts in the Library of St. John's College, Cambridge* (Cambridge, 1913).

Jennings, B., *Yorkshire Monasteries: Cloister, Land and People* (Otley, 1999).

Jones, M., *Ducal Brittany, 1364–1399: Relations with England and France during the Reign of Duke John IV* (Oxford, 1970).

Knight, H., and N. Jeffries, *Medieval and Later Urban Development at High Street, Uxbridge* (London, 2004).

Knowles, D., and R. N. Hadcock, *Medieval Religious Houses: England and Wales* (London, 1971).

Lawne, P., *Joan of Kent: The First Princess of Wales* (Stroud, 2015).

Le Patourel, J. H., *The Medieval Administration of the Channel Islands, 1199–1399* (London, 1937).

Leyser, H., *Medieval Women: A Social History of Women in England, 450–1500* (London, 1996).

Lindenbaum, S., 'The Smithfield Tournament of 1390', *Journal of Medieval and Renaissance Studies*, 20 (1990), 1–20.

Little, A. G., *The Grey Friars in Oxford*, Oxford Historical Society, 20 (Oxford, 1892).

Luce, S., *Histoire de Bertrand du Guesclin et de son époque: la jeunesse de Bertrand (1320–1364)* (Paris, 1876).

McFarlane, K. B., *Lancastrian Kings and Lollard Knights* (Oxford, 1972).

—— *The Nobility of Later Medieval England* (Oxford, 1973).

McHardy, A. K., 'Richard II: A Personal Portrait', in *The Reign of Richard II*, ed. G. Dodd (Stroud, 2000), 11–32.

McKisack, M., *The Fourteenth Century, 1307–1399* (Oxford, 1959).

Macklin, H. W., *The Brasses of England* (London, 1907).

Maddicott, J. R., 'Thomas of Lancaster and Sir Robert Holland: A Study in Noble Patronage', *EHR*, 86 (1971), 449–72.

Matthew, H. C. G., and B. H. Harrison (eds), *The Oxford Dictionary of National Biography*, 60 vols (Oxford, 2004).

Maxwell Lyte, H. C., *A History of Dunster and of the families of Mohun and Luttrell*, 2 vols (London, 1909).

Millea, N., *The Gough Map: The Earliest Road Map of Great Britain?* (Oxford, 2007).

Newton, S. M., *Fashion in the Age of the Black Prince: A Study of the Years 1340–1365* (Woodbridge, 1980).

Nicholson, R., *Edward III and the Scots: The Formative Years of a Military Career* (Oxford, 1965).

Ormrod, W. M., 'In Bed with Joan of Kent: The King's Mother and the Peasants' Revolt', in *Medieval Women: Texts and Contexts in Late Medieval Britain. Essays for Felicity Riddy*, ed. J. Wogan-Brown, R. Voaden, A. Diamond, A. Hutchison, C. Meale and L. Johnson (Turnhout, 2000), 277–92.

—— *Edward III* (London, 2011).

Ormrod, W. M., G. Dodd and A. Musson (eds), *Medieval Petitions: Grace and Grievance* (York, 2009).

Palmer, J. J. N. (ed.), *Froissart: Historian* (Woodbridge, 1981).

Pearsall, D., *The Life of Geoffrey Chaucer: A Critical Biography* (Oxford, 1992).

Pépin, G., 'Towards a New Assessment of the Black Prince's Aquitaine: A Study of the Last Years (1369–1372)', *Nottingham Medieval Studies*, 50 (2006), 59–114.

Perroy, É., *The Hundred Years War*, trans. W. B. Wells (London, 1951).

Petit, J., *Charles de Valois, 1270–1325* (Paris, 1900).

Pevsner, N., *Yorkshire: York and the East Riding* (Harmondsworth, 1972).

Phillips, J. R. S., *Edward II* (London, 2010).

Phillips, K. M., *Medieval Maidens: Young Women and Gender in England, 1270–1540* (Manchester, 2003).

Poulson, G., *The History and Antiquities of the Seigniory of Holderness*, 2 vols (Hull, 1840–41).

Prestwich, M., *The Three Edwards: War and State in England, 1272–1377* (London, 1980).

—— *Edward I* (London, 1988).

Prince, A. E., 'A Letter of Edward the Black Prince describing the Battle of Nájera in 1367', *EHR*, 41 (1926), 415–18.

Ralegh Radford, C. A., *Restormel Castle* (London, 1977).

—— *Tintagel Castle* (London, 1987).

Renouard, Y. (ed.), *Bordeaux sous les rois d'Angleterre* (Bordeaux, 1965).

——'L'apogée politique au temps du prince Noir (1355–1372)', in *Bordeaux sous les rois d'Angleterre*, ed. Y. Renouard (Bordeaux, 1965), 369–404.

——'Nouvelles crises et dévastations', in *Bordeaux sous les rois d'Angleterre*, ed. Y. Renouard (Bordeaux, 1965), 407–18.

Richmond, C., and E. Scarff (eds), *St. George's Chapel, Windsor, in the Late Middle Ages* (Windsor, 2001).

Rickard, P., *Britain in Medieval French Literature, 1100–1500* (Cambridge, 1956).

Rickert, E., Olson, C. C., and M. M. Crow, *Chaucer's World* (London, 1948).

Rosenthal, J. T., 'Aristocratic Marriage and the English Peerage, 1350–1500: Social Institution and Personal Bond', *Journal of Medieval History*, 10 (1984), 181–94.

Roskell, J. S. [with L. Clark and C. Rawcliffe] (eds), *The House of Commons, 1386–1421*, 4 vols (Stroud, 1992).

Royal Commission on Historical Monuments, *An Inventory of the Historical Monuments in the Town of Stamford* (London, 1977).

Russell, P. E., *The English Intervention in Spain and Portugal in the Time of Edward III and Richard II* (Oxford, 1955).

—— 'The War in Spain and Portugal', in *Froissart: Historian*, ed. J. J. N. Palmer (Woodbridge, 1981).

Sandler, L. F., *Gothic Manuscripts, 1285–1385*, A Survey of Manuscripts Illuminated in the British Isles, 5 (London and Oxford, 1986).

Saul, N., *Richard II* (London, 1997).

—— *The Three Richards: Richard I, Richard II and Richard III* (London, 2006).

Shakespeare, William, *King Henry IV, Part One*, Arden Shakespeare, 3rd series (London, 2002).

Sherborne, J. W., 'Indentured Retinues and Expeditions to France, 1369–1380', *EHR*, 79 (1964), 718–46.

Simpson, C., *Wallingford: The Archaeological Implications of Development. A Survey* (Oxford, 1974).

Strickland, A., *Lives of the Queens of England*, 6 vols (London, 1906).

Sumption J., *The Hundred Years War*, 4 vols (London, 1990–2015).

Thompson, E. M., *The Carthusian Order in England* (London, 1930).

Thurston H. J., and D. Attwater (eds), *Butler's Lives of the Saints*, 2nd edn (London, 1981).

Tierney, M. A., *The History and Antiquities of the Castle and Town of Arundel*, 2 vols (London, 1834).

Toynbee, M. R., *St Louis of Toulouse and the Process of Canonisation in the Fourteenth Century* (Manchester, 1929).

Tuck, A., *Richard II and the English Nobility* (London, 1973).

Tucoo-Chala, P., *Gaston Fébus, prince des Pyrénées (1331–1391)* (Pau, 1993).

Uytterbrouck, A., *Le gouvernement du duché de Brabant au bas Moyen Âge (1355–1430)*, 2 vols (Brussels, 1975).

Vale, J., *Edward III and Chivalry: Chivalric Society and its Context, 1270–1360* (Woodbridge, 1982).

Vale, M. G. A., *The Angevin Legacy and the Hundred Years War, 1250–1340* (Oxford, 1990).

Vaughan, R., *John the Fearless: The Growth of Burgundian Power*, new edn (Woodbridge, 2002).

—— *Philip the Bold: The Formation of the Burgundian State*, new edn (Woodbridge, 2002).

—— *Philip the Good: The Apogee of Burgundy*, new edn (Woodbridge, 2002).

Victoria County History, *Berkshire*, 4 vols (London, 1906–24).

—— *Buckinghamshire*, 4 vols (London, 1905–27).

—— *Hampshire and the Isle of Wight*, 5 vols (London, 1900–12).

—— *Lincolnshire* (London, 1906).

—— *Yorkshire: East Riding*, 9 vols (London, 1969–2012).

—— *Yorkshire: North Riding*, 2 vols (London, 1914–23).

Walker, S., *The Lancastrian Affinity 1361–1399* (Oxford, 1990).

Ward, J. C., 'Joan de Bohun, Countess of Hereford, Kent and Northampton, c. 1370–1419: Family, Land and Social Networks', *Essex Archaeology and History*, 32 (2001), 146–53.

Watson, A. G., *Catalogue of Dated and Datable Manuscripts c. 700–1600 in the Department of Manuscripts in the British Library*, 2 vols (London, 1979).

Webb, D., *Pilgrimage in Medieval England* (London, 2000).

Weever, J., *Ancient Funeral Monuments of Great Britain, Ireland and the Islands Adjacent* (London, 1631).

Weir, A., *Katherine Swynford: The Story of John of Gaunt and His Scandalous Duchess* (London, 2007).

Wentersdorf, K. P., 'The Clandestine Marriages of the Fair Maid of Kent', *JMH*, 5 (1979), 203–31.

Wood, M., *Donnington Castle, Berkshire* (London, 1964).

Zutshi, P., 'Petitions to the Pope in the Fourteenth Century', in *Medieval Petitions: Grace and Grievance*, ed. W. M. Ormrod, G. Dodd and A. Musson (York, 2009), 82–98.

Acknowledgements

OVER THE PAST MONTHS cumulative health problems made it increasingly difficult to bring this book to completion. My wife Jackie came to the rescue. The text was complete but needed proofreading and some editing; the notes for each chapter existed but were not typed up and some were incomplete or not clearly related to the text. We read the text many times at regular intervals, assessing what still needed to be done and discussing refinements of content and style until a final version emerged. The same procedure was applied to the notes and bibliography. It was a big task for her to undertake and I am very grateful for her determination in sifting and sorting endless piles of papers, checking and typing for hours whilst urging me to listen to and comment on finished chapters.

I also owe thanks to Professor Christopher Allmand for his detailed comments on a chapter and helpful telephone discussion on a wide range of points.

Thanks too are due to Owen Dudley Edwards who scrutinised the whole text and then fed back his comments page by page whilst interspersing these comments with highly entertaining relevant quotations from a vast range of literary sources, transforming a chore into an enjoyable experience.

A special thanks must go to Alison Weir who never ceased encouraging me to complete the book and was most generous in sharing her research.

I am grateful for the references which Professors Michael Jones and Christopher Given-Wilson passed on to me. Professor Michael Angold also helped to keep me on the right track with his helpful suggestions about a Richard unknown to me.

The information about the ransom of the count of Denia was mainly helped by the generous translations of the archive material from Valencia made by Dr Jorge Saiz Serrano. Dr Nicholas Bennet and Mark Christodolou gave me very helpful information relating to ecclesiastical and architectural details, so thanks are due to them.

My good friend Dr Christopher Cameron, a retired GP, offered me helpful insights during our numerous discussions about the possible causes of the Black Prince's fatal illness.

I am sure that over my long teaching career the contacts and discussions I have had with so many colleagues and friends have contributed much to my overall knowledge and appreciation of the fourteenth century. Thanks therefore to them and apologies for not naming them individually.

Finally I must thank Taylor & Francis for allowing me to reproduce maps and tables.

❖   ❖   ❖

SADLY MY HUSBAND did not live to see the publication of his book. However, thanks to the prompt response of those concerned at Boydell & Brewer, he did see the jacket, tangible proof that his work would be published. My thanks go to the cover designer. Indeed, in these somewhat exceptional circumstances, the book would not have seen the light of day without the extra effort of so many. I would particularly like to thank Robert Kinsey at Boydell & Brewer for his dedicated attention to the text, his willingness to go the extra mile to ensure the book stayed on track, for dealing with the illustrations and for patiently coping with my questions. It has been a steep learning curve for me but he helped to smooth the process. I would like to thank Caroline Palmer for her continued faith in the project. I am also grateful to Professor Christopher Allmand for his painstaking scrutiny of the text, making me aware of inconsistences, possible confusions and infelicities and for keeping my spirits up.

Jackie Goodman
Edinburgh, February 2017

Index

Index

Index

Printed and bound by CPI Group (UK) Ltd, Croydon, CR0 4YY

09/06/2025

14685773-0001